Indian
FOR Everyone

THE **HOME COOK'S GUIDE** TO **TRADITIONAL FAVORITES**

Anupy Singla

S
SURREY
BOOKS

AN AGATE IMPRINT

CHICAGO

Printed in China

All photographs © Brave New Pictures and Gregg Lowe
Photo art direction by Mary Valentin

Library of Congress Cataloging-in-Publication Data

Singla, Anupy.
 Indian for everyone : the home cook's guide to traditional favorites / Anupy Singla.
    pages cm
 Includes index.
 Summary: ""Over 100 Indian cuisine recipes along with many adaptations for vegan,
vegetarian, and gluten-free diets"--Provided by publisher"-- Provided by publisher.
 ISBN 978-1-57284-162-8 (hardback) -- ISBN 1-57284-162-1 (hard cover) -- ISBN
978-1-57284-745-3 (ebook)
 1. Cooking, Indic. 2. Vegetarian cooking. 3. Gluten-free diet--Recipes I. Title.
 TX724.5.I4S5348 2014
 641.5954--dc23
                    2014017605

14 15 16 17 18   10 9 8 7 6 5 4 3 2 1

Surrey Books is an imprint of Agate Publishing. Agate books are available in bulk at
discount prices. For more information, go to agatepublishing.com.

This book is for my wonderful family—especially my husband, Sandeep, who always helps me think bigger and better even when I can't see it. I love to cook. He loves to eat. We make a great team! It's also in memory of my Sneh *bua*, who helped me create some of my most cherished food memories—your contagious laugh is sorely missed.

Contents

Introduction

You picked up this cookbook, and I'm so glad that you did! I know that you're probably wondering if it's the right Indian cookbook for you. Rest assured—it is. I wrote it with you and your family in mind. The title says it all—this is an Indian cookbook for *everyone*.

It's for Indian-food lovers who live for the diversity of this amazing cuisine. Although many of the recipes are native to the region I am from—Punjab—I have included some from other states and areas as well.

It's for skeptics who claim they hate the taste of curry. Fantastic! Read on—you'll learn that Indians typically don't use curry powder as a spice.

It's for cooks who are new to Indian cooking and eating. You'll find step-by-step instructions and photographs on spices, legumes, and your favorite Indian recipes.

It's for seasoned Indian cooks to serve as a reference point for their favorite Indian dishes. In this book, you'll find the instructions and cooking times our mothers and grandmothers followed in a forthright and easy-to-understand style.

It's for the meat eaters (like my husband) who can't resist *tandoori* chicken, minced lamb, and fish.

It's for vegans and vegetarians (my mother, my mother-in-law, and I fall into this group) who want real, road-tested meatless alternatives to traditional Indian meat recipes. This book celebrates our plant-based choices and preferences, rather than making them just a sidebar.

It's for healthy eaters who want to know whether you can bake a *samosa* instead of frying it, whether you can substitute quinoa for rice when grinding *dosa* batter, and whether there are gluten-free Indian bread options. *The short answer is "yes" to all of the above.*

It's for the Indian-food lovers who occasionally like to indulge, who crave a touch of cream in their *dal makhani* when they make it at home.

It's for folks with allergies and/or dietary preferences. If you maintain a gluten-free (GF) diet, know that virtually all of these recipes will work for you (save the wheat-based recipes in the bread section, of course, but that section has many GF options as well).

It's for the little girls (like me) who left India at a very young age but want to preserve their food heritage for sons and daughters who are growing up in America. Despite our hectic and sometimes overwhelming schedules, we busy moms share the crazy notion that every child deserves good, wholesome food.

And, most of all, it's for those who love Indian restaurants—the folks who experience a delicious meal out and want to replicate it at home.

Opening this book is akin to opening a menu at your favorite Indian eatery. Along with the recipes to your beloved dishes, you'll find tips on how to make them healthier and even how to "veganize" them.

What I think you'll also find intriguing about this book—and indicative of the times we live in—is that you'll likely recognize the Hindi names for many of the recipes and ingredients. To me, this means that Indian food has really hit the mainstream in the United States. Today, few people (even in the Midwest, where I reside) need an explanation of what *Tandoori* Chicken, *Dal Makhani*,

Aloo Gobi, or Chicken *Tikka Masala* (see recipes on pp. 189, 124, 98, and 192) are. But they do need an explanation of how to make them—and that's what *Indian for Everyone* provides.

Indian food becoming ubiquitous in the United States is a trend I don't take lightly. As someone who came to this country at the age of three and was largely raised in King of Prussia, which at the time was a fairly culturally limited town located just outside Philadelphia, I am excited that Indian food is quickly becoming so widely accepted. When my parents and I moved into our neighborhood back in the 1970s, I used to get a lot of harsh comments about the "funny" smell of curry. And those were just some of our neighbors.

But times are changing. Our world is becoming more global and more willing to celebrate differences rather than letting them divide us. That's a trend that I'll never take for granted, having grown up navigating the challenges of "otherness." Even King of Prussia has come a long way since then.

If any of the previous descriptions apply to you, this book is for you. Thank you for joining me on my delicious and fulfilling journey to demystify all of the Indian recipes I grew up eating and now make successfully at home, from a decidedly Indian–American point of view.

This book is not an anthology of every single Indian recipe ever concocted— instead, it's a reference full of your favorites. As with my two previous books, *The Indian Slow Cooker* and *Vegan Indian Cooking,* my goal is to never overwhelm or intimidate you, but to get your creative juices flowing and to get your confidence up.

The recipes within this book include both conventional and metric measurements for ingredients. We even took extra care to measure every spice blend ourselves for better accuracy. Please note that the recipes were tested with conventional measurements; if you note differences in the metric yields as you put my recipes to use in your own kitchen, keep me posted at my website, indianasapplepie.com.

I know that there will invariably be a few favorites I have missed. Don't worry: They'll come in the next book, most likely. I test my recipes at least a dozen times each, and if I can't perfect the recipe and fine-tune the process, it doesn't make it into my books. So I'm probably still trying.

Once you start making a few of these recipes you'll immediately want to rush off and make more. Use this book as your guide and launching point to more delicious things to come.

Anupy Singla
Chicago, IL

Getting Started

Tools of the Trade

Get your key kitchen tools together and you'll be cooking with ease soon after. Indian cooking does not require much in the way of special gear, so a well-stocked kitchen with basic, quality items will take you far.

Blender, food processor, and immersion blender: It's essential to have a strong, heavy-duty blender. I have a Vitamix and love how it instantly breaks down chutneys and curries, but any quality blender will do. A food processor helps break down ingredients like ginger, garlic, onions, and tomatoes with ease. I have two—a large one and a small one. I also like to whip up dough for my *roti* in the large one. Keep an immersion blender on hand for a quick and easy way to blend down curries without having to transfer them from the pot you're cooking in.

***Idli* mold:** A stainless steel *idli* mold will help you make the steamed South Asian rice and lentil dumplings found in the bread section. You'll use it for only this recipe, but I think you'll find it's worth making the small investment. You can purchase one at an Indian grocery store.

Kettle: If you need to add water to a dish while it's cooking, it's best to add boiling water so you don't lose precious cooking time or bring down your cooking temperature. I always keep my electric kettle handy; I've had the same one for more than 14 years.

Pots and pans: Heavy-bottomed stockpots and pans are ideal for Indian cooking. Cast-iron pans work well, especially the small ones, for dry roasting whole spices. For making flatbreads, use a ***tava,*** a concave or flat metal pan. For deep frying, try using a ***kadhai,*** India's take on the wok. If you don't have these items on hand, just use a flat cast-iron pan for making breads and any deep, heavy pot for deep frying. A quality **Dutch** or **French oven** will serve you well, especially when making lentils. My 5-quart Le Creuset French oven was a wonderful investment that works great on days I haven't thought ahead to put lentils or other foods in the slow cooker to prepare in advance. Just note that when using a Dutch oven, your cooking time may decrease and the amount of water needed may alter slightly from these recipes because of how well these pots retain heat.

Serrated peeler: I always keep this tool close by to easily peel tomatoes without a drop of water. You'll never go back to peeling the traditional way. It's also great for peaches and plums.

Slow cooker: Always keep a slow cooker or two on hand to help cook whole beans and lentils. Even though I have not included many slow cooker recipes in this book (my book *The Indian Slow Cooker* is full of nothing but, and there's

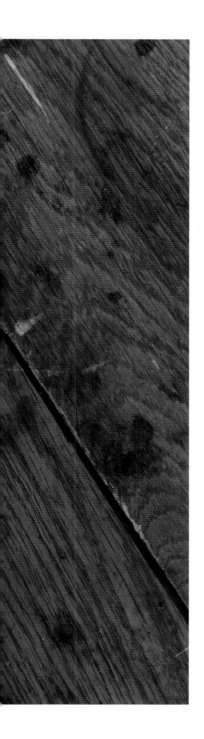

also a section in my book *Vegan Indian Cooking),* it's an important tool. *The Indian Slow Cooker,* along with this book, will give you all the information you need to easily make several dishes at the same time, especially when you are cooking for guests. I typically recommend that folks have one 5-quart / 5-L and one 3½-quart / 3-L cooker. It's even better if they have timers.

Spice Tiffin: Known in India as a *masala dabba,* or spice box, the Spice Tiffin is my amped-up version of this handy tool. Every home should have several; I have 12. Why? Think about it. You prep your ingredients before you cook, right? The French call that *mise en place.* Why not do the same for your spices? Keep them organized by cuisine. Imagine having small amounts of key spices for each cuisine on hand ready for immediate, efficient use, without having to fiddle with lids or go searching for spices in the back of overfilled cabinets. That's what the Spice Tiffin enables you to do. In my house, we have a separate box for every group of spices we use, from Mexican to Chinese—and there's even one each for baking, soups, sundae sprinkles, and oatmeal toppings.

To purchase your own—which will revolutionize your cooking experience—head to my website, indianasapplepie.com. The container is stainless steel (you should always house spices in metal or glass containers, because they can eat away at other materials) and holds seven round bowls for each individual spice. The small containers in my Spice Tiffins include a metal bar that lets you level your measure of a spice without having to grab another utensil and a tablespoon and teaspoon measure, in order to make precise measurements. The Spice Tiffin was featured in *Food & Wine Magazine's* trendspotting column in August 2013.

Spice grinder: To successfully make delicious Indian food, you should plan to blend your own spices in small batches. To do this effectively, you need an electric coffee grinder reserved for spices (or a powerful blender) for the big jobs and a **mortar and pestle** for the small jobs. I've started grinding all of my spice blends down in my Vitamix (both the dry and wet containers work) because it easily breaks down cinnamon sticks and other hard spices. One tip—when grinding a blend that requires turmeric, add it after you finish grinding and have transferred your blend to a bowl, so that your jug does not discolor.

Vegetable scrubber: Investing in this little tool will pay dividends. I always wash my nonleafy vegetables as soon as I purchase them, and a scrubber helps clean the potatoes, carrots, and other items fast and easily. Often, if you are buying quality organic produce, you can use this tool and avoid peeling things like carrots, cucumbers, and daikon (radishes).

CUMIN SEEDS

GROUND CUMIN

ROASTED CUMIN, GROUND

CORIANDER SEEDS

GROUND CORIANDER

ROASTED CORIANDER SEEDS

GREEN CARDAMOM

BLACK CARDAMOM

TURMERIC POWDER

GARAM MASALA

BLACK MUSTARD SEEDS

CINNAMON STICKS

CLOVES

FENUGREEK SEEDS

**KALA NAMAK/
BLACK SALT**

AJWAIN/CAROM SEEDS

FENNEL SEEDS

**WHOLE DRIED
RED CHILES**

CASSIA LEAF

AMLA

**AMCHUR/DRIED
MANGO POWDER**

HING/ASAFETIDA

**ANARDANA/DRIED
POMEGRANTE SEEDS**

DRIED TAMARIND

Indian Spices and Herbs

Finding Indian spices and groceries today is so much easier than when I was growing up in Pennsylvania, back in the 1980s. An Indian grocery store was a rare find, and one for which we were constantly on the lookout. I still remember making a weekly jaunt to a dark, slightly unkempt store with a steep, curved driveway in Norristown, Pennsylvania. Now, most basic Indian ingredients are well stocked in mainstream grocery stores—so much so, in fact, that many Indian grocers are scrambling for business.

If you have trouble finding spices, head to my website, indianasapplepie.com, where I stock basic Indian spices and blends. More are added every day.

Amla (Phyllanthus emblica): Also known as an Indian gooseberry, *amla* is a round, pale, greenish-yellow-colored fruit that is extremely tart and high in vitamin C. I bring back the dried variety from my mother's childhood home in Chandigarh, but if you can find dried *amla* in an Indian grocery store, it's worth adding to Mom's Morning Cleanse (see recipe on p. 53). The frozen kind is a terrific and easy addition to my Indian as Apple Pie Green Juice Smoothie (see recipe on p. 54).

Asafetida (hing, Ferula assafoetida): Also known as devil's dung, likely because of its sharp smell, this gum-like resin is ground into a powder and added sparingly to hot oil to help with digestion. It tastes like leeks once cooked in hot oil but should be used carefully—it is very strong. Buy it preground and keep it in a tightly sealed container.

Black salt *(kala namak):* My favorite spice, mined from soft-stone quarries in northern India and Pakistan, is *kala namak.* It has a sulfuric tang and is used in salads and street foods to help boost flavor. Sprinkle it, along with lemon juice, over fresh veggies like raw onions and cucumbers for an addictive side salad and/or snack. This tangy spice is how I got my young girls hooked on veggies.

Cardamom, green *(elaichi, Elletaria cardamomum):* Known as the queen of spices, *hara* (green) cardamom grows as pods on a six-foot-tall shrub. One of the most valued and costliest spices in the world, it contains 25 volatile oils. Key among these is cineole, which is also found in bay leaves. Cineole is being studied for its many benefits, which may include aiding digestion, getting rid of bad breath, inhibiting the growth of ulcers, and preventing colon cancer. It's the primary flavor in Indian teas, rice pudding, basmati rice, and meat stews. Buy it whole in pods and crush it gently (discard the hull before eating) or take the seeds out and crush them into a powder (it's used this way in many desserts). You can also purchase cardamom seeds already removed from the hull.

Cardamom, black *(kali* or *badi elaichi, Amomum subulatum* or *costatum*):* This large, woody pod is used in Indian cuisine to spice rice, curries, and meat dishes. I love its warm and comforting taste and always add it to my *chai* to help ward off coughs for my kids. You'll likely have to visit an Indian grocer to find this spice. If a recipe calls for it and you don't have it, just leave it out.

Carom seeds *(ajwain, ajowan, Trachyspermum copticum):* These small, beige, pungent seeds come from an annual shrub from the same family as cumin and caraway. They look like cumin seeds, but have a more distinct flavor and are also used for their soothing digestive properties. They are a key addition to lentil dishes like *Kitchari* (see recipe on p. 145); snacks made from *besan* (chickpea flour), like *pakoras;* and biscuits. (See recipes on pp. 81 and 243.)

Cassia leaves *(tej patta):* Often mistaken for bay leaves, cassia leaves are also referred to as Indian bay leaves, but they differ from their European counterpart

in look and taste. They are bigger and longer and come from the tropical laurel tree that produces cassia bark. Fry them in hot oil to release their inherent woody flavor and aroma. If you don't have them on hand, just use regular bay leaves—I use both interchangeably.

Chile *(mirch):* Since its discovery by Christopher Columbus in the Americas, the chile pepper has become one of the most widely consumed spices in the world. Chiles derive their heat and healing properties from capsaicin, an alkaloid found mostly in their seeds and inner membranes. In this book, I spell chiles with an "e" rather than an "i" (chili), which in the United States is generally used in reference to a Tex-Mex blend of spices. In Indian cooking, use peppers with thin skins, like Thai, serrano, or cayenne chiles.

In just about every recipe in this book, I suggest a range of chiles to use (say, 1 to 4 chiles). Keep in mind that when you see those higher numbers, I'm referring to Thai chiles, which are smaller. Reduce the amount of chiles you use according to your preferred heat level. Also feel free to remove the chiles' seeds and membranes to reduce the heat even more but still get the flavor. I use whole chiles and always want and need more in our typical Punjabi household, where everyone (including my kids) loves heat. Always remember that if you are a true beginner, there's no harm in leaving chiles out completely. Also, mincing chiles releases more capsaicin and makes your dish spicier. Keep your chiles whole or slice them in half lengthwise for a milder dish.

WHOLE DRIED RED CHILES: These are used extensively in Indian cooking to make spice blends and round out curries. In stores, you'll find thick, long chiles as well as short, round ones. Try them out and see what you like best.

RED CHILE POWDER: With this ingredient, I am referring to powdered red chiles found in large bags in most Indian grocery stores. You can substitute cayenne powder, but the Indian red chile powder packs more flavor and heat. Adjust accordingly.

Cilantro *(dhaniya, Coriandrum sativum):* This herb (also referred to as coriander leaf) is used extensively in Indian cooking, especially in the north. Use both the leaves and the stem, which is tender enough to be crushed into chutneys and chopped and sprinkled over stews.

Cinnamon *(dalchini, Cinnamomum zeylanicum, verum,* or *cassia):* Cinnamon is derived from the inner bark of the upper branches of a tree native to Sri Lanka. In Indian cooking, cinnamon is not just reserved for dessert. It is primarily used to subtly spice savory dishes and is a key component in many spice blends.

Clove *(laung, Syzygium aromaticum):* Cloves are dried, unopened flowers from a tropical evergreen. They are used to subtly spice rice, stir-fries, curries, and *chai.* The essential oil from cloves can be used to help alleviate toothaches.

Coriander seeds *(sabut dhaniya, Coriandrum sativum):* Coriander refers to the seed and cilantro refers to the herb that grows from that seed, but in India, we sometimes use the words interchangeably. These green-yellow grassy seeds impart a wonderfully subtle, lemony taste to a dish. The seeds are used in various spice blends, dry roasted, or heated in oil to release their essential oils. Try grinding your own—it's a much better product than the preground spice found in most stores. Especially in North Indian cooking, you'll find coriander seeds paired with cumin seeds in various recipes and spice blends.

Cumin seeds *(jeera, Cuminum cyminum):* Indian cuisine, especially in the north, depends on these little brown-beige seeds. On their own, they seem dull and uninteresting, but heated in oil or dry roasted and ground, cumin seeds are purely amazing and the root of almost all of my childhood food memories. In scientific studies, cumin has been shown to fight diabetes and cancerous tumors, and it may help prevent bone loss.

ROASTED CUMIN *(BHUNA JEERA):* I call this getting double duty from your spices. You can dry roast your cumin and grind it into a powder. Use it in *Kheera Raita* (see recipe on p. 50) and even in soups and stews.

Curry leaves *(kari patta, Murraya koenigii):* Curry leaves are to South Indian cuisine what cilantro is to North Indian: ubiquitous. To dispel any misunderstandings, these leaves have little—if anything—to do with curry powder. They are added to hot oil in everything from vegetable stir-fries to rice dishes. Their addictive, grassy flavor is a cross between lemongrass and tangerines. The fresh leaves can be found at Indian grocers.

Fennel seeds *(saunf, Foeniculum vulgare):* These tiny seeds, which look like curled-up green cumin seeds, are the dried seeds of the yellow flower from a large dill-like perennial plant. They are typically found at the entrance of an Indian restaurant as a post-meal breath freshener and digestive aid. When my girls had bellyaches as babies, I would boil a little in water and give them small sips of the cooled fennel water.

Fenugreek seeds *(methi dana, Trigonella foenum-graecum):* Small, hard, and square, these beige seeds are powerful in terms of flavor and nutrition. Derived from the pod of the fenugreek plant, the seeds are considered legumes. Their slightly bitter taste not only adds flavor to Indian dishes but is also an indication of their nutritional power. They're reputed to do everything from aiding digestion to controlling diabetes to aiding in weight loss by suppressing appetite. Try them in Mom's Morning Cleanse (see recipe on p. 53), which also includes lemon juice, turmeric, hot water, and cayenne pepper.

DRIED FENUGREEK LEAVES *(KASOORI METHI):* These are the dried leaves of the fenugreek plant. Use them in all sorts of curries to lend a more full-bodied flavor. You can also use the fresh leaves (found at Indian grocers) for quick stir-fries with other vegetables, including potatoes.

Ginger, ground *(adarak, Zingiber officinale):* Ginger is a root-like rhizome whose flavor depends on how it is prepared. It can go from mildly sweet and lemony pungent when fresh to twice as pungent when dried. It becomes aromatic and less pungent when cooked. The powdered form of the ginger root is useful to keep on hand if you don't have fresh ginger. You can also use it in *chai,* some spice blends, and stir-fries.

Idli **rice:** This rice, also known as parboiled rice, is used to make steamed fermented rice dumplings. Find it at any Indian grocery store.

Kokum (*Garcinia indica*): Use this dried rind of the fruit of a large evergreen tree to add tartness to a dish much as you would tamarind. Soak it in hot water first to extract its flavor. In this book, it's used only in my *Toor Dal* recipe (see p. 131), but you can experiment by adding it to fish and other lentil dishes.

Mango powder (*amchur, Mangifera indica*): This tart, beige powder is made from uncooked, dried, and unripe green mangoes. It functions like lemon juice or vinegar in your dishes and is usually added toward the end of the cooking process. It's essential in my okra dishes.

Masala: By definition, *masalas* are spice blends. There are many out there and all are specific to their uses. *Chana Masala* (see recipe on p. 36) is used in a chickpea curry to make it more tart, while *Garam Masala* (see recipe on p. 35) gives dishes a warm, earthy flavor. *Sambhar* Powder (see recipe on p. 38) flavors a South Indian dish by the same name. Try these blends in their traditional ways and then start experimenting and mixing them up a bit. I often sprinkle a favorite blend over freshly made stovetop popcorn for a healthy snack with a kick.

Mint (*pudina, podina, Mentha spicata*): Grown in the backyards of many Indian families who immigrated to the United States, fresh mint is a key element in North Indian cooking. The mint used for chutneys and marinades is typically spearmint, which has a darker, more jagged leaf than other varieties.

Mustard seeds (*rai, Brassica juncea*): These tiny, hard seeds are to South Indian cuisine what cumin seeds are to North Indian. They are added to hot oil and popped to release their flavor. In Indian cooking, we typically use the black or brown seeds. Mixed with curry leaves, they make one heck of a base for a curry. I sometimes substitute the two in my North Indian Chicken Curry (see recipe on p. 212) for a South Indian take on a North Indian classic and use it traditionally in *Sambhar* Powder (see recipe on p. 38). The different-colored seeds (brownish-black, reddish-brown, and yellowish) are produced from different varieties of mustard plants. The first two are used most often in Indian cuisine, but if you can't find them, use the yellowish seeds more commonly found in Western grocers.

Nigella seeds (*kalonji, Nigella sativa*): These tiny black seeds are the product of an annual flowering plant. The seeds are sometimes referred to as onion seeds or black cumin, but are not related to either. When sizzled in hot oil, they taste a bit like onions and look like onion seeds—hence the misleading reference. They are added to Indian pickles and used in curries and Indian breads, including *Naan* (see recipe on p. 238).

Paprika *(deghi mirch, Capsicum)*: Paprika is made from dried sweet peppers from Kashmir. The powder is used to give *tandoori* chicken and curries a reddish color without adding a ton of heat or red food dye.

Pomegranate seeds, dried *(anardana, Punica granatum)*: From wild Indian pomegranates, these seeds are dried and used to add a touch of tartness to various dishes and spice blends like *Chana Masala* (see recipe on p. 36). They are sold as whole, sticky seeds and as a powder.

Salt *(namak):* The type of salt you use can make or break your interpretation of a recipe. In this book, I have used Redmond's Real Salt (extra fine). If using coarse sea salt or kosher salt, keep in mind that these types have larger crystals than finer varieties. If you question the salt level in a recipe, start with about half the recommended level and add more if you need it. It's always better to start conservatively—yet another advantage to making your own meals. Consult the chart below to determine how much salt you should use in these recipes developed with Redmond's Real Salt, depending on which brand you use.

Weight in Grams for Various Brands or Types of Salt, 1 Cup

Table salt	304 g
Redmond's Real Salt (extra fine)	266 g
Morton's Kosher Salt	240 g
Supermarket-brand coarse sea salt	185 g
Maldon Sea Salt	125 g
Diamond Kosher Salt	120 g

Tamarind *(imlee, imli, Tamarindua indica):* Key to many Indian dishes and sides, dark brown tamarind pods grow in tall trees all over India. The seeds and pulp are scraped out of the pods and sold in blocks. This pulp is then soaked in hot water until all of the tartaric and malic acids are extracted. The resulting tart and sour juice is used for cooking, and the pulp and seeds are discarded.

TAMARIND PASTE: A concentrated form of dried tamarind. It is a wonderful shortcut to the soaking process, but it can be very strong. Add it to recipes slowly, so as not to overpower them.

Turmeric powder *(haldi, Curcuma longa)*: If there is one wonder spice, I'd say it's *haldi*. I drink it in the morning in my Mom's Morning Cleanse (see recipe on p. 53), gargle with it to relieve coughs, and make a paste out of it to heal minor cuts. A rhizome, turmeric grows underground and looks like orange-yellowish ginger. It is washed, peeled, dried, and ground into the bright yellow-orange powder you likely know. Although fresh turmeric is not easily found in the United States, I have seen it quite regularly in Indian grocery stores and even in some mainstream grocers in Chicago. Peel it and grate it over salads, use it in a Green Juice Smoothie (see recipe on p. 54), or slice it thin and pickle it with vinegar or mustard oil, fresh chiles, and salt. I love prepping it the latter way in a small glass jar to eat with my meals.

The Fridge and Pantry

If your pantry and fridge are well stocked, there's nothing you can't conquer in the kitchen. On my website and my Facebook fan page, I always urge folks to prep a few things ahead of time to save minutes—even hours—during the week, when your life is in full swing.

Always reserve some time after grocery shopping to clean and prep your produce. After a trip to the grocery store or farmers' market, I arrange some dish towels on the kitchen counters, put a large salad spinner (perfect because you can soak things and also drain them by pulling out the inner plastic bowl with holes) or bowl in the sink, squeeze some lemon juice (a natural cleanser) into the bowl, and add water.

I wash everything from the cucumbers to the ginger—even going so far as to scrub what I can down with a vegetable scrubber and peel all my onions (but I do leave them whole so they don't stink up my vegetable drawer). I leave everything out to dry and then arrange it carefully in the fridge, often lining the bottom drawer with either paper towels or dish cloths. It's a perfect setup for the kids to grab veggies and fruit quickly on their own and for me to quickly prep any meal.

Some discourage you to wash fruits like strawberries ahead of time, because they'll spoil sooner. I find that if I don't wash and trim them, they'll go bad in the fridge because no one wants to take time during the week to do it. More delicate fruits, like raspberries, should be eaten quickly if washed and stored.

If you're feeling really ambitious, pull out your food processor and grind up small batches of ginger and garlic. You can grind them separately or together and use it during the week in your cooking. I also like to place the ground-up mixture in ice cube trays (without oil or water) and pop a few out into a bowl to thaw in the morning, giving them a good long time to defrost before dinnertime. If I want to use the slow cooker that day, I can just pop in the frozen cube (such a small amount won't affect the cooking time).

For onions, I typically slice one and mince another to have on hand to dress quick Indian salads or to sprinkle on *dals*. I do the same with fresh chiles, which I either finely dice or put through a food processor and keep on hand to use during the week. Remember, these fresh ingredients will keep for just a little less than two weeks, so they need to be used up fast.

Butter/*ghee*, vegan spreads: You can go the traditional route with my recipes and use butter, or you can go the vegan route and use Earth Balance or Spectrum butter substitutes. These substitutes are made from soy, coconut, or olive oils and can be found in tubs or sticks in most mainstream grocers. In our house, we don't use traditional butter at all; I lean toward a vegan diet, and no one misses it.

Ghee is clarified butter, or butter that has been boiled. The milk solids collect at the top and are skimmed off and discarded. Since the milk solids are gone, *ghee* does not need to be refrigerated and has a higher smoke point than butter. *Ghee* can be purchased in mainstream grocers and in Indian grocery stores.

Coconut *(narial, nariyal, Cocos nucifera):* What we know as white, fleshy coconut is actually the interior nut of the large, brown, and hairy fruit of coconut palm trees. Shredded and unsweetened, the interior flesh of the ripe coconut is used extensively in South Indian cooking and in some North Indian desserts. More and more grocers are starting to carry fresh coconut, but if you cannot find it, use prepackaged unsweetened coconut. My local Whole Foods Market will halve a whole coconut for me, and then I can shred the coconut myself using techniques and tools I acquired on a 2012 visit to the state of Kerala. Inquire at your local Indian grocer about frozen shredded coconut—it's much better than the dried stuff you find in the baking aisle.

Coconut water: When you shake a coconut, you'll hear liquid inside. This is coconut water, which is often sipped through straws right from the fruit on the streets of India. For the water to be drinkable, the coconut must be young and green.

Coconut milk: Many don't realize that coconut milk is different from coconut water. It is obtained by passing hot water through coarsely grated coconut (the white, fleshy meat) contained in muslin or cheesecloth. Squeezing the bundle with your hands helps extract the oils and aromatic compounds.

The traditional method of extraction yields several different batches of coconut milk, which is then used in different ways. The first is naturally a thicker product, while subsequent batches are thinner and lighter, as they contain more water. Once the water begins to run clear, the grated coconut is discarded, as you have literally squeezed out the entire flavor.

In the West, this process is more cumbersome. In the interest of time and effort, simply buy the canned version of coconut milk—but know that the taste will never match freshly squeezed.

As coconut milk sits, its fat rises to the top. It is often skimmed off and sold as ...

Coconut cream: Coconut cream is a great alternative to dairy cream in curries. If you are using a canned variety, shake it well before using. Regular coconut cream is thicker and more flavorful, and "lite" varieties are, unsurprisingly, thinner.

Flour *(atta)* wheat and gluten-free alternatives: In Indian cuisine, countless types of flour can be used—anything from wheat-based to gluten-free alternatives. The most important is *chapati* flour, a finely milled, stoneground whole durum wheat flour used to make *roti* (also called *chapati* or *phulka),* an unleavened flat bread. Though *chapati* is traditionally a whole-wheat flour *(atta),* some manufacturers have started offering a more processed, less nutritious all-purpose flour called *maida.* While it makes lighter bread, it also has little nutrition. Why compromise? When you buy *chapati* flour, make sure the label clearly states that it is "100 percent whole wheat."

Also, know that *chapati* flour is different from whole-wheat flours found in regular grocery stores. If you try making *rotis* with regular whole-wheat flour, they will be heavier, darker, and somewhat bitter, because flours made in the United States are made with hard red winter wheat. *Chapati* flour is without question worth searching for if you plan to make your own Indian breads.

If you can't find *chapati* flour at your grocer, look for white whole-wheat flour. You can also substitute a mixture of one part regular whole-wheat flour and one part all-purpose flour.

CHICKPEA, GRAM FLOUR *(BESAN):* High-protein *besan* is made from skinned, split, and ground black chickpeas. This option is a vegan and gluten-free eater's dream, because it's naturally wheat-free. *Besan* is added to many savory items, like *Pakoras* (see recipe on p. 81). It acts as a binding agent and makes eggs completely unnecessary.

It's also delicious blended with water and spices to make a gluten-free pancake that can be eaten on its own or as a wrap. If you follow a gluten-free diet for medical reasons, I urge you to purchase chickpea flour from mainstream, trusted grocers. (Their chickpea flour is most likely made from white chickpeas and thus a little softer in texture—just use a little less water when mixing the batter.) Indian manufacturers often don't isolate gluten-free products from those with gluten, which could expose you to contaminants.

Garlic *(lassan, Allium sativum):* Garlic, like ginger and turmeric, is essential in my home—it's downright powerful. Obviously, it's a key ingredient in Indian cooking, but it's also an amazing healing aid and a natural antibiotic. Garlic is the first thing my girls ask for when they are sick. If you have a cold, fever, or sore throat, mince one clove and swallow it with a glass of water (no chewing—use honey to make it more palatable). You'll feel better instantly. Just make sure you eat something first—it can upset an empty stomach.

Because I use it in large quantities, I often purchase garlic already peeled. Just make sure it's fresh. I also grind up a large batch in the food processor over the weekend for use during the week. It can keep for up to a week in the fridge. You can also freeze some in an ice cube tray (no water or oil needed) and pop out a cube in the morning for use that evening.

Ginger *(adarak, Zingiber officinale):* Ginger, a key element to most Indian cooking, is a rhizome that grows close to the ground. The best ginger, which is hard to find, is young with a thin, pinkish skin. Avoid ginger that looks shriveled, dried up, and old. Once you grate it or cut into it, the threads will be thick and chewy, and it won't work well in your dishes. You want ginger that looks fresh, vibrant, plump, and smooth. The easiest ways to peel ginger are with a paring knife, a spoon, or, better yet, a grapefruit spoon.

Chop it up or grate it if you have kids (like mine) who don't like to chomp on pieces of ginger. For a great sore throat cure, grate a 2-inch / 5-cm piece of peeled ginger and squeeze out as much juice as you can with one hand. Add lemon juice and honey to the ginger juice and stir well. Drink it up, and that sore throat will disappear. My kids beg for it even when they don't have sore throats. Discard the ginger pulp.

Gur (jaggery): *Gur,* one of the least refined forms of sugar, is made from sugarcane stalks that are pressed to extract all of their juice. This juice is then boiled until it becomes brown and sticky; at that point, it's poured into molds to cool and solidify. The first time I saw this process was in the village of Bhikhi—dried, discarded sugarcane husks were everywhere.

Use *gur* as a sweetener if you can find it, or substitute dark or light brown sugar. I also like to use the Sucanat brand, which is dried pure sugar cane juice.

Karela (bitter melon or gourd, *Momordica charantia):* I always keep this funny-looking green, wrinkled fruit handy. In North India, it's typically stuffed with spices and baked. *Karela* is coveted for its naturally bitter flavor, which is a bit of an acquired taste. I like it in my morning green juice, and it's fantastic for diabetics because it reduces blood sugar levels. It can also aid digestion and can help clear up some skin conditions. Just be sure to remove and discard the seeds before using.

Oil *(thel):* Whenever I teach a cooking class, the first thing everyone wants to know is what oil I prefer to use. North Indian cooks traditionally use *ghee,* or clarified butter. As people have gravitated toward healthier diets, they've moved away from *ghee* in favor of vegetable oils.

When I was a child, my mother always cooked with oil (usually olive). I recommend using an oil with a clean taste and high smoke point, like grapeseed. You can also choose canola, vegetable, corn, or safflower oils.

South Indian cooks use peanut oil quite a bit. In many North Indian homes, more pungent mustard oil is used for some specific dishes. In Kerala, coconut oil is widely used. In my recipes, I will indicate a specific oil only if it's key to the dish. Otherwise, feel free to experiment. And if you love butter? By all means, incorporate *ghee* into your cooking.

Onions *(pyaz):* Indians love onions—cooked or raw and sprinkled with lemon juice and spices like *kala namak* (black salt) and red chile powder. It's a great thing, because this smelly vegetable is actually rich in a powerful antioxidant called quercetin, which may reduce the risk of cancer by reducing inflammation.

The crunch of raw onion is the perfect accompaniment to an Indian meal. Likewise, cooked onions blend beautifully with cumin seeds, ginger, and garlic.

The best onions for Indian cuisine are yellow and red. White, sweet onions tend to be too sweet for cooking, but they're delicious in raw onion salads. If you find that the onion you're cutting up is a bit too sharp, soak it in water for 15 minutes.

Rice *(chawal)*: Basmati, one of the most coveted varieties of rice in the world, means "fragrant" in Sanskrit. Its grains are thin, slender, and delicious when paired with Indian curries. When cooked, true basmati grains will never stick together—that's the sign of a quality brand.

You can now find quality brown basmati rice on the market as well—and you'll find it's just as delicious. I cook the brown variety during the week and use the white as a treat on weekends. I also like to blend basmati rice with quinoa (see recipe on p. 49), a high-protein seed, which helps cut the carbs and adds protein to our largely vegetarian Indian diet.

Tofu/tempeh/seitan: All fantastic vegan alternatives to meat, these substitutes are delicious as long as you know how to prep them. For soy tofu, be sure to bake it first to achieve the best consistency in curries. Tempeh, a fermented soybean cake, is best when sliced thin and pan-fried. Seitan is made from wheat gluten and has a meatier texture, which some prefer. If you follow a gluten-free diet, you'll obviously want to avoid seitan.

Tomatoes (*tamatar***):** Tomatoes in Indian cuisine are not super sweet. We want tomatoes with a little tartness to add that flavor profile to our cooking. I often use plum tomatoes, which are just the right size and taste for Indian cuisine.

Many of my dishes call for peeled tomatoes, which are easy to prep. The traditional method is to cut an X into the nonstem end of each tomato with a sharp knife and blanch them. To do so, drop them in boiling water for a little less than a minute, until the peel starts to pull away. Pull the tomatoes out of

the water using tongs, drop them in an ice bath, and once they've cooled, they will peel easily. The fastest way to peel tomatoes without blanching is to use a serrated peeler, one of my favorite gadgets.

Yogurt (*dahi*): Indians have a cultural affinity for yogurt. It's present at every meal. The kind we typically eat is homemade and is thinner and more tart than the kind sold in supermarkets. If you are going store-bought, look for unsweetened, plain yogurt. If you have the patience to make it at home (it's not hard—check out my recipe in *The Indian Slow Cooker),* and have an Indian friend who can give you some culture, you'll never, ever go back, and you'll save a ton of money.

The Basics
Spice Blends, Chutneys, Shortcuts, and Beverages

1

I n my cooking classes, I always say that for successful Indian cooking, you should be less concerned about the slicing and dicing and instead stay focused on the spicing. Keeping key spice blends on hand will mean that you can whip up a delicious Indian meal in minutes. Making batches of chutneys ahead of time can also help ensure a delicious, authentic Indian meal in no time. It's not hard to cook Indian food, but it does take a little planning and an understanding that several side dishes are essential to a perfectly complete Indian meal.

In this section, you'll also find suggestions on how to make substitutions for meat and dairy in the recipes that follow. Make a batch of Baked Tofu or Cashew Cream (see recipes on pp. 46 and 47) a few days ahead of time, and you'll be well prepared to tackle all of your weekday meals without a mad scramble.

Tandoori Masala

YIELD: 2 CUPS / 230 G

TOOLS: You'll need a shallow, heavy pan; a plate; a spice grinder or powerful blender, such as a Vitamix; a large mixing bowl; and a whisk.

This is one of the most versatile spice blends. Mix it with yogurt to make a fantastic marinade for virtually any protein before it hits the grill—you can use it to make everything from *tandoori* chicken to tofu. It's also fantastic as a dry rub on meats, sprinkled on fish, or even as a healthy seasoning for popcorn. The nice thing about my version is that it gets its red hue from natural ingredients, rather than red food dye.

1 cup / 40 g whole dried red chiles
½ cup / 40 g coriander seeds
½ cup / 50 g cumin seeds
¼ cup / 35 g whole black peppercorns
¼ cup / 20 g whole cloves
2 tablespoons green cardamom pods
1 tablespoon *ajwain* (carom seeds)

2 teaspoons fenugreek seeds
3 (3-inch / 8-cm) sticks cinnamon
1 heaping tablespoon dried ginger powder
2 teaspoons garlic powder
2 teaspoons turmeric powder
½ cup / 50 g unsmoked paprika

1. Combine the dried chiles, coriander and cumin seeds, peppercorns, cloves, cardamom pods, *ajwain*, fenugreek seeds, and cinnamon in a shallow, heavy pan over medium heat and dry roast the spices for 4 minutes. During the entire cooking time, shake the pan every 15 to 20 seconds to prevent the spices from burning. The mixture should be just toasted and aromatic. Remove from the heat, transfer to a plate, and set aside to cool for 15 minutes.

2. Place the cooled, roasted spices in a spice grinder or a powerful blender, such as a Vitamix, and process into a fine powder. *Take your time, as this may take a few minutes. If your spice grinder is small, you may need to grind it in several small batches.* Sift after grinding to refine the powder or use as is. Transfer to a large mixing bowl.

3. Add the ginger, garlic, turmeric, and paprika to the mixing bowl and whisk to combine. *If you add the turmeric when grinding, it can discolor the blender jug.*

4. Store in an airtight (preferably glass) jar in a cool, dry place for up to 6 months.

Pav Bhaji Masala

YIELD: 2 CUPS / 250 G

TOOLS: You'll need a shallow, heavy pan; a plate; a spice grinder or powerful blender, such as a Vitamix; a large mixing bowl; and a whisk.

This spice blend is necessary to make the beloved Mumbai street food classic *Pav Bhaji* (see recipe on p. 90), a mash of vegetables served on toasted hamburger buns, but you can (and should) use this blend on all kinds of vegetables. Steam your veggies, drizzle them with Cashew Cream (see recipe on p. 47), and sprinkle this *masala* over the whole dish: Voilà! You'll have a simple, delicious meal in no time for the whole family. Substitute this blend for *Garam Masala* or other spice blends in a curry to come up with your own creations.

1 cup / 90 g coriander seeds
⅓ cup / 30 g cumin seeds
⅓ cup / 40 g whole black peppercorns
10 black cardamom pods
¼ cup / 25 g fennel seeds
20 whole dried red chiles

5 (3-inch / 8-cm) sticks cinnamon
6 medium cassia or bay leaves
1 tablespoon whole cloves
1 tablespoon *ajwain* (carom seeds)
1 tablespoon turmeric powder
2 tablespoons *amchur* (dried mango powder)

1. Combine the coriander and cumin seeds, peppercorns, cardamom pods, fennel seeds, dried chiles, cinnamon, cassia leaves, cloves, and *ajwain* in a shallow, heavy pan over medium heat and dry roast the spices for 4 minutes. During the entire cooking time, shake the pan every 15 to 20 seconds to prevent the spices from burning. The mixture should be just toasted and aromatic. Remove from the heat, transfer to a plate, and set aside to cool for 15 minutes.

2. Place the cooled, roasted spices in a spice grinder or a powerful blender, such as a Vitamix, and process into a fine powder. *Take your time, as this may take a few minutes. If your spice grinder is small, you may need to grind it in several small batches.* Sift after grinding to refine the powder or use as is. Transfer to a large mixing bowl.

3. Add the turmeric and *amchur* to the mixing bowl and whisk to combine. *If you add the turmeric when grinding, it can discolor the blender jug.*

4. Store in an airtight (preferably glass) jar in a cool, dry place for up to 6 months.

Garam Masala

YIELD: 2½ CUPS / 300 G

TOOLS: You'll need a shallow, heavy pan; a plate; and a spice grinder or powerful blender, such as a Vitamix.

Garam masala is the quintessential North Indian spice blend. Every household in the region has its own version, and this is my family's take on it. In Hindi, *garam* means "warm" or "hot," and *masala* means a "blend of spices." The combination is a warm, woody taste that adds depth and texture to any dish.

1 cup / 100 g cumin seeds
½ cup / 40 g coriander seeds
¼ cup / 25 g black cardamom pods
12 (3-inch / 8-cm) sticks cinnamon
¼ cup / 20 g whole cloves
¼ cup / 35 g whole black peppercorns

1. Combine all the ingredients in a shallow, heavy pan over medium heat and dry roast the spices for 4 minutes. During the entire cooking time, shake the pan every 15 to 20 seconds to prevent the spices from burning. The mixture should be just toasted and aromatic. Remove from the heat, transfer to a plate, and set aside to cool for 15 minutes.

2. Place the cooled, roasted spices in a spice grinder or a powerful blender, such as a Vitamix, and process into a fine powder. *Take your time, as this may take a few minutes. If your spice grinder is small, you may need to grind it in several small batches.* Sift after grinding to refine the powder or use as is.

3. Store in an airtight (preferably glass) jar in a cool, dry place for up to 6 months.

Chana Masala

YIELD: 1½ CUPS / 190 G

TOOLS: You'll need a shallow, heavy pan; a plate; and a spice grinder or powerful blender, such as a Vitamix.

This is the perfect spice blend for the spicy chickpea curry also called *Chana Masala* (see recipe on p. 152). (It's a little confusing, but the dish and the spice blend go by the same name.) The key to this spice blend is dried pomegranate seed, which lends a distinctive, tasty tartness.

¼ cup / 20 g coriander seeds
¼ cup / 25 g cumin seeds
¼ cup / 30 g *anardana* (dried pomegranate seeds)
2 teaspoons black mustard seeds
2 teaspoons fenugreek seeds
10 whole cloves
2 black cardamom pods
4 green cardamom pods
3 (3-inch / 8-cm) sticks cinnamon
1 teaspoon *ajwain* (carom seeds)
1 tablespoon whole black peppercorns

5 medium cassia or bay leaves, broken into pieces
10 whole dried red chiles, broken into pieces
1 tablespoon *kasoori methi* (dried fenugreek leaves)
2 tablespoons *amchur* (dried mango powder)
1 tablespoon dried ginger powder
1 tablespoon *kala namak* (black salt)

1. Combine the coriander and cumin seeds, *anardana,* mustard and fenugreek seeds, cloves, black and green cardamom pods, cinnamon, *ajwain,* peppercorns, cassia leaves, dried chiles, and *kasoori methi* in a shallow, heavy pan over medium heat and dry roast the spices for 4 minutes. During the entire cooking time, shake the pan every 15 to 20 seconds to prevent the spices from burning. The mixture should be just toasted and aromatic. Remove from the heat, transfer to a plate, and set aside to cool for 15 minutes.

2. Place the cooled, roasted spices in a spice grinder or a powerful blender, such as a Vitamix. Add the *amchur,* ginger, and *kala namak* and process into a fine powder. *Take your time, as this may take a few minutes. If your spice grinder is small, you may need to grind it in several small batches.* Sift after grinding to refine the powder or use as is.

3. Store in an airtight (preferably glass) jar in a cool, dry place for up to 6 months.

Chaat Masala

YIELD: 2 CUPS / 220 G

TOOLS: You'll need a shallow, heavy pan; a plate; and a spice grinder or powerful blender, such as a Vitamix.

Most North Indian street foods get their addictive taste in part from *chaat masala*. It's a delicious combination of tart and spicy that helps elevate the flavor of any fruit or vegetable it's sprinkled on. Use it simply, over cucumbers with lemon juice, or as an interesting boost of flavor on sautéed potatoes. It's a spice blend worth keeping on hand and experimenting with over and over again.

½ heaping cup / 45 g coriander seeds

2 heaping tablespoons cumin seeds

2 heaping tablespoons fennel seeds

8 whole dried red chiles, broken into pieces

½ cup / 70 g whole black peppercorns

2 tablespoons *kala namak* (black salt)

2 heaping teaspoons *amchur* (dried mango powder)

2 heaping teaspoons dried ginger powder

2 heaping teaspoons *ajwain* (carom seeds)

1. Combine the coriander, cumin, and fennel seeds; dried chiles; and peppercorns in a shallow, heavy pan over medium heat and dry roast the spices for 4 minutes. During the entire cooking time, shake the pan every 15 to 20 seconds to prevent the spices from burning. The mixture should be just toasted and aromatic. Remove from the heat, transfer to a plate, and set aside to cool for 15 minutes.

2. Place the cooled, roasted spices in a spice grinder or a powerful blender, such as a Vitamix. Add the *kala namak, amchur,* ginger, and *ajwain* and process into a fine powder. *Take your time, as this may take a few minutes. If your spice grinder is small, you may need to grind it in several small batches.* Sift after grinding to refine the powder or use as is.

3. Store in an airtight (preferably glass) jar in a cool, dry place for up to 6 months.

Sambhar Powder

YIELD: 1 CUP / 188 G

TOOLS: You'll need a shallow, heavy pan; a plate; a spice grinder or power-ful blender, such as a Vitamix; a large mixing bowl; and a whisk.

This is the perfect spice blend to add to the South Indian lentil and veg-etable stew that shares its name, *sambhar*. It's also a great blend to keep on hand when you want to change the flavor profiles of a curry chicken or *dal makhani*. It's also delicious sprinkled over rice or homemade popcorn.

1 tablespoon *dhuli urad* (dried, split, and skinned black *dal*), picked over and washed

1 tablespoon *dhuli moong* (dried, split, and skinned green *dal*), picked over and washed (they look yellow)

¼ cup / 50 g *chana dal*, (dried, split, and skinned gram or black chickpeas), picked over and washed

½ cup / 40 g coriander seeds

½ cup / 40 g whole dried red chiles, broken into pieces

½ cup / 10 g firmly packed fresh curry leaves

1 heaping tablespoon cumin seeds

1 heaping tablespoon black mustard seeds

1 tablespoon fenugreek seeds

2 (3-inch / 8-cm) sticks cinnamon

20 whole black peppercorns

1 heaping tablespoon white poppy seeds

3 tablespoons / 20 g turmeric powder

1. Combine all the ingredients, except the turmeric, in a shallow, heavy pan over medium heat and dry roast the spices for 7 minutes. *It is very important to start with the* dals, *so they remain closest to the heat and cook thoroughly.* During the entire cooking time, shake the pan every 15 to 20 seconds to prevent the spices from burning. *You have to be extra careful with the poppy seeds, which can burn easily. They can also be added at the end of the cook time.* The *dals* should be slight-ly brown, the curry leaves should start to curl, and the spices should be aromatic. Remove from the heat, transfer to a plate, and set aside to cool for 15 minutes.

2. Place the cooled, roasted ingredients in a spice grinder or a powerful blender, such as a Vitamix, and process into a fine powder. *Take your time, as this may take a few minutes. If your spice grinder is small, you may need to grind it in several small batches.* Sift after grinding to refine the powder or use as is. Transfer to a large mixing bowl.

3. Add the turmeric to the mixing bowl and whisk to combine. *If you add the turmeric when grinding, it can discolor the blender jug.*

4. Store in an airtight (preferably glass) jar in a cool, dry place for up to 6 months.

Chai Masala

YIELD: ¾ CUP / 140 G

TOOLS: You'll need a spice grinder or a powerful blender, such as a Vitamix.

Chai is very easy to make once you have the right spices on hand. This is also a great blend of flavors to cook and bake with. Mix it into pies, muffins, or cookies, or sprinkle it over baked potatoes and even spiced nuts. My girls even bake it into Indian flatbreads and sprinkle it into their soup concoctions. Talk about fusion!

1 tablespoon whole black peppercorns
9 (3-inch / 8-cm) sticks cinnamon
1 tablespoon whole cloves
½ teaspoon fennel seeds

2 tablespoons whole green cardamom pods
3 black cardamom pods
2 tablespoons dried ginger powder

1. Combine all the ingredients in a spice grinder or a powerful blender, such as a Vitamix, and process into a fine powder. *Take your time, as this may take a few minutes. If your spice grinder is small, you may need to grind it in several small batches.* Sift after grinding to refine the powder or use as is.

2. Store in an airtight (preferably glass) jar in a cool, dry place for up to 6 months. *I always add a pinch of turmeric to my chai if someone in the house has a cold.*

TO MAKE *CHAI* (TEA): To make traditional *chai*, place 1 teaspoon of this mix (or more if you prefer), 4 cups / 950 mL boiling water, 2 black tea bags, ½ cup / 120 mL milk or milk alternative, and honey or agave nectar, to taste, in a medium saucepan over medium–high heat. Bring to a boil and allow to boil for 3 to 4 minutes. Remove from the heat. Remove and discard the tea bags, strain, and serve immediately, piping hot. For richer flavor, add grated or thinly sliced ginger while the mixture is boiling.

Bhuna Jeera
Roasted
Ground Cumin

YIELD: 1 CUP / 100 G

TOOLS: You'll need a shallow, heavy pan; a plate; a spice grinder, mortar and pestle, or powerful blender, such as a Vitamix; and a large mixing bowl.

NOTE: If you don't have a grinder, a powerful blender, or a mortar and pestle, you can place the roasted whole cumin seeds between 2 paper towels or dish towels and roll over the top sheet with a rolling pin. Press hard and continue to roll until the seeds are crushed into a fine powder. This is best done in small batches.

Roasted cumin seeds have a uniquely nutty flavor that is the key to a perfectly spiced *raita* or yogurt. It's also essential to many Indian street foods. I often roast a batch, store it whole, and then grind it up as needed so that it's as fresh as possible.

1 cup / 100 g cumin seeds

1. Combine the cumin seeds in a shallow, heavy pan over medium heat and dry roast for 3 minutes, until the cumin seeds are reddish-brown. During the entire cooking time, shake the pan constantly to prevent burning (just like roasting pine nuts). *The key here is to never step away, so the seeds don't burn.* The mixture should be just toasted and aromatic. *If they burn (and it's OK—I've been there many times) discard them and start again.* Remove from the heat, transfer to a plate, and set aside to cool for 15 minutes.

2. Place the cooled, roasted seeds in a spice grinder, mortar and pestle, or a powerful blender, such as a Vitamix, and process into a fine powder. *Take your time, as this may take a few minutes. If your spice grinder is small, you may need to grind it in several small batches.* Sift after grinding to refine the powder or use as is. Transfer to a large mixing bowl.

3. Store in an airtight (preferably glass) jar in a cool, dry place for up to 6 months.

Pudina ki **Chutney** Mint Chutney

YIELD: 2 CUPS / 470 ML

TOOLS: You'll need a blender (a Vita-mix works best) or food processor.

NOTE: Add 1 bunch of fresh cilantro to make Mint–Cilantro Chutney. A spoonful of yogurt or cream added to the mix will give it some extra tanginess.

PICTURED ON P. 30

If you love Indian cuisine, you're familiar with mint chutney, which is found at the side of most North Indian meals. What you likely *don't* know is how incredibly easy it is to make. Whip it up over the weekend and it will last you through the week. Eat it as we did when we were little, layered over a slice of buttered bread.

4 cups / 80 g packed fresh mint leaves, leaves removed and stems discarded
1 small yellow or red onion, roughly chopped
1 (1-inch / 3-cm) piece ginger, peeled and roughly chopped
1 clove garlic, peeled
1–3 fresh Thai, serrano, or cayenne chiles, stems removed

1 teaspoon salt
1 teaspoon red chile powder or cayenne pepper
1 teaspoon *gur* (jaggery) or light brown sugar
Juice of 1 lemon
1–2 tablespoons water (optional)

1. Combine all the ingredients, except the water, in a blender or food processor and blend until smooth.

2. If you prefer the chutney to be even smoother, add the water.

3. Store in an airtight (preferably glass) jar in the refrigerator for up to 1 week.

Imlee ki **Chutney** Tamarind– Date Chutney

YIELD: 2 CUPS / 470 ML

TOOLS: You'll need a heavy-bottomed, 4-quart / 4-L sauté pan and a blender.

PICTURED ON P. 31

This dark brown, sweet chutney is delicious especially when paired with street foods and snacks like *samosas* and spinach *pakoras*. Make it ahead of time and keep it on hand for up to 2 weeks. It goes especially well when paired with mint chutney and is delicious with lamb or beef as well.

3 cups / 710 mL tamarind juice*
1 cup / 150 g pitted dates, roughly chopped
¾ cup / 170 g *gur (jaggery)* or dark brown sugar
1 tablespoon grated ginger
½ teaspoon *kala namak* (black salt)
1 teaspoon salt

1 teaspoon red chile powder or cayenne pepper
1 teaspoon *Garam Masala* (see recipe on p. 35)
2 teaspoons roasted cumin, ground (see *Bhuna Jeera* recipe on p. 40)

1. Combine the tamarind juice, dates, *gur,* and ginger in a heavy-bottomed, 4-quart / 4-L sauté pan over medium–high heat and bring the mixture to a boil.

2. Reduce the heat to medium and simmer, uncovered, for 15 minutes. Remove from the heat.

3. Once the mixture is cool enough to handle, transfer to a blender and process until smooth.

4. Return the mixture to the sauté pan over medium–high heat and add the *kala namak,* salt, red chile powder, *Garam Masala,* and cumin. Stir well and bring to a boil.

5. Reduce the heat to medium–low and simmer for 2 minutes, until the mixture thickens and large, sticky bubbles start to form on the surface. Stir well. Remove from the heat and set aside to cool for 10 minutes.

6. Store in an airtight (preferably glass) jar in the refrigerator for up to 2 weeks.

*To make the tamarind juice, place 1 (7-ounce / 200-g) block of dried tamarind and 6 cups / 1.4 L of boiling water in a deep bowl and soak for at least 1 hour. With the back of a fork, break apart as much of the pulp as possible and then squeeze the water out of the pulp. Discard the pulp and strain the liquid through cheesecloth or a strainer. Use part of it for the chutney and store the rest for later.

Coconut Chutney

YIELD: 2 CUPS / 470 ML

TOOLS: You'll need a shallow, heavy pan; a powerful blender, such as a Vitamix; and a large mixing bowl.

PICTURED ON P. 30

No South Indian meal is complete without coconut chutney. Freshly grated coconut is best but is hard to find. The best substitute is frozen grated coconut from an Indian grocer. If you are not close to an Indian grocer, use dried, unsweetened, grated coconut from your grocer's baking aisle. My version includes mint and cilantro. For a more authentic South Indian version, omit both.

1 tablespoon *chana dal* (dried, split, and skinned gram or black chickpeas), picked over and washed
1 cup / 240 mL boiling water
2 cups / 160 g fresh unsweetened grated coconut
1 (1-inch / 3-cm) piece ginger, peeled and coarsely chopped
1–2 fresh Thai, serrano, or cayenne chiles, stems removed
6–7 mint leaves

1 tablespoon chopped fresh cilantro
1 teaspoon salt
1 teaspoon red chile powder or cayenne pepper
1¼ cups / 300 mL room-temperature water
2 tablespoons vegetable oil (I use peanut)
1 teaspoon black mustard seeds
5–6 curry leaves, roughly chopped
3 whole dried red chiles

1. Combine the *chana dal* in a shallow, heavy pan over medium–high heat and dry roast for 1 to 2 minutes. During the entire cooking time, shake the pan every 15 to 20 seconds to prevent burning. The *chana dal* should be slightly brown. Remove from the heat, cover with boiling water, and set aside to soften.

2. In a powerful blender, such as a Vitamix, combine the coconut, ginger, fresh chiles, mint, cilantro, drained *chana dal,* salt, red chile powder, and room-temperature water and blend until smooth. Transfer to a large mixing bowl.

3. Return the pan used in Step 1 to medium–high heat and warm the oil. Add the mustard seeds, curry leaves, and dried chiles and cook for 40 seconds, until lightly browned. Remove from the heat.

4. Add the contents of the pan to the mixing bowl and stir gently until combined.

5. Store in an airtight (preferably glass) jar in the refrigerator for up to 2 weeks. Serve as a side to any meal, especially with *Dosa* and *Idli* (see recipes on pp. 253 and 258).

Paneer

YIELD: 2 CUPS / 470 ML OF 1-INCH /
3-CM CUBES

TOOLS: You'll need a heavy-bottomed,
6-quart / 6-L (and preferably nonstick) saucepan with a lid; a small
spatula; a colander; a large mixing
bowl; a 2½- × 1½-foot / 75- × 45-cm
piece of double-lined cheesecloth; a
long-handled strainer; a large plate; a
heavy plate or cutting board; various
cans and pots, for pressing; a large,
wide spatula; and a sharp knife or
pizza cutter.

NOTE: Instead of the buttermilk,
you can use ½ cup / 120 mL plain,
unsweetened yogurt plus 2 tablespoons of fresh lemon juice. I find that
buttermilk makes a slightly thicker
paneer. Experiment with both options.
Don't get discouraged if this takes
time to perfect. I have been making
paneer for years, and sometimes it
still doesn't work out perfectly. If it's
too watery, you can blend it up with
a curry and pour it over your meat
or vegetables—I once had to do that
ahead of time for a very large dinner
party, and it ended up being the
crowd favorite.

Homemade cubed cheese is a staple of the North Indian diet, providing
much-needed protein for vegetarians. Make a big batch and freeze half of it
for use later. It's great in curries or stuffed in *samosas,* or fry it up as a snack
for the kids after school. Making *paneer* is not hard, but it takes patience to
squeeze out all the moisture.

½ gallon / 2 L whole or 2% milk | 1½ cups / 350 mL regular or
reduced-fat buttermilk

1. In a heavy-bottomed, 6-quart / 6-L saucepan over medium heat, warm the
milk. Bring to a slow boil and reduce the heat to medium–low. *Keeping the heat
low is important. If the milk boils too fast, it can burn. Stir it slowly and occasionally to ensure it does not stick to the pot. Using a nonstick pot helps.*

2. The moment the milk starts to boil and foam starts to rise, reduce the heat to
the lowest setting possible and add the buttermilk. As the milk begins to separate, use a small spatula to slowly pull the curds away from the sides of the pan.
*I like to leave the rest of the curds intact in the middle so that they form a nice solid
layer on top of the whey.* Stir gently and cook for 2 to 3 minutes, until the milk
separates completely. *Some recipes recommend turning the heat off immediately
after the milk boils. I find it helps to keep the heat on and continue stirring gently.
The milk will start to separate immediately, but you want it to separate completely,
which takes an extra few minutes.*

3. Once solid-looking curds form and the remaining liquid (whey) looks thin
and watery, turn the heat off, cover the pan completely, and allow to cool
slightly for 10 to 15 minutes. *If you have a gas stove, leave it on the same burner
on which you cooked it. If you have an electric stove and if the coils remain hot,
remove the pot from the burner. Excessive heat can burn the bottom of the pot.*

4. Place a colander in a large mixing bowl and lay a 2½- × 1½-foot / 75- × 45-cm
piece of double-lined cheesecloth inside it. Drape the ends of the cheesecloth
over the sides of the colander so you can twist them easily. Using a long-handled
strainer, gently scoop up pieces of the curds and transfer them to the cheesecloth-
lined colander. Continue until you have transferred all of the curds—scrape the
bottom of the pan to pick up any remaining curds. *I prefer doing this to dump-
ing the entire mixture into the cheesecloth, which can be messy. You can discard the
whey, or reserve it to add to curries later. Freeze it if you're not using it right away.*
Set the colander aside to allow the curds to cool and slowly drain the remaining
liquid for 15 minutes.

5. Gather all sides of the cheesecloth and tie the bundle into a knot as close to the cheese as possible. Squeeze as hard as you can in order to extract as much moisture as possible from the curds. Be careful—the curds may still be hot. *When I was younger, my mother would hang the cheesecloth on the faucet all day so that the liquid would slowly drip away into the sink. I press the curds to speed up the process.*

6. Remove the *paneer* from the cheesecloth (discard the cheesecloth) and place it on a large plate. *I prefer to use a large, stainless steel Indian* thali, *which has raised edges that prevent liquid runoff.* Place a heavy plate or cutting board on top of the *paneer* and a heavy pot or flat-bottomed skillet on top of the plate. Next, stack large, heavy unopened cans (I use canned tomatoes) inside the pot. *No need to open the cans. They are for stacking only. Keep adding weight if you can keep it balanced—I use up to 15 pounds / 6.8 kg.* Set aside to drain for at least 2 to 3 hours.

7. Remove the weights and drain any remaining moisture from the plate containing the *paneer.* Place the plate in the freezer for 15 minutes. *My Yog* mamaji *(uncle) taught my mom this trick, which helps set the cheese so you can cut it easily later.*

8. Using a large, wide spatula, carefully transfer the *paneer* (now a disc roughly 6 inches / 15 cm wide) from the plate to a cutting board. Cut into 1-inch / 3-cm cubes with a sharp knife or pizza cutter. You can also crumble and store to use later either in curries or as a fun topping for any Indian dish.

9. Use immediately or transfer to an airtight container and store in the refrigerator for up to 1 week. You can also freeze it for up to 3 months.

Baked Tofu

YIELD: 2 CUPS / 470 ML OF 1-INCH /
3-CM CUBES

TOOLS: You'll need a baking sheet,
a wire rack, a cutting board, and a
sharp knife.

Most Indians I know turn up their noses at tofu whenever I talk about adding it to an Indian dish. But when I make them a curry with baked tofu, they usually devour it (all the men in my life would fall into this category). The key is to get the right consistency. The firmer the tofu, the better it holds up in an Indian curry, and the more it starts to taste like *paneer,* only lighter. Try it yourself and you'll likely find your toughest critics in line for seconds.

Vegetable oil, for greasing
1 (14-ounce / 400-g) package
   extra-firm organic tofu, sliced into
   ½-inch-thick / 1-cm-thick slices
   (I find that organic tofu has better
   consistency and flavor)

Salt, as needed (optional)
Garam Masala (see recipe on p. 35),
   as needed (optional)

1. Set the oven rack at the highest position, preheat the oven to 400°F / 200°C, and lightly oil a baking sheet.

2. Place the tofu slices on the baking sheet and spray their tops with oil. Bake for 40 minutes, flipping the pieces over after the first 20 minutes of cooking time. *Cook longer if you want the tofu to be crispier. Also, if you want to add flavor, sprinkle the tofu with a little salt and* Garam Masala *on both sides before cooking.* Remove from the oven. Remove the tofu from the pan and set on a wire rack to cool.

3. Transfer the tofu to a cutting board and slice into 1-inch / 3-cm cubes.

4. Use the tofu immediately or store in an airtight container in the refrigerator for up to 1 week. You can also freeze it for up to 3 months.

Cashew Cream

YIELD: 2½ CUPS / 590 ML

TOOLS: You'll need a powerful blender, such as a Vitamix.

Cashew cream is one of the best vegan substitutes for dairy. Use it to add robust flavor to a lentil dish, to give some depth to your *Rajmah* (see recipe on p. 126), or in place of dairy in your *Chicken Makhani* (see recipe on p. 193). I use it to make Italian alfredo sauce and often just drizzle it over steamed vegetables. It's the best way to add a little nutrition while taking dairy out of a meal.

1 cup / 140 g raw cashews, soaked overnight and drained

1¼ cups / 300 mL water, plus more as needed

1. Place the cashews in a powerful blender, such as a Vitamix. Add the water and blend on the highest speed until the mixture becomes smooth and creamy. *If it's still too thick, add more water, 1 tablespoon at a time.*

2. Use immediately or transfer to an airtight container and store in the refrigerator for up to 2 weeks.

Jeera Chawal
Cumin Rice

YIELD: 8 CUPS / 1.9 L

TOOLS: You'll need a heavy-bottomed, 4- or 6-quart / 4- or 6-L stockpot or Dutch oven with a lid.

NOTE: You can also substitute brown rice—just increase the amount of water to 5 cups / 1.2 L and cook, partially covered, for 13 minutes. When finshed, cover completely, turn the heat off, and let it sit for at least 5 minutes. When we make everyday rice at home, we often omit the onion.

PICTURED ON P. 31

This is a recipe for the most basic rice accompaniment to North Indian meals. My mom cooked it nearly every day for me when I was growing up. She also made *roti* for everyone else, but I always preferred rice to bread.

1 tablespoon vegetable oil
1 heaping teaspoon cumin seeds
4 whole cloves
2 black cardamom pods
1 (3-inch / 8-cm) stick cinnamon

1 small yellow onion, thinly sliced
2 cups / 370 g uncooked white
 basmati rice, washed
½ teaspoon salt
4 cups / 950 mL water

1. In a heavy-bottomed, 4- or 6-quart / 4- or 6-L stockpot or Dutch oven over medium–high heat, warm the oil. Add the cumin seeds, cloves, cardamom, and cinnamon and cook for 40 seconds, until the cumin seeds sizzle and turn reddish-brown.

2. Add the onion and sauté, stirring occasionally, for 2 minutes, until the onion has slightly browned and is opaque. Add the rice and salt and sauté for 1 minute, stirring gently to ensure the rice does not stick to the bottom of the pot. Add the water and bring to a boil.

3. Reduce the heat to low, partially cover, and simmer for 8 minutes, until the moisture just evaporates. Remove from the heat and set aside, fully covered, for at least 5 minutes. *I find that this step really helps the rice absorb the extra moisture and fluffs it up.*

4. Remove and discard the whole spices and fluff the rice with a fork before serving. *You can also leave the whole spices in as a decorative touch, as long as your guests know not to chomp down on them.*

5. Transfer to a serving bowl and use immediately or transfer to an airtight container and store in the refrigerator for up to 1 week.

Brown Rice–Quinoa *Palau*

YIELD: 6 CUPS / 1.4 L

TOOLS: You'll need a large strainer and a heavy-bottomed, 3-quart / 3-L stockpot with a lid.

In our house, we like to eat healthy and gravitate toward plant-based proteins. Quinoa, a high-protein seed, is just about the perfect source of protein, and it's whole-family friendly when it's hidden away in rice. Use white quinoa if you want it to blend in, or the multicolored variety if you want a prettier dish. When the family gobbles it up with their curry or *dal,* you'll do as I do—sit back and smile.

1 cup / 190 g uncooked brown basmati rice, washed	1 cup / 170 g white quinoa 3½ cups / 830 mL water

1. In a large strainer, rinse the rice and quinoa. *Quinoa sometimes has a bitter coating that has to be rinsed off, so this step is important. Some brands come pre-rinsed. Check the package.*

2. Combine all the ingredients in a heavy-bottomed, 3-quart / 3-L stockpot over medium–high heat and bring to a boil.

3. Reduce the heat to low, partially cover the pot, and simmer for 15 minutes, until the moisture evaporates. Remove from the heat and set aside, fully covered, for at least 5 minutes. *I find that this step really helps the rice absorb the extra moisture and fluffs it up.*

4. Transfer to a serving bowl and use immediately in your favorite curries and stir-fries or transfer to an airtight container and store in the refrigerator for up to 1 week. *I like to freeze a batch to always have this mix on hand; it can be stored frozen for up to 3 months.*

Kheera Raita
Cucumber Yogurt

YIELD: 2 CUPS / 470 ML

TOOLS: You'll need a large, deep mixing bowl and a whisk.

VEGANIZE IT! It's hard to replicate the taste of dairy yogurt, but you can substitute plain, unsweetened soy or coconut yogurt. Just add the juice of a ½ lemon for tartness.

PICTURED ON P. 31

Growing up, we always required yogurt on the side of our meal to help cool the fieriness of the curries on our plate. A good *raita* takes yogurt one step further with spices and chopped or grated veggies. My kids take turns deciding what to put in their yogurt. Try everything from grated cucumber to carrots, zucchini, or even boiled potato.

2 cups / 470 mL plain, unsweetened yogurt
1 tablespoon milk or water, plus more as needed
1 small cucumber, peeled and grated
1 teaspoon roasted cumin, ground
¼ teaspoon *kala namak* (black salt)
¼ teaspoon red chile powder or cayenne pepper
¼ teaspoon ground black pepper
¾ teaspoon salt

1. In a large, deep mixing bowl, combine the yogurt and milk and whisk until smooth. *I find store-bought yogurt to be too thick, and like to add water or milk to thin it out a bit, so feel free to use more than the 1 tablespoon if you like. If you are using homemade yogurt, there is no need to do this; Indians prefer thinner, tangier, homemade yogurt.*

2. Add the remaining ingredients to the bowl and whisk again until well blended. *Some like to squeeze the moisture out of the cucumber before adding it, but I prefer the extra moisture.*

3. Transfer to a serving bowl and use immediately or transfer to an airtight container and store in the refrigerator for up to 3 days. *To make this restaurant-style, add 1 teaspoon of* Pudina ki *Chutney (see recipe on p. 41).*

North Indian Onion Salad

YIELD: 4 SERVINGS

TOOLS: You'll need a large, deep mixing bowl.

PICTURED ON P. 31

Most Indian food lovers don't realize that North Indians—especially Punjabis—cannot and will not eat their dinner without raw, spiced salads on the side. We need that extra crunch and texture with every bite. I always ask waiters to make me a plate, and even go and cut my own at Indian friends' houses if they happen to overlook this cardinal rule. Our typical salads include onion, cucumber, and tomatoes, with whole green chiles on the side. I'm giving you just the onion version, but feel free to add the rest and adjust the spices.

1 large yellow, red, or white onion, sliced in thin rings
Juice of 1 lemon
½ teaspoon salt
½ teaspoon *kala namak* (black salt)

½ teaspoon red chile powder or cayenne pepper
½ teaspoon *Chaat Masala* (optional; see recipe on p. 37)

1. In a large, deep mixing bowl, submerge the onion in water. Set aside to soak for 15 minutes. Drain and pat the onion dry. *This step removes bitterness.*

2. Return the onion to the bowl and add all the remaining ingredients. Mix until well combined.

3. Transfer to a serving bowl and serve immediately as a side salad. *Be prepared to hear "I call the water!" from your kids. My girls fight over the spicy lemon water left over at the bottom of the bowl.*

Kachumber
Indian Salsa

YIELD: 5 CUPS / 1.2 L

TOOLS: You'll need a large, deep mixing bowl.

PICTURED ON P. 31

This easy salad is traditionally served as a side at Indian meals, but it's versatile. Use it more creatively as a stand-in to Mexican salsa with chips, or on top of a *dal* or black bean soup with a touch of sour cream.

1 large yellow or red onion, diced
4 medium tomatoes, diced
4 medium cucumbers, peeled
  and diced
1–3 fresh Thai, serrano, or cayenne
  chiles, stems removed, finely
  sliced

Juice of 2 limes
¼ cup / 5 g fresh cilantro, chopped
1 teaspoon salt
1 teaspoon *kala namak* (black salt)
1 teaspoon red chile powder or
  cayenne pepper

1. In a large, deep mixing bowl, combine all the ingredients and mix well.

2. Transfer to a serving bowl and serve immediately. *Keep in mind that like any other combination of lime juice and tomatoes, this salad doesn't have a very long shelf life.*

Mom's Morning Cleanse

YIELD: 1½ CUPS / 350 ML

NOTE: Eat the fenugreek seeds that drift to the bottom of the mug at the end—they will be soft by then. I keep a spoon in the cup to stir as I go in case the turmeric settles. *My mother insists that the pinch of sugar boosts your brain activity in the morning. If you're feeling really ambitious, do as I do and add a couple pieces of dried* amla *(Indian gooseberry) to give you a vitamin C boost, too.*

I always give credit where it is due, and this recipe is my mother's. She has been making us drink this concoction for years—despite our protests. I finally listened and tried it in my own home. Now, my husband and I are addicted. Drink it first thing in the morning on an empty stomach and you'll flush your liver of toxins with the lemon juice, boost your immune system with the turmeric, boost your metabolism with the red chile powder, and help suppress your appetite with the fenugreek seeds.

Juice of 1 small lemon (fresh is best)
¼–½ teaspoon turmeric powder
¼ teaspoon red chile powder or cayenne pepper
½–1 teaspoon dried fenugreek seeds
Pinch of raw cane sugar, such as Sucanat (optional)
1½ cups / 350 mL boiling water

1. Combine all the ingredients in the order listed above in a large mug. Stir well and drink up.

Indian as Apple Pie Green Juice Smoothie

YIELD: 4 CUPS / 950 ML

TOOLS: You'll need a powerful blender, such as a Vitamix.

3 stalks kale, cleaned and trimmed (discard hard inner vein)
½ small cucumber, peeled and trimmed
1 (1-inch / 3-cm) piece *karela* (bitter melon), skin-on and deseeded* (optional)
5–6 sprigs parsley
1 small carrot, cleaned and trimmed
1 (1½-inch / 4-cm) piece fresh turmeric, peeled
1 (2-inch / 5-cm) piece ginger, peeled
2 small key limes or 1 regular lime, peeled
3 pineapple chunks
1 tangerine, peeled
1 clove garlic, peeled
1 tablespoon flax seeds
5 ice cubes
3 cups / 710 mL cold water

1. Combine all the ingredients in the order listed above in a powerful blender, such as a Vitamix, and blend at the highest setting for 2 to 3 minutes, until completely smooth and slightly frothy. *If you don't have a Vitamix, you can make this in any quality blender, but you may need to add more water to help smooth it out. Remember, this is more of a smoothie than juice from a juicer—it still has pulp and fiber, so it's a little thick.*

2. Transfer to serving glasses and serve immediately or store in the refrigerator for up to 2 days. *This makes enough for my family to have a little as well. I keep leftovers in a glass in the fridge to sip throughout the day or the next morning. After 2 days, it will start to get bitter.*

*Although bitter melon has many amazing healing properties, it can have adverse effects for people on diabetes medication. Please consult your doctor before adding it to your regular diet.

Neha's *Chai* Spiced Indian Tea

YIELD: 4 CUPS / 950 ML

TOOLS: You'll need a mortar and pestle, a medium pot, and a strainer.

PICTURED ON P. 31

As a young girl, I associated waking up on the weekends with a cup of steaming, fragrant *chai*. It was my job to make it for my parents, and I took my task very seriously. Now my girls make it for me. Neha, my older daughter, has been making *chai* since she was four and loves it with extra cardamom. It's what good *chai* should be—a perfect balance of spice, milk, and sweetness. It's a shame that in the West, *chai* is associated with syrup and layers of sugar. I've only had it that way in Indian train stations. In Indian homes, the *chai* is just kissed with a hint of honey or sweetener.

20 green cardamom pods (yes, 20!)
6 whole cloves
4 whole black peppercorns
1 (3-inch / 8-cm) stick cinnamon
1 (2-inch / 5-cm) piece ginger, peeled and thinly sliced or grated
4 cups / 950 mL water
2 black tea bags or 2 tablespoons loose tea

½ cup / 120 mL milk or milk alternative (soy, almond, or hemp)
2–4 teaspoons granulated or raw cane sugar, such as Sucanat; honey; or agave nectar (plus more, to taste)

1. Using a mortar and pestle, grind the cardamom, cloves, and peppercorns into a powder. *Enlist the kids—they love this part. Using a lot of cardamom is key to this version of* chai, *but if your tastes differ, feel free to tone it down.*

2. In a medium pot over medium–high heat, combine the freshly ground spices (retain the broken cardamom husks), the cinnamon, the ginger, the water, and the tea. Bring to a boil.

3. Reduce the heat to medium–low and simmer, uncovered, for 3 minutes.

4. Raise the heat to medium–high, add the milk, and bring to a boil. Allow the mixture to boil for 2 minutes. Remove from the heat, cover, and set aside for 1 minute.

5. Strain the contents of the pot into 4 mugs. Add ½ to 1 teaspoon of the sugar to each mug and serve.

Mango *Lassi*

YIELD: 8 SERVINGS

TOOLS: You'll need a powerful blender, such as a Vitamix.

NOTE: You can also make this *lassi* an "adult" drink by adding 2 to 3 ounces / 60 to 90 mL of vodka or rum.

VEGANIZE IT! This is so simple to make vegan! Just substitute soy or coconut yogurt and milk alternatives for the dairy yogurt and milk. I make it vegan-style for many of my cooking classes, and no one misses the dairy!

I love *lassi*. It's a delicious drink that is at once tart and refreshing. Though most Indian home cooks make theirs as a thin and savory drink, many restaurants offer this sweeter version.

2 cups / 470 mL plain, unsweetened yogurt
1 cup / 240 mL milk
3 cups / 500 g fresh or frozen mango, diced
1 teaspoon cardamom seeds
1–3 cups / 140–420 g crushed ice (as needed)

2–3 tablespoons granulated or raw cane sugar, such as Sucanat, or agave nectar
8 mint leaves, for garnish
1 teaspoon ground pistachios, for garnish

1. In a powerful blender, such as a Vitamix, combine all the ingredients except the mint leaves and pistachios in the order listed above. Process at the highest setting for 2 to 3 minutes, until completely smooth and slightly frothy.

2. Transfer to 8 glasses and garnish each with a mint leaf and a pinch of the pistachios. Serve immediately.

Street Foods and Snacks

India has some of the best and most delicious street food traditions in the world. I still remember visiting as a little girl and begging my grandfather to let me eat from the carts of vendors lined up in the dusty market of his village, Bhikhi.

The carts were loaded with fried mini *puris* stuffed with potatoes and dunked in spicy water, crispy stuffed *samosas* plated with spiced chutneys, and even chopped fruit doused with lemon juice and *chaat masala* arranged in little paper bowls with toothpicks as utensils.

The only thing that held my cousins (Papla, Sunil, Dolly, and Vickie) and me back from ruining every meal with these tempting snacks were my grandmother's threats that we—especially me with my American tummy—would get sick. It was a real deterrent, because not only was it always true, it would keep me in bed for most of my visit.

So, knowing my obsession with street foods, my aunts would make them for me at home. Suraj *massi* (my mom's sister) would fry up hundreds of little *puris* for *papdi chaat,* while my Sheela *bua* (my dad's sister)—using just a few ingredients—would roll out fresh *samosa* dough and have us dunking and eating in no time. I shamelessly put both to work on their respective trips to America. But they loved doing it— both were the best cooks on either side of the family.

I still have my obsession with street foods, so conquering all of the recipes in this section brought back countless food memories. I won't lie to you—you will

have to work to make Indian street food. Although most Indian cuisine is very easy to make, these snacks have so many little components that they often take time, energy, and planning to make perfectly. To get a head start, make the chutneys from the previous section (*Pudina ki* and *Imlee ki,* see recipes on pp. 41 and 42) ahead of time. But don't worry! With my clear instructions, you can do it. Take it from me—the effort is more than worth it. My young girls are growing up in America, but they have as much of an appreciation and obsession for Indian snack foods as I do. It's history repeating itself—minus all the bellyaches.

Vegetable *Samosas*

YIELD: 20 MEDIUM *SAMOSAS*

TOOLS: You'll need a deep mixing bowl; a sifter; plastic wrap; a heavy-bottomed, 4-quart / 4-L sauté pan with a lid; a damp cloth; a rolling pin; a knife or pizza cutter; a small bowl filled with water; a baking sheet; a small *kadhai*, wok, or saucepan; a slotted spoon, and a wire rack.

NOTE: The type of flour used is key. Most *samosa* recipes call for all-purpose flour, but I find that 100% whole-wheat *chapati* flour, a stone-milled, durum whole-wheat flour, works just fine. See my notes on *chapati* flour on p. 26. To save time, you can also freeze the stuffed but uncooked *samosas*. Simply take them out of the freezer a day or so before your party, defrost them completely, and fry them to perfection.

Samosas are known the world over. Ask anyone from England to the Caribbean about them, and you'll inspire daydreams of these stuffed and fried fritters. Make the filling and dough ahead of time and stuff them a day later for an easier time. Better yet—ask your kids to help stuff them. They'll have a ball.

FOR THE DOUGH:
2 cups / 280 g whole-wheat *chapati* flour
1 tablespoon rice flour (optional)
1 teaspoon salt
¼ cup / 60 mL vegetable oil
⅔ cup / 160 mL lukewarm water

FOR THE FILLING:
1 tablespoon vegetable oil
1 teaspoon cumin seeds
1 teaspoon turmeric powder
1 small yellow onion, minced
1 fresh Thai, serrano, or cayenne chile, stem removed and minced
1 large russet potato, peeled, finely diced, immersed in water until ready to use, and drained

½ cup / 75 g peas, fresh or frozen
1 teaspoon *Garam Masala* (see recipe on p. 35)
1 teaspoon ground coriander
1 teaspoon red chile powder or cayenne pepper
1 teaspoon *amchur* (dried mango powder)
1 teaspoon salt
1 tablespoon *kasoori methi* (dried fenugreek leaves), lightly hand crushed to release flavor
2 cups / 470 mL vegetable oil, optional, if frying

TO MAKE THE DOUGH:

1. In a deep mixing bowl, sift together the flours and salt. *The rice flour helps make* samosas *a little crispier.* Add the oil to the bowl. Using your hands, gradually mix in the oil until the dough becomes slightly crumbly.

2. Add the water. Using your hands, knead the dough until all the ingredients come together into a smooth ball. *If the dough is a little wet and sticky, add a little more flour. If it's too hard, add a little more oil.*

3. Tightly wrap the dough in plastic wrap so it does not dry out. Set aside for at least 30 minutes while you prep the filling.

TO MAKE THE FILLING:

1. In a heavy-bottomed, 4-quart / 4-L sauté pan over medium–high heat, warm the oil. Add the cumin seeds and cook for 40 seconds, until the cumin seeds sizzle and turn reddish-brown. Add the turmeric, onion, and fresh chile. Cook, stirring occasionally to prevent sticking, for 2 minutes, until the onion is slightly opaque.

2. Add the remaining ingredients, except the oil, in the order listed above. Cook, stirring occasionally, for 2 to 3 minutes. *Be careful to work quickly, as the ingredients can burn easily—the slight moisture from the potatoes will help. If you need more moisture, add 1 tablespoon of water.*

3. Reduce the heat to low and partially cover the pan. Cook, stirring frequently, for 5 minutes, until the potatoes soften. Remove from the heat, remove the cover, and set aside to cool. *The mixture must be completely cool before stuffing the* samosas, *or the dough will soften.*

TO ASSEMBLE AND COOK THE *SAMOSAS:*

1. Divide the dough into 10 balls and roll them between your hands until they are as smooth as possible. *Cover them with a damp cloth or paper towel as you work so they don't dry out.* Flatten out each ball with the palms of your hands.

2. On a clean, dry, and flat work surface, use a lightly oiled rolling pin to roll out 1 ball into a thin 6-inch-wide / 15-cm-wide round. *The thinner it is, the crispier it will be. The dough contains a good bit of oil, so you should be able to work with it easily.* Pull the round up and turn it without adding any flour to the work surface. *To make cocktail-sized* samosas, *roll the dough out to half this size and follow the steps below, using only ½ as much filling.*

3. With a knife or a pizza cutter, slice 1 round exactly in half, making 2 semicircles. *This will make 2* samosas.

4. Dip a finger in a small bowl of water and moisten the edges of the round sides of the semicircles. Pick up 1 edge of the half circle and bring it to the other edge, creating a cone shape. Gently press the moistened edges of the rounded side together with your fingers, sealing them. *I can't stress how important this step is. If the dough is not pressed together it will open up during frying and oil will collect inside the* samosas—*I learned this one the hard way.*

5. Using your other hand, stuff about 2 tablespoons of the filling into the open end of the cone. Tap the filling down with 1 finger at the end, making sure that about ¼ inch / 6 mm of dough is showing at the top. Dip a finger in the bowl of water and moisten the open inside edges of the dough. Seal them together gently with your fingertips. *You should now have a stuffed triangle.* Gently place the *samosa* on a baking sheet and cover with a damp cloth or paper towel.

6. Repeat Steps 2, 3, 4, and 5 until you finish stuffing all of the *samosas. You may need another baking sheet. The* samosas *should not touch.*

Continued

7. **To fry the *samosas*:** In a *kadhai*, wok, or saucepan over medium–high heat, warm 2 cups / 470 mL of the oil. *I use a small* kadhai *because I don't like to use too much oil, and cooking the* samosas *just 2 to 3 at a time ensures they cook more evenly.* The oil should be about 1 inch / 3 cm deep in the deepest part of the *kadhai* or pan. Cook the *samosas* for a total of 20 to 40 seconds, until golden brown. Carefully remove with a slotted spoon, draining the oil, and transfer the *samosas* to a wire rack to allow them to cool slightly. Continue to fry the *samosas* in batches until finished. *One trick? Reduce the heat slightly as you cook. If the oil is too hot, the* samosas *will burn on the outside and not warm through nor will the dough crisp up.*

To bake the *samosas*: Brush both sides of the *samosas* lightly with oil or spray them with cooking spray. Set the oven rack at the middle position and preheat the oven to 425°F / 220°C. Bake the *samosas* for 15 minutes. Flip over the *samosas,* spray them lightly with cooking spray, and bake for 6 to 7 minutes, until lightly browned on both sides. Remove from the oven.

8. Serve the *samosas* with a side of *Pudina ki* and/or *Imlee ki* Chutney (see recipes on pp. 41 and 42).

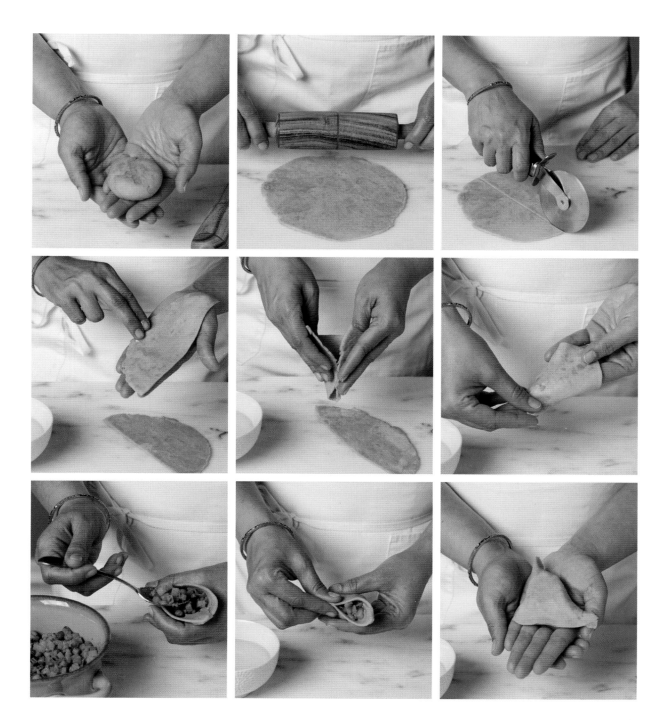

Keema Samosas Minced Lamb *Samosas*

YIELD: 20 MEDIUM *SAMOSAS*

TOOLS: You'll need a deep mixing bowl; a sifter; plastic wrap; a food processor; a heavy-bottomed, 4-quart / 4-L sauté pan with a lid; a damp cloth; a rolling pin; a knife or pizza cutter; a small bowl filled with water; a baking sheet; a small *kadhai,* wok, or saucepan; a slotted spoon; and a wire rack.

VEGANIZE IT! I always make a vegan version of this *samosa* for myself by substituting textured vegetable protein or ground seitan. You can also use the various frozen meat substitutes on the market, but if you truly are vegan, keep in mind some do contain egg whites. If using this substitution, you'll only have to cook the filling in Step 4 for 8 minutes.

Minced lamb is one of the most popular meat fillings for *samosas* and a perfect combination with the fried dough shell. If you're not a fan of lamb, just substitute minced chicken, turkey, or even vegetarian crumbles. I've made them all with great success.

FOR THE DOUGH:
2 cups / 280 g whole-wheat *chapati* flour
1 tablespoon rice flour (optional)
1 teaspoon salt
¼ cup / 60 mL vegetable oil
⅔ cup / 160 mL lukewarm water

FOR THE FILLING:
1 small yellow onion, coarsely chopped
1 (2-inch / 5-cm) piece ginger, peeled and coarsely chopped
10 cloves garlic, peeled
4–6 fresh Thai, serrano, or cayenne chiles, stems removed
¼ cup / 60 mL vegetable oil

1 teaspoon cumin seeds
1 (3-inch / 8-cm) stick cinnamon
2 cassia or bay leaves
1½ pounds / 680 g ground lamb
1 tablespoon tomato paste
½ cup / 120 mL water
1 tablespoon *Garam Masala* (see recipe on p. 35)
2 teaspoons salt
1 teaspoon red chile powder or cayenne pepper
¼ cup / 5 g *kasoori methi* (dried fenugreek leaves), lightly hand crushed to release flavor
2 cups / 470 mL vegetable oil, optional, if frying

TO MAKE THE DOUGH:

1. In a deep mixing bowl, sift together the flours and salt. *The rice flour helps make* samosas *a little crispier.* Add the oil to the bowl. Using your hands, gradually mix in the oil until the dough becomes slightly crumbly.

2. Add the water. Using your hands, knead the dough until all the ingredients come together into a smooth ball. *If the dough is a little wet and sticky, add a little more flour. If it's too hard, add a little more oil.*

3. Tightly wrap the dough in plastic wrap so it does not dry out. Set aside for at least 30 minutes while you prep the filling.

TO MAKE THE FILLING:

1. In the bowl of a food processor, grind the onion, ginger, garlic, and fresh chiles into a smooth paste.

2. In a heavy-bottomed, 4-quart / 4-L sauté pan over medium–high heat, warm the oil. Add the cumin seeds, cinnamon, and cassia leaves and cook for 40 seconds, until the cumin seeds sizzle and turn reddish-brown.

3. Add the onion paste from Step 1 to the sauté pan and cook, stirring constantly, for 1 to 2 minutes, until slightly browned.

4. Add the lamb, tomato paste, water, *Garam Masala,* salt, and red chile powder to the sauté pan and stir well. Reduce the heat to medium and cook, uncovered and stirring occasionally, for 18 minutes, until the lamb is completely cooked through. Toward the end of the cooking time, add the *kasoori methi* and stir well. Remove from the heat, cover, and set aside for 5 minutes to allow the flavors to come together.

5. Remove the cover and remove and discard the whole spices. Allow the mixture to cool completely before filling the *samosas*.

TO ASSEMBLE AND COOK THE *SAMOSAS:*

1. Divide the dough into 10 balls and roll them between your hands until they are as smooth as possible. *Cover them with a damp cloth or paper towel as you work so they don't dry out.* Flatten out each ball with the palms of your hands.

2. On a clean, dry, and flat work surface, use a lightly oiled rolling pin to roll out 1 ball into a thin 6-inch-wide / 15-cm-wide round. *The thinner it is, the crispier it will be. The dough contains a good bit of oil, so you should be able to work with it easily.* Pull the round up and turn it without adding any flour to the work surface. *To make cocktail-sized samosas, just roll the dough out to half this size and follow the steps below, using only half as much filling.*

3. With a knife or a pizza cutter, slice 1 round exactly in half, making 2 semicircles. *This will make 2* samosas.

4. Dip a finger in a small bowl of water and moisten the edges of the round sides of the semicircles. Pick up 1 edge of the half circle and bring it to the other edge, creating a cone shape. Gently press the moistened edges of the rounded side together with your fingers, sealing them. *I can't stress enough how important this step is. If the dough is not pressed together it will open up during frying and oil will collect inside the* samosas—*I learned this one the hard way.*

5. Using your other hand, stuff about 2 tablespoons of the filling into the open end of the cone. *Lamb tends to give off oil, so when you fill the* samosas, *use a slotted spoon and leave that oil behind.* Tap the filling down with 1 finger at the end, making sure that about ¼ inch / 6 mm of dough is showing at the top. Dip a finger in the bowl of water and moisten the open inside edges of the dough. Seal them together gently with your fingertips. *You should now have a stuffed triangle.* Gently place the *samosa* on a baking sheet and cover with a damp cloth or paper towel.

Continued

6. Repeat Steps 2, 3, 4, and 5 until you finish stuffing all of the *samosas*. *You may need an extra baking sheet.* The samosas *should not touch.*

7. To fry the *samosas*: In a *kadhai,* wok, or saucepan over medium–high heat, warm 2 cups / 470 mL of the oil. *I use a small* kadhai *because I don't like to use too much oil, and cooking the* samosas *just 2 to 3 at a time ensures they cook more evenly.* The oil should be about 1 inch / 3 cm deep in the deepest part of the *kadhai* or pan. Cook the *samosas* for a total of 20 to 40 seconds, until golden brown. Carefully remove with a slotted spoon, draining the oil, and transfer the *samosas* to a wire rack to allow them to cool slightly. Continue to fry the *samosas* in batches until finished. *One trick? Reduce the heat slightly as you cook. If the oil is too hot, the* samosas *will burn on the outside and not warm through nor will the dough crisp up.*

To bake the *samosas*: Brush both sides of the *samosas* lightly with oil or spray them with cooking spray. Set the oven rack at the middle position and preheat the oven to 425°F / 220°C. Bake the *samosas* for 15 minutes. Remove from the oven. Flip over the samosas, spray them lightly with cooking spray, and bake for 6 to 7 minutes, until lightly browned on all sides. Remove from the oven.

8. Serve the *samosas* with a side of *Pudina ki* and/or *Imlee ki* Chutney (see recipes on pp. 41 and 42).

Paneer Tikka

YIELD: 6–8 SERVINGS

Whenever we light the grill we always have something vegetarian on hand for half the family. *Paneer Tikka* is easy to make and delicious enough that the meat eaters will even ask for a taste. Save the leftovers for the kids to stuff into pitas or eat as sandwiches during the week.

TOOLS: You'll need a food processor, a large mixing bowl, bamboo or metal skewers, and a baking sheet or grill.

VEGANIZE IT! You can easily make this dish vegan by substituting extra-firm organic tofu for the *Paneer* and soy or coconut yogurt for the dairy yogurt.

PICTURED ON P. 70

1 (3-inch / 8-cm) piece ginger, peeled and coarsely chopped
10 cloves garlic, peeled
2 cups / 470 mL plain, unsweetened yogurt
1 heaping tablespoon *Tandoori Masala* (see recipe on p. 33)
2 teaspoons *amchur* (dried mango powder)
2 teaspoons *Chaat Masala* (see recipe on p. 37), plus more if desired
1 teaspoon *kala namak* (black salt)
1 teaspoon ground black pepper
1 tablespoon salt
⅓ cup / 10 g *kasoori methi* (dried fenugreek leaves), lightly hand crushed to release flavor
Juice of ½ lemon, plus more if desired
2 pounds / 910 g *Paneer*, diced into 1-inch to 1½-inch / 3-cm to 4-cm cubes (see recipe on p. 44)
1 large red bell pepper, diced into 8 pieces
1 large green bell pepper, diced into 8 pieces
1 large yellow bell pepper, diced into 8 pieces
1 large yellow or red onion, diced into 8 pieces
1 tablespoon *ghee* or vegetable oil, for brushing
2 tablespoons chopped fresh cilantro, for garnish

1. In the bowl of a food processor, grind the ginger and garlic into a smooth paste.

2. In a large mixing bowl, combine the ginger paste from Step 1, the yogurt, the *Tandoori Masala,* the *amchur,* the *Chaat Masala,* the *kala namak,* the black pepper, the salt, the *kasoori methi,* and the lemon juice and stir well.

3. Slowly fold the *Paneer* and vegetables into the yogurt marinade. Mix gently, cover, and refrigerate for at least 2 hours to overnight.

4. Set the oven rack at the second-highest position and preheat the oven to 350°F / 180°C or a grill to medium–high heat.

5. Remove the *Paneer* and vegetable mixture from the refrigerator and set aside for at least 20 minutes to rise to room temperature.

6. Skewer the *Paneer* and vegetables alternately on the skewers and place the skewers on a baking sheet. Discard the remaining marinade.

7. Brush the *Paneer* and vegetables with the *ghee* and bake in the oven for 40 minutes or on the grill for 20 minutes. No matter which option you choose, be sure to turn the skewers over halfway through the cooking time. *If baking in the oven, I don't even bother using the skewers. I just place the ingredients on the baking sheet and spray them with cooking oil.* Remove from the oven or grill.

8. Serve on the skewers or remove and arrange on a serving platter. If desired, sprinkle the *Paneer* and vegetables with a touch more *Chaat Masala* and a dash of lemon juice. Garnish with the cilantro. Serve immediately as an appetizer.

Pani Puri or *Gol Gappa*

YIELD: 22-25 (2-INCH / 5-CM) *PURIS*

TOOLS: You'll need a small mixing bowl; a damp cloth; a lightly oiled rolling pin; a 2¼-inch-wide / 6-cm-wide round metal lid or cookie cutter; 2 baking sheets; a small *kadhai*, wok, or saucepan; a slotted spoon; a plate lined with dry paper towels; a blender; 2 large mixing bowls; and a pitcher.

NOTE: To store cooked *puris*, place them in an airtight container for up to 1½ weeks. They tend to go stale after that. *Most Indian grocery stores sell premade* puris—*a real time saver.*

TRY THIS! Got a little leftover *pani*? For a fun twist on an adult beverage, add a few ounces of vodka to it and make *pani puri*-tinis.

There's no way I can convey how much *pani puris* (also called *gol gappas*) mean to me. *Gol* means round and *gappa* refers to chatting or talking, while *pani* means water and *puris* are fried round crisps. All over northern India, you'll find carts surrounded by people stuffing these mini *puris* into their mouths, one after another. When I'd visit India as a little girl, it was the one snack I would wail about for hours until my grandfather would finally give in. Be warned: Once you eat one, you'll be hard-pressed to stop.

FOR THE *PURIS:*
- 1 cup / 170 g fine *sooji* (semolina or cream of wheat)
- 2 teaspoons whole-wheat *chapati* flour or all-purpose flour
- ½ teaspoon salt
- 3-4 / 45-60 mL tablespoons club soda
- 2 cups / 470 mL vegetable oil, for frying

FOR THE *PANI* (SPICY WATER):
- 2 cups / 50 g packed fresh mint leaves
- ½ cup / 10 g fresh cilantro, chopped
- 1 (2-inch / 5-cm) piece ginger, peeled and coarsely chopped
- 1-3 fresh Thai, serrano, or cayenne chiles, stems removed
- 2 teaspoons tamarind paste

- 2 teaspoons *amchur* (dried mango powder)
- 1 tablespoon *kala namak* (black salt)
- 1 tablespoon roasted cumin, ground
- 1 teaspoon red chile powder or cayenne pepper
- 1 teaspoon ground black pepper
- 2 teaspoons light brown sugar
- 6 cups / 1.4 L cold water

FOR THE FILLING:
- 1 boiled russet potato, peeled and diced
- 1 cup / 160 g cooked chickpeas or black chickpeas
- 1 medium yellow or red onion, minced
- 1 tablespoon chopped fresh cilantro
- 1 teaspoon *Chaat Masala* (see recipe on p. 37)

TO MAKE THE DOUGH:

1. In a small mixing bowl, combine the *sooji, chapati* flour, salt, and club soda and stir the ingredients together with your hands until they clump together into a ball of dough. Cover with a damp cloth or paper towel and set aside for at least 15 minutes. *Letting the dough sit is key—helping it harden slightly and making it easier to roll out.*

TO COOK THE *PURIS:*

1. Divide the dough in half. Return the other half to the bowl and keep the bowl covered with the damp cloth. Roll the half you are working with between your hands until it is as smooth as possible. Flatten out the ball of dough with the palms of your hands.

Continued

2. On a clean, dry, and flat work surface, use a lightly oiled rolling pin to roll out the ball into a very thin 8½- to 9-inch-wide / 22- to 23-cm round. Using a round metal lid or cookie cutter 2¼ inches / 6 cm wide, cut out as many rounds as you can from the dough. *Try to work as close to the edge of the dough as possible to make as many rounds as you can.* Place the rounds on a baking sheet in a single layer and cover them with a damp cloth or paper towel until they are ready to be fried.

3. Gather the remaining scraps of dough and roll them into a ball. Flatten the ball and roll the dough out again to the same thickness as before. Continue to make more rounds until you have as many as you can make, and discard any leftover dough.

4. Repeat Steps 2 and 3 with the other half of the dough, placing the rounds on a second baking sheet covered with a damp cloth or paper towel.

5. In a *kadhai,* wok, or saucepan over medium–high heat, warm the oil. *I use a small* kadhai *because I don't like to use too much oil, and cooking the* puris *3 to 4 at a time ensures they cook more evenly.* The oil should be about 1 inch / 3 cm deep in the deepest part of the *kadhai.* You'll know the oil is hot enough if you drop in *a tiny ball of dough and it rises to the top immediately. The key to successfully frying these up is to ensure that the oil is not too hot.* As soon as you see that the oil is ready, reduce the heat slightly. *If it starts to smoke, it's too hot. Just pull the* kadhai *away from the heat to let the oil cool down a bit.*

6. Carefully place 3 to 4 uncooked *puri* rounds into the oil, 1 at a time, and cook for 20 to 30 seconds on 1 side, until each has puffed up and is slightly browned. Use a slotted spoon to press down on each *puri* as it rises to the top of the oil; it will puff up beautifully. Turn over each of the *puris* and cook for 10 to 20 seconds more. Remove from the heat.

7. Remove the cooked *puris* from the oil and transfer to a plate lined with dry paper towels.

8. Repeat Steps 6 and 7 until you have finished frying all the *puris.* Set aside the *puris* to cool for at least 20 minutes before stuffing. *This is essential for them to crisp.*

TO MAKE THE *PANI:*

1. Combine all the ingredients, except the water, in a blender and grind into a paste. *Take your time, as it takes a few minutes for them all to blend to a smooth texture. I sometimes add 1 tablespoon of water to help the process, but the moisture from the mint, cilantro, and tamarind paste is usually enough to do the trick.*

2. In a large mixing bowl, combine the paste with the water. Stir well until the paste has completely dissolved into the water. Transfer to a pitcher. *Instead of wasting the paste that gets stuck in the blades of the blender after transferring it, I typically pour 1 cup / 240 mL of water over the blades and run the blender on low. Then, I pour that spicy water into the pitcher containing the rest of the* pani.

TO MAKE THE FILLING:

1. In a separate large mixing bowl, combine the potato, chickpeas, onion, and cilantro and sprinkle with the *Chaat Masala.*

TO SERVE:

1. Place the *puris* on a serving tray. Transfer the *pani* into individual serving bowls.

2. To eat, pop your thumb gently into 1 *puri,* making a tiny hole. Fill the hole with a few tablespoons of the filling. Dip the filled *puri* into the *pani,* filling each one with the water. *The art is in getting the filled* puri *into your mouth before the water has a chance to soak through! Ready, set, go!*

Angoor Chaat Tangy Grape Salad

YIELD: 2 CUPS / 470 ML

TOOLS: You'll need a large mixing bowl.

Combining sweet fruits with Indian spices and lemon juice is common not only in Indian kitchens but also on the streets, where vendors mix these combinations for their customers. Feel free to substitute any fruit, such as papaya, cantaloupe, banana, or even mango, for the grapes to make a healthy treat that your whole family will enjoy.

1 pound / 450 g green or red grapes, cut in half
Juice of 1 medium lemon
½ teaspoon *kala namak* (black salt)
½ teaspoon *Chaat Masala* (see recipe on p. 37)
½ teaspoon salt
½ teaspoon ground black pepper
½ teaspoon red chile powder or cayenne pepper
1 heaping tablespoon minced fresh cilantro

1. In a large mixing bowl, combine all the ingredients and stir well to combine. Refrigerate for at least 1 hour.

2. Transfer into individual serving bowls and serve as a side salad.

Matthi
Spiced Indian Crackers

YIELD: 24 (2-INCH / 5-CM) CRACKERS

TOOLS: You'll need a food processor; a rolling pin; a baking sheet; a fork; a *kadhai,* wok, or saucepan; a mortar and pestle; and a slotted spoon.

NOTE: Believe it or not, I tried baking these and they came out even crispier and tastier. If you choose to bake them, place them on a well-oiled baking sheet (spray them lightly with oil across the top as well) and bake at 350°F / 180°C for 20 to 25 minutes, until golden brown. There's no need to flip them. Remove from the oven and place on a tray to cool.

I remember piles of these beautifully round, flaky crackers sitting in a large plastic bin in my Mattu *massi's* (aunt's) pantry in Chandigarh. We would always sneak in the pantry to grab a couple in between meals and slather them with spicy Indian pickle.

1 cup / 140 g whole-wheat *chapati* flour*
¼ cup / 40 g *sooji* (semolina or coarse cream of wheat)
½ teaspoon salt
½ teaspoon black peppercorns, coarsely ground in a mortar and pestle
¼ teaspoon *ajwain* (carom seeds)
2 cups / 470 mL plus 2½ tablespoons vegetable oil, divided
3 tablespoons / 45 mL warm water

1. In the bowl of a food processor, combine the flour, the *sooji,* the salt, the ground peppercorns, the *ajwain,* and the 2½ tablespoons of oil. Process until the mixture forms a coarse texture. *The coarser the black pepper, the better. Pound the peppercorns in a mortar and pestle just a few times.*

2. As the processor is running, add the water very slowly, 1 tablespoon at a time, to the food processor. Continue processing until all the ingredients come together into a coarse ball. *This dough should be slightly hard and crumbly. You don't want it to be too smooth, or the end product will be too soft, like a* puri, *when frying in the oil.*

3. Using a tablespoon measure, carve small balls out of the dough and roll them between your hands until they are as smooth as possible. Flatten out each ball with the palms of your hands.

4. On a clean, dry, and flat work surface, use a rolling pin to roll out 1 ball into a thin round that is 2 inches / 5 cm wide. *The thinner it is, the crispier it will be. The dough will crumble at the edges.*

5. Repeat with the remaining balls of dough until all have been rolled out. Place the rounds of dough on a baking sheet. Using a fork, prick the centers of each round a few times to make sure they don't puff up when you fry them.

6. In a small *kadhai,* wok, or saucepan over medium–high heat, warm 2 cups of the oil. The oil should be about 1 inch / 3 cm deep in the deepest part of the *kadhai. You'll know the oil is hot enough if you drop in a tiny ball of dough and it rises to the top immediately. The key to successfully frying these up is to ensure that the oil is not too hot; if it is too hot, the crackers will burn on the outside and won't cook through.* As soon as you see that the oil is ready, reduce the heat to medium or medium–low. *If it starts to smoke, it's too hot. Just pull the* kadhai *away from the heat to let the oil cool down a bit.*

7. Carefully place 7 to 8 uncooked *matthi* into the oil at a time, depending on the size of the pan. *Don't overcrowd them.* Cook for 2 minutes on each side, turning them over once to be sure they brown evenly. Remove from the heat.

8. Remove the *matthi* with a slotted spoon and transfer to a baking sheet lined with a paper towel to absorb the extra oil. Set aside to cool completely. *This step is important to make sure they remain crisp.*

9. Repeat Steps 7 and 8 until you have finished frying all the *matthi.* Set aside to cool for at least 20 minutes.

10. Transfer to an airtight container for up to 2 weeks. *Try eating these with a little mango pickle and a cup of tea—amazingly addictive!*

*If you are not near an Indian grocer who stocks *chapati* flour, you can substitute white whole-wheat flour. Most recipes and commercial takes on this snack use white all-purpose flour *(maida),* but I prefer to use whole-wheat flour. Use all-purpose flour if you prefer a lighter, flakier texture. See my notes on *chapati* flour on p. 26.

Spinach *Pakoras*

YIELD: 17–20 PIECES

TOOLS: You'll need 2 large mixing bowls; a *kadhai,* wok, or saucepan; a slotted spoon; a baking sheet; and a small, flat bowl.

I'm going to be honest: I grew up having *pakoras* made for me all the time. I'd never made them myself—never had to—until I had my own family. I had to ask my aunts in Chandigarh to show me how they were able to whip them up for company so quickly—they'd have them mixed, cooked, and plated in minutes. Turns out, it's not that complicated—it's just a matter of having a few key spices handy to get the true Punjabi flavors.

2 cups / 90 g packed, chopped fresh spinach
1 medium red onion, diced
1 (2-inch / 5-cm) piece ginger, peeled and grated or minced
1–3 fresh Thai, serrano, or cayenne chiles, stems removed and finely sliced
1 cup / 110 g *besan* (gram or chickpea flour)

1 teaspoon salt
1 teaspoon red chile powder or cayenne pepper
½ teaspoon turmeric powder
½ teaspoon *ajwain* (carom seeds)
½ cup / 120 mL plus 1 tablespoon warm water
2 cups / 470 mL vegetable oil, for frying

1. In a large mixing bowl, combine the spinach, onion, ginger, and fresh chiles and mix well to combine. Set aside.

2. In a separate large mixing bowl, combine the *besan,* salt, red chile powder, turmeric, and *ajwain* and stir well to combine. *You can also add other spices, including* garam masala, *ground black pepper, and so on. Be as creative as you like.* Add the water to the *besan* mixture and stir until smooth. *This mixture should be slightly thick and not too watery. Make sure that there are no lumps in the batter.*

3. Slowly fold the spinach mixture into the batter.

4. In a small *kadhai,* wok, or saucepan over medium–high heat, warm the oil. The oil should be about 1 inch / 3 cm deep in the deepest part of the *kadhai. You'll know the oil is hot enough if you drop in a cumin seed and it sizzles and rises to the top immediately.*

5. Using a tablespoon measure, carefully place 4 tablespoons / 60 mL of batter into the oil, 1 at a time, and cook for about 30 seconds on 1 side, until lightly browned but just shy of being cooked through. Turn over each of the *pakoras* and cook for 30 seconds more.

6. Remove the *pakoras* with a slotted spoon and transfer to a baking sheet lined with a paper towel to absorb extra oil. Place a small, flat bowl on top of each *pakora* and press down lightly.

Continued

7. Return the *pakoras* to the hot oil and cook for 30 to 40 seconds on each side, until golden brown. Remove from the heat. Remove the *pakoras* with a slotted spoon and transfer to the baking tray lined with fresh paper towels to absorb the oil. *My aunts in Chandigarh insist on doing this to ensure the* pakoras *are extra crispy. It also helps to make sure they cook through. Don't worry: You can fry them just once as well. Just cook them a little longer to ensure they cook through.*

8. Repeat Steps 5, 6, and 7 until you have finished frying all the *pakoras*. Remove from the heat.

9. Transfer the *pakoras* to a serving platter and serve them with a side of *Pudina ki* and/or *Imlee ki* Chutney (see recipes on pp. 41 and 42).

COOKING TIPS: The oil should be about 350°F / 180°C, but not much hotter than that. If you feel like the *pakoras* are frying too quickly, reduce the heat to low. You don't want them to cook too quickly on the outside and then remain uncooked on the inside.

You can also make a batch and keep them in the oven on the warm setting to serve later, or pan fry or bake them. If baking, place 1 tablespoon of batter in each section of an oiled or nonstick muffin pan and bake for 25 minutes at 350°F / 180°C. Flip them over and bake for 1 to 2 minutes for extra crispiness. Remove from the oven.

Masala Egg Scramble

YIELD: 2-3 SERVINGS

TOOLS: You'll need an 8-inch / 20-cm skillet (nonstick helps) and a whisk or blender if using the method mentioned in the Note.

VEGANIZE IT! You can easily make this dish vegan by substituting 1 (14-ounce / 400-g) package of extra-firm tofu (crumbled by hand) for the eggs. If you're doing so, add ½ teaspoon of *kala namak* (black salt) toward the end of the cooking time. Its sulfuric notes will give the dish the slight taste of eggs.

NOTE: You can also include chopped tomato and/or any other vegetables you like. My mother often whips the eggs in a blender and then pours them into the skillet in individual portions. The result: very thin omelets, which are even more delicious. In this case, cook up the ingredients and spices, remove them from the skillet, and portion them out evenly into each omelet.

Can you believe that eggs are considered an Indian street food? You'll see them everywhere, stacked seemingly a mile high, in cardboard crates on the back of bikes. Vendors will whip up everything from egg sandwiches to spicy *masala* omelets. This recipe is hard to resist, especially when it's cooked thin and sandwiched between two slices of freshly buttered toast.

1 tablespoon vegetable oil
1 teaspoon cumin seeds
½ teaspoon turmeric powder
1 small yellow or red onion, finely diced
1 (1-inch / 3-cm) piece ginger, peeled and grated
1 fresh Thai, serrano, or cayenne chile, stem removed and thinly sliced

½ teaspoon salt
¼ teaspoon red chile powder or cayenne pepper
1 tablespoon chopped fresh cilantro
5 eggs, whisked (or make the dish lighter by using 1 whole egg and 4 egg whites)

1. In an 8-inch / 20-cm nonstick skillet over medium–high heat, warm the oil. Add the cumin seeds and turmeric and cook for 40 seconds, until the cumin seeds sizzle and turn reddish-brown. Add the onion and cook for 1 minute.

2. Add the ginger, fresh chile, salt, red chile powder, and cilantro to the skillet. Cook for 1 minute.

3. Reduce the heat to medium and add the eggs to the skillet. Cook for 2 minutes on 1 side and flip and cook until the eggs cook through on the other side, or gently scramble the eggs until they are cooked through. Remove from the heat.

4. Serve immediately with buttered toast. *In North India, this dish is served rolled up in stuffed Indian bread or* Paratha *(see recipe on p. 236).*

Aloo Tikki
Spicy Potato Patties

YIELD: 15–17 (2½-INCH-WIDE) PATTIES

TOOLS: You'll need a large mixing bowl, a potato masher, an 8-inch / 20-cm sauté pan, 2 baking sheets, a 10-inch / 25-cm frying pan, and a spatula.

Spicy potato patties make a great sandwich in a nation where about 30 percent of the population is vegetarian. These patties are sold everywhere—on the street, in trains, and in movie theaters. In some recipes, the potatoes are mashed together with white bread, but I prefer to make them this way and let the potatoes shine.

3 large russet potatoes, boiled, drained, and peeled (1½ pounds / 680 g)
1 tablespoon vegetable oil, plus more for greasing
1 heaping teaspoon cumin seeds
1 teaspoon turmeric powder
1 medium red or yellow onion, minced, divided
2 teaspoons plus 1 pinch salt, divided
1 (1-inch / 3-cm) piece ginger, peeled and grated (1 tablespoon)
2–3 fresh Thai, serrano, or cayenne chiles, stems removed and minced

⅔ cup / 90 g frozen peas, defrosted
1 heaping teaspoon ground coriander
1 heaping teaspoon *Garam Masala* (see recipe on p. 35)
1 teaspoon red chile powder or cayenne pepper
1 teaspoon *amchur* (dried mango powder)
2 teaspoons salt
1 heaping tablespoon *besan* (gram or chickpea flour)
1 tablespoon fresh lemon juice

1. Place the potatoes in a large mixing bowl and mash them until there are no lumps. *You'll end up with about 4 cups / 950 mL of mashed potatoes.* Set aside.

2. In an 8-inch / 20-cm sauté pan over medium–high heat, warm the oil. Add the cumin seeds and turmeric and cook for 30 seconds, until the seeds sizzle. Add ⅔ cup / 110 g of the onion and the pinch of salt and cook, stirring constantly to avoid sticking, for 2 minutes.

3. Add the ginger and fresh chiles to the sauté pan and cook for 1 minute. Add the peas and cook for 1 minute. Remove from the heat. Add the contents of the sauté pan to the bowl containing the potatoes.

4. Add the remaining 2 teaspoons of salt, the coriander, the *Garam Masala,* the red chile powder, the *amchur,* the *besan,* and the remaining onion to the mixing bowl and stir well, ideally with your hands or the back of a fork, until combined. Add the lemon juice and stir again until well combined.

5. Using your hands, shape ¼ cup / 60 mL of the mixture into a flat, 2½-inch / 6-cm patty and place the patty on a baking sheet (you'll probably need 2). Continue until you have used all of the mixture and have all the patties in a single layer on the baking sheets; you should have 15 to 17 patties.

Continued

6. Lightly grease a 10-inch / 25-cm or larger frying pan and warm it over medium–high heat. Carefully place 4 to 5 patties in the pan. *Be careful not to overcrowd them or they will be tougher to flip.* Cook for 3 minutes on each side, until browned on both sides. *Yes, you will be tempted to turn them over right away, but trust me—give them time to brown and caramelize. Once they move easily rather than stick to the pan, they are ready to be flipped. Just reduce the heat a little if you need to. You don't want them to burn.* Remove from the heat.

7. Remove the patties with a spatula and transfer to a baking sheet lined with a paper towel to absorb the extra oil.

8. Repeat Steps 6 and 7 until you have finished frying all the patties. Remove from the heat.

9. Transfer to a serving platter and serve with a side of *Pudina ki* and/or *Imlee ki* Chutney (see recipes on pp. 41 and 42).

Veggie Kabobs

YIELD: 20–25 (2-INCH-LONG / 5-CM-LONG) KABOBS

TOOLS: You'll need a food processor; a large, deep mixing bowl; a small bowl filled with water; a baking sheet; a griddle, frying pan, or grill (depending on how you are cooking); kabob skewers; tongs; and a large lid.

NOTE: These kabobs are great stuffed inside hot dog buns for the kids. I also love molding these into small patties and serving them on mini buns as sliders.

PICTURED ON. P. 88

I dreamed up this recipe one day while making lamb kabobs. I just knew the chewy texture of black chickpeas along with tofu would be firm enough to grill. This is one recipe you'll keep on hand to make regularly, especially for the kids.

2 cups / 380 g *kala chana* (dried black chickpeas), soaked overnight and drained
8 ounces / 230 g extra-firm organic tofu, crumbled
⅔ cup / 110 g finely minced yellow or red onion
¼ cup / 25 g grated ginger
1–2 fresh Thai, serrano, or cayenne chiles, stems removed and thinly sliced

¼ cup / 5 g chopped fresh cilantro
2 tablespoons *kasoori methi* (dried fenugreek leaves), lightly hand crushed to release flavor
2 teaspoons *Garam Masala* (see recipe on p. 35)
2 teaspoons ground coriander
2 teaspoons salt
½–1 teaspoon red chile powder or cayenne pepper

1. In the bowl of a food processor, grind together the *kala chana* and tofu until the mixture forms a dough-like ball. *Be patient. This may take some time because of the meaty texture of the chickpeas, which are soaked but uncooked. If necessary, stop the machine, push the ingredients down from the sides, and process again.* If the food processor is small, divide the ingredients and blend in small batches. Transfer to a deep mixing bowl.

2. Add the remaining ingredients, except the water, to the mixing bowl. Using your hands, stir until fully combined (using your hands is the best way to make sure all the ingredients are well blended).

3. Dip 1 hand in a small bowl of water. Using your wet hand, mold 1 tablespoon of the mixture into a 2-inch / 5-cm log. Set the log down on a baking sheet.

4. Repeat with the remainder of the mixture until you have used all of it.

5. **If grilling:** Mold the logs onto skewers. Cook over medium heat for 10 minutes, turning once during the cooking time, until the kabobs are cooked through.

If cooking on a griddle: Warm a well-oiled griddle over medium–high heat. Place 8 kabobs on the griddle and cook, turning every 2 minutes or so with tongs and keeping covered with a large lid, for a total of 9 minutes, until they are browned on all sides. *Because the black chickpeas were soaked and not cooked through, it helps to cover the kabobs as they cook so the steam will help them cook. I always keep cooking spray handy to add a little oil if needed.*

6. Transfer to a serving platter and serve with a side of *Pudina ki* and/or *Imlee ki* Chutney (see recipes on pp. 41 and 42).

Poha

YIELD: 5 CUPS / 1.2 L

TOOLS: You'll need a colander and a 4-quart / 4-L sauté pan with a lid.

Using the dry, flattened rice called *mota poha* is key for this dish. Prepping it in this manner is a fun and unique way to make rice. It's also a nutritious snack to keep on hand post school or over the weekend in between meals.

4 cups / 330 g *mota poha* (thick *poha*)

2 tablespoons vegetable oil (I use peanut)

½ teaspoon black mustard seeds

½ teaspoon coriander seeds

1 teaspoon turmeric powder

¼ cup / 40 g raw, unroasted peanuts

1 tablespoon grated ginger

1 small yellow or red onion, diced

1 small russet potato, peeled and diced small, and submerged in water to avoid browning

2 medium carrots, diced small

½ cup / 70 g frozen or fresh peas or edamame

½–1 fresh Thai, serrano, or cayenne chile, stem removed and minced

2 teaspoons salt

2 tablespoons lime juice

2 heaping tablespoons chopped fresh cilantro

1. In a colander with small holes, wash the *poha* in cold water. Set aside to drain for 10 to 15 minutes, until you finish prepping the remainder of the ingredients. *Be careful to use thick* poha *and to make sure it drains well, as it can break down and get mushy while cooking.*

2. In a 4-quart / 4-L sauté pan over medium–high heat, warm the oil. Add the mustard seeds and cook, covered, for 1 minute, until the seeds sizzle and pop slightly. Add the coriander seeds and turmeric and cook for 30 seconds.

3. Add the peanuts to the sauté pan. Stir well and cook for 50 seconds, until the nuts are browned. Add the ginger and onion and cook for 1 minute, until the onions are slightly browned.

4. Add the drained potato to the sauté pan. Stir well and cook, stirring occasionally, for 2 minutes, until they brown. Add the carrots and cook for 1 minute. Add the peas, fresh chile, and salt and cook for 2 minutes, until heated through. Remove from the heat.

5. Add the soaked *poha* to the sauté pan and mix well, until all the ingredients come together and the turmeric has coated the mixture. Add the lime juice and cilantro and stir to combine.

6. Transfer to a serving bowl and serve warm as a snack or side dish.

PICTURED AT LEFT

1 *Poha*
2 Veggie Kabobs (p. 87)

Pav Bhaji
Veggie Sloppy
Joe

YIELD: 8 CUPS / 1.9 L (16 OPEN-FACED SANDWICHES)

TOOLS: You'll need a medium pot with a steamer insert; a heavy-bottomed, 6-quart / 6-L sauté pan; a spoon; a potato masher or immersion (stick) blender; and a frying pan or griddle.

Pav means bread, while *bhaji* means vegetables. The story goes that street vendors in Mumbai came up with this popular street food as a lunch option for workers who wanted something lighter and faster than the traditional Indian fare. They simply mashed and spiced up vegetables and served them on buttered, toasted bread.

1 heaping cup / 140 g chopped carrots
1 heaping cup / 140 g frozen peas
2 green bell peppers, diced
3 tablespoons / 45 g butter or vegan margarine, divided, plus more for spreading
1 medium yellow or red onion, minced
4 cloves garlic, peeled and minced
2–4 fresh Thai, serrano, or cayenne chiles, stems removed and chopped
3 large tomatoes, diced
1 cup / 240 mL water

3 large russet potatoes, boiled, peeled, and mashed
1 teaspoon turmeric powder
2 tablespoons *Pav Bhaji Masala* (see recipe on p. 34), plus more for sprinkling
1 teaspoon red chile powder or cayenne pepper
1 tablespoon salt
Juice of 1 small lime, divided
8 hamburger buns (any kind of roll will do)
Chopped onion and chopped fresh cilantro, for garnish

1. In a medium pot with a steamer insert over medium–high heat, combine the carrots, peas, and bell peppers and steam for 5 to 6 minutes, until they soften. Remove from the heat and set aside.

2. In a heavy-bottomed, 6-quart / 6-L sauté pan over medium–high heat, warm 2 tablespoons of the butter. Add the onion, garlic, and fresh chiles and cook for 2 minutes, until the onions turn opaque. Stir well.

3. Add the tomatoes to the sauté pan and stir well to combine. Cook for 3 minutes, until they start to break down (use the back of the spoon to break them down further). Add the water and cook for 5 minutes.

4. Add the steamed vegetables from Step 1, the potatoes, the turmeric, the *Pav Bhaji Masala,* the red chile powder, and the salt to the sauté pan. Cook, stirring occasionally, for 5 minutes, and use the back of the spoon to mash the ingredients slightly. Remove from the heat.

5. Using a potato masher or immersion (stick) blender, mash the ingredients together until most of the larger vegetables are broken up. *I like a little bit of texture, but that's up to you.*

6. Return the sauté pan to medium–high heat. Add the remaining 1 tablespoon of butter and ¾ of the lime juice and cook for 1 minute. Remove from the heat and set aside, covered.

7. Slice each of the buns in half and on each half, spread the butter and sprinkle with the *Pav Bhaji Masala*. Place each half on a frying pan or griddle and toast them until they are lightly browned. Repeat until all the bun halves are toasted.

8. Place about ½ cup / 120 mL of the *bhaji* on the flatter side of each bun, making 16 open-faced sandwiches. Place the open-faced sandwiches on a very large serving platter. Garnish each with the chopped onion and cilantro and sprinkle the remaining lime juice over each. Serve immediately.

Sabji
Vegetable Stir-Fries

Very few cuisines can boast that among their dishes, vegetables shine more than meat. Indian is one of the few that can. It's the reason why I grew up leaning toward vegetarianism and was able to transition to a vegan lifestyle with very little struggle. Along this journey, I never had to substitute highly processed foods or ingredients for wholesome, real vegetables and legumes.

This section is very special to me, because it's a reflection of how vegetarians and vegans who eat Indian food regularly can maintain a very balanced and fulfilling diet. These recipes not only satisfy folks who love meat—they leave them wanting more.

Indian cuisine is celebrated for its gravy-based dishes, which are also known as curries. But what many newcomers to Indian cuisine don't realize is that stir-fried vegetables are always present on the table as well—and in fact, they're easier to whip up than meat curries.

I've included my family's favorite dishes in this section. Most can be made for dinner one night and then sandwiched between bread the next day for a quick lunch. Experiment with any of these dishes by substituting your own favorite vegetables.

Aloo Mattar
Potatoes and
Peas

YIELD: 6 CUPS / 1.4 L

TOOLS: You'll need a heavy-bottomed, 4-quart / 4-L sauté pan with a lid.

Nothing says homestyle Indian better than a simple mix of potatoes and peas. Whenever we visited my aunt in Delhi, we always looked forward to having this dish. There, it's made with freshly shelled peas—a treat, if you can find them.

2 tablespoons *ghee* or vegetable oil
1 teaspoon cumin seeds
½ teaspoon mustard seeds
1 medium yellow or red onion, finely diced
1½ teaspoons plus 1 pinch salt, divided
1 (1-inch / 3-cm) piece ginger, peeled and grated
3 cloves garlic, peeled and minced
12 small red potatoes with skin, each chopped in 8 pieces
1 teaspoon turmeric powder

1 teaspoon *Garam Masala* (see recipe on p. 35)
1 teaspoon ground coriander
1 teaspoon red chile powder or cayenne pepper
1 (16-ounce / 450-g) bag frozen peas (no need to defrost)
1–2 fresh Thai, serrano, or cayenne chiles, stems removed and thinly sliced
Brown or white basmati rice, *Roti,* or *Naan* (see recipes on pp. 230 and 238), for serving

1. In a heavy-bottomed, 4-quart / 4-L sauté pan over medium–high heat, warm the *ghee.* Add the cumin and mustard seeds and cook for 40 seconds, until the cumin seeds sizzle and turn reddish-brown. *Be careful, as the mustard seeds may pop out of the pan. Keep a lid handy.*

2. Add the onion and the pinch of salt to the sauté pan and cook for 1 minute, until the onion has slightly browned and is opaque. Add the ginger and garlic and cook, stirring constantly, for 2 minutes.

3. Add the potatoes, turmeric, *Garam Masala,* coriander, and red chile powder to the sauté pan and cook, stirring well, for 1 minute, until cooked through.

4. Raise the heat to high and add the peas, the remaining 1½ teaspoons of salt, and the fresh chiles to the sauté pan, stirring well to combine. Cook, uncovered, for 5 minutes.

5. Reduce the heat to low, cover, and cook for 20 minutes, until the potatoes have softened.

6. Remove the cover and raise the heat to medium–high. Cook for 2 minutes, until the moisture from the peas dries up a bit. Remove from the heat.

7. Transfer to a serving bowl and serve immediately with the brown or white basmati rice, *Roti,* or *Naan. This recipe is also delicious stuffed in a pita.*

Palak Aloo
Spinach and Potatoes

YIELD: 3 CUPS / 710 ML

TOOLS: You'll need a heavy-bottomed, 4-quart / 4-L sauté pan with a lid.

I can't tell you how many people have emailed me asking that I include this recipe in this cookbook. Apparently it's a favorite even beyond our household.

2 tablespoons *ghee* or vegetable oil
1 teaspoon cumin seeds
½ cup / 80 g minced yellow or red onion
1½ teaspoons plus 1 pinch salt, divided
1 (1-inch / 3-cm) piece ginger, peeled and grated
3 cloves garlic, peeled and minced
12 small red potatoes with skin, each chopped in 8 pieces
1 teaspoon turmeric powder
1 teaspoon *Garam Masala* (see recipe on p. 35)

1 teaspoon red chile powder or cayenne pepper
8 ounces / 230 g fresh or frozen spinach, chopped (should yield 4 cups / 950 mL)
1–2 fresh Thai, serrano, or cayenne chiles, stems removed and thinly sliced
1 tablespoon water (optional)
Brown or white basmati rice, *Roti,* or *Naan* (see recipes on pp. 230 and 238), for serving

1. In a heavy-bottomed, 4-quart / 4-L sauté pan over medium–high heat, warm the *ghee.* Add the cumin seeds and cook for 40 seconds, until the cumin seeds sizzle and turn reddish-brown.

2. Add the onion and the pinch of salt to the sauté pan and cook for 1 minute, until the onion has slightly browned and is opaque. Add the ginger and garlic and cook for 4 minutes, until the mixture is browned. *You'll want to be sure to mix this as it cooks so that it does not stick to the bottom of the pan. If it starts to stick, just add a little water about a teaspoon at a time. You don't want to add too much.*

3. Add the potatoes to the sauté pan and cook, stirring well, for 2 minutes, until cooked through. Add the turmeric, *Garam Masala,* and red chile powder. Stir well and cook for 1 minute.

4. Add the spinach, the remaining 1½ teaspoons of salt, and the fresh chiles to the sauté pan. Stir well and cook for 2 to 3 minutes. If the vegetables start to stick to the pan, add the water.

5. Raise the heat to high and cook for 2 minutes to remove any excess moisture.

6. Reduce the heat to low, cover, and cook for 20 minutes, until the potatoes are soft. Remove from the heat. Stir well.

7. Transfer to a serving bowl and serve immediately with the brown or white basmati rice, *Roti,* or *Naan.*

PICTURED AT LEFT

1 *Palak Paneer* (p. 158)
2 Baked *Tandoori* Cauliflower (p. 107)
3 *Palak Aloo*

Aloo Gobi
Potatoes and
Cauliflower

YIELD: 7 CUPS / 1.7 L

TOOLS: You'll need a heavy-bottomed, 4-quart / 4-L sauté pan with a lid.

NOTE: This dish is even more delicious if you add 1 cup / 130 g of frozen or fresh peas just after the potato in Step 2. You can also boost its protein by substituting edamame for the peas.

One of the better known North Indian vegetarian dishes outside of India, *Aloo Gobi* is a mainstay in any Indian household. It's also quite the surprise. On paper, cauliflower and potatoes sounds boring. But combine them with the right spices, and you'll have a dish that leaves you wanting more. This recipe was hailed a 2013 favorite by the *Chicago Tribune's* Good Eating section.

3 tablespoons / 45 mL *ghee* or vegetable oil
½ teaspoon *hing* (asafetida)
2 teaspoons cumin seeds
1 teaspoon turmeric powder
1 large yellow or red onion, roughly chopped
2 teaspoons plus 1 pinch salt, divided
2 heaping tablespoons grated or minced ginger
4 cloves garlic, peeled and grated or minced
4 fresh Thai, serrano, or cayenne chiles, stems removed and finely sliced

1 large potato (russet or red), peeled, diced, and submerged in water to avoid browning
1 medium head cauliflower, trimmed and cut into florets
2 teaspoons *Garam Masala* (see recipe on p. 35)
1 teaspoon ground coriander
1 teaspoon red chile powder or cayenne pepper
¼–½ cup / 60–120 mL water
1 heaping tablespoon minced fresh cilantro
Brown or white basmati rice, *Roti,* or *Naan* (see recipes on pp. 230 and 238), for serving

1. In a heavy-bottomed, 4-quart / 4-L sauté pan over medium–high heat, warm the *ghee.* Add the *hing,* cumin seeds, and turmeric and cook for 40 seconds, until the cumin seeds sizzle and turn reddish-brown.

2. Add the onion and the pinch of salt to the sauté pan. Stir well and cook for 2 minutes, until the onion is slightly browned. Add the ginger, garlic, and fresh chiles and cook, stirring occasionally, for 40 seconds. Add the drained potato and cook for 1 minute, until it softens slightly.

3. Add the cauliflower, *Garam Masala,* coriander, red chile powder, and the remaining 2 teaspoons of salt to the sauté pan. Cook, uncovered and stirring constantly, for 3 minutes. If the ingredients start to stick to the bottom of the pan, add the water, 1 tablespoon at a time. *Be sure to do so carefully; don't add too much water, or the vegetables will get soggy.*

4. Reduce the heat to medium or medium–low, cover, and cook, stirring occasionally, for 10 to 12 minutes. *Use your judgment—if you like the vegetables softer, cook a little longer.*

5. Add the cilantro to the sauté pan. Cover and remove from the heat. Set aside for 5 minutes to allow the flavors to blend.

6. Transfer to a serving bowl and serve immediately with the brown or white basmati rice, *Roti,* or *Naan.*

Punjabi *Bhindi Masala* Punjabi Okra

YIELD: 5 CUPS / 1.2 L

My favorite vegetable growing up was—hands down—okra. I know it's not commonly on teens' lists of favorite veggies, but I was lucky enough to have it at my *Nani's* (grandmother's) home in India, where I could pick it right from the garden. It would then be quickly prepped with spices and some key ingredients, and the result was a dish that is irresistible. Try the recipe below, and it will make okra one of your favorites, too.

TOOLS: You'll need a heavy-bottomed, 4-quart / 4-L sauté pan with a lid and a plate.

70 medium-sized okra pods (about 1¼ pounds / 580 g)
4 tablespoons / 60 mL vegetable oil, divided
1 teaspoon *amchur* (dried mango powder), divided
1 teaspoon cumin seeds
1 teaspoon turmeric powder
1 medium yellow or red onion, coarsely chopped
1 (1-inch / 3-cm) piece ginger, peeled and grated or minced
6 cloves garlic, peeled and grated or minced
1–4 fresh Thai, serrano, or cayenne chiles, stems removed and finely sliced
1 teaspoon red chile powder or cayenne pepper
1 teaspoon *Garam Masala* (see recipe on p. 35)
1 teaspoon ground coriander
2 teaspoons salt
Brown or white basmati rice, *Roti,* or *Naan* (see recipes on pp. 230 and 238), for serving

1. Wash the okra thoroughly and dry it with a dish cloth. *This step is critical—drying the okra helps prevent sliminess later.* Trim off the stem end of the okra and cut it into ½-inch / 1-cm rounds. *The smaller and fresher the okra, the better.*

2. In a heavy-bottomed, 4-quart / 4-L sauté pan over medium–high heat, warm 2 tablespoons of the oil. Add the okra and sauté for 4 minutes, stirring constantly. *At this point, the okra will start to get a little lacy.* Sprinkle it with ½ teaspoon of the *amchur* and cook for 6 minutes. Remove from the heat, transfer to a plate, and set aside.

3. Return the sauté pan to medium–high heat and warm the remaining 2 tablespoons of oil. Add the cumin seeds and turmeric and cook for 40 seconds, until the cumin seeds sizzle and turn reddish-brown.

4. Add the onion to the the sauté pan and cook for 3 minutes, until the onions are slightly browned. Stir well. Add the ginger, garlic, and fresh chiles. Cook, stirring constantly, for 1 minute.

5. Add the red chile powder, *Garam Masala,* coriander, salt, and the remaining ½ teaspoon of *amchur* to the the sauté pan and stir until combined. Cook for about 1 minute. Add the okra from Step 2 and cook for 2 minutes, until cooked through. Remove from the heat.

6. Transfer to a serving bowl and serve immediately with the brown or white basmati rice, *Roti,* or *Naan.*

Masala Bharwan Bhindi
Stuffed Okra

YIELD: 3–4 SERVINGS

TOOLS: You'll need a very small mixing bowl; a paring knife; a small spoon; a baking sheet; and a heavy-bottomed, 4-quart / 4-L sauté pan with a lid.

In Indian cooking, "stuffing" vegetables often involves just spices. My *Nani* (grandmother) made her okra this way—simple and to the point.

1 teaspoon turmeric powder
1 teaspoon *amchur* (dried mango powder)
1 teaspoon red chile powder or cayenne pepper
1 teaspoon salt

40 medium-sized okra pods (about 13 ounces / 350 g)
1–2 tablespoons vegetable oil
Brown or white basmati rice, *Roti*, or *Naan* (see recipes on pp. 230 and 238), for serving

1. In a very small mixing bowl, combine the turmeric, *amchur,* red chile powder, and salt, making a *masala.* Stir until well blended. Set aside.

2. Wash the okra thoroughly and dry it with a dish cloth. *This step is critical—drying the okra helps prevent sliminess later.* Trim off the stem end of the okra and, with a paring knife, slit the okra lengthwise from end to end, being careful not to cut all the way through. Each okra pod should have a slit on 1 side but should remain intact on the other side. *You are not cutting the okra into separate pieces. Rather, you are making a slit just big enough to pry it open slightly and drop the* masala *inside.* Some okra may split apart completely, and that's okay. Just rub the inside with the filling and place the pod in the pan along with the others. *The goal is to keep most pods intact. Always remember, the smaller and fresher the okra, the better.*

3. Hold 1 of the okra pods over the bowl (so you don't lose any of the spice mixture) and, using a small spoon, drop a few pinches of the *masala* into the slit. Place the stuffed pod on a baking sheet. Continue until you have finished filling all the pods.

4. In a heavy-bottomed, 4-quart / 4-L sauté pan over medium–low heat, warm the oil. Once the oil is hot, remove from the heat and carefully place each okra pod, slit side up, in the pan in a single layer. *It helps to pull the pan from the hot burner for this step because it takes time and you want the okra to cook evenly.* If any *masala* is left in the bowl, sprinkle it over the okra. *It's okay if you don't have enough room for all the okra to be in a single layer; simply place some pods on top of others.*

5. Return the sauté pan to the heat and cook, uncovered and without moving the okra, for 5 minutes. *Don't raise the heat. If it's any higher, the* masala *that falls out of the okra will burn, and you'll make a mess on the bottom of the pan.*

6. Stir the pods gently and then place the lid on the sauté pan slightly ajar. Cook, stirring occasionally, for 10 minutes. *At this point, it's okay if the okra pieces get turned around. Some of the* masala *will spill, but most will cook inside the okra.*

7. Remove the cover and cook for 3 minutes, until any remaining moisture has cooked off. Remove from the heat, cover, and set aside for 3 to 5 minutes, allowing the okra to absorb the flavors.

8. Serve immediately with the brown or white basmati rice, *Roti,* or *Naan. My kids love this dish rolled up in a fresh* roti, *with a tiny piece of raw onion tucked inside for crunch.*

Besan Bharwan Bhindi
Okra Stuffed with Chickpea Flour

YIELD: 6–8 SERVINGS

TOOLS: You'll need a paring knife; a large, deep mixing bowl; a small frying pan; a small spoon; a baking sheet; and a heavy-bottomed, 6-quart / 6-L sauté pan with a lid.

A common take on okra in Rajasthani cuisine, this dish is just plain addictive. The first time I made it, the pods literally disappeared in minutes. The earthy combination of chickpea flour with the spices and okra is delicious—and worth the extra prep time.

70 medium-sized okra pods (about 1¼ pounds / 580 g)
2 heaping tablespoons *besan* (gram or chickpea flour), sifted
2 tablespoons ground coriander
1 tablespoon *amchur* (dried mango powder)
1 teaspoon dried ginger powder
1 teaspoon turmeric powder
1 teaspoon red chile powder or cayenne pepper
2 teaspoons salt
5 tablespoons / 75 mL vegetable oil, divided
Brown or white basmati rice, *Roti*, or *Naan* (see recipes on pp. 230 and 238), for serving

1. Wash the okra thoroughly and dry it with a dish cloth. *This step is critical—drying the okra helps prevent sliminess later.* Trim off the stem end of the okra and, with a paring knife, slit the okra lengthwise from end to end, being careful not to cut all the way through. Each okra pod should have a slit on 1 side but should remain intact on the other side. *You are not cutting the okra into separate pieces. Rather, you are making a slit just big enough to pry it open slightly and drop the* besan *mixture inside.* Some okra may split apart completely, and that's okay. Just rub the inside with the filling and place the pod in the pan along with the others. *The goal is to keep most pods intact. Always remember, the smaller and fresher the okra, the better.*

2. In a large, deep mixing bowl, combine the *besan,* coriander, *amchur,* ginger powder, turmeric, red chile powder, and salt and stir well.

3. In a small frying pan over medium–high heat, warm 3 tablespoons / 45 mL of the oil. Once it is hot, remove from the heat and pour it into the spiced *besan* mixture. Stir well, until all the ingredients come together and the mixture forms a paste. *It may not look like it's going to be enough to fill all of the okra pods, but trust me—it will be. You need just a little filling in each pod.*

4. Hold 1 of the okra pods over the bowl (so you don't lose any of the *besan* mixture) and, using a small spoon, place a small amount of the *besan* mixture into the slit. Place the stuffed pod on a baking sheet. Continue until you have finished filling all the pods.

5. In a heavy-bottomed, 6-quart /6-L sauté pan over medium–low heat, warm the remaining 2 tablespoons of oil. Once the oil is hot, remove from the heat and carefully place each okra pod, slit side up, in the pan in a single layer. *It helps to pull the pan from the hot burner for this step because it takes time and you want the okra to cook evenly.* If any *besan* mixture is left in the bowl, sprinkle it over the okra. *It's okay if you don't have enough room for all the okra to be in a single layer; simply place some pods on top of others.*

6. Return the sauté pan to medium–low heat and cook, uncovered and without moving the okra, for 5 minutes. *If the heat is any higher, the* besan *mixture that falls out of the okra will burn, and you'll make a mess on the bottom of the pan.*

7. Stir the pods gently and then place the lid on the sauté pan slightly ajar. Cook, stirring occasionally, for 10 minutes. *At this point, it's okay if the okra pieces get turned around. Some of the* besan *mixture will spill, but most will cook inside the okra.*

8. Reduce the heat to low, cover, and cook for 4 minutes. Stir well. Remove from the heat, cover, and set aside for 5 minutes, allowing the okra to absorb the flavors.

9. Serve immediately with the brown or white basmati rice, *Roti,* or *Naan.*

Baingan Aloo Eggplant and Potatoes

YIELD: 4 CUPS / 950 ML

TOOLS: You'll need a heavy-bottomed 4-quart / 4-L sauté pan with a lid.

This is the very first Indian recipe I learned how to make. It was taught to me by my *Babaji* (paternal grandfather) who was visiting us in America from his tiny Punjabi village. You could say this is where my love of cooking started. Try this recipe as is or substitute a sweet potato for the regular kind.

2 tablespoons *ghee* or vegetable oil
½ teaspoon *hing* (asafetida)
1 teaspoon cumin seeds
½ teaspoon turmeric powder
1 (1-inch / 3-cm) piece ginger, peeled and cut into matchsticks ½ inch / 1 cm long
4 cloves garlic, peeled and roughly chopped
1 medium russet potato, peeled and roughly chopped, and submerged in water to avoid browning
1 medium yellow or red onion, roughly chopped
1–2 fresh Thai, serrano, or cayenne chiles, stems removed and finely sliced

1 medium tomato, roughly chopped
2 medium eggplants with skin, roughly chopped
2 teaspoons salt
2 teaspoons *Garam Masala* (see recipe on p. 35)
2 teaspoons ground coriander
1 teaspoon red chile powder or cayenne pepper
2 tablespoons water
2 tablespoons chopped fresh cilantro, for garnish
Roti or *Naan* (see recipes on pp. 230 and 238), for serving

1. In a heavy-bottomed, 4-quart / 4-L sauté pan over medium–high heat, warm the *ghee*. Add the *hing*, cumin seeds, and turmeric and cook for 40 seconds, until the cumin seeds sizzle and turn reddish-brown. Add the ginger and garlic and cook, stirring constantly, for 30 seconds. *Both will brown and slightly caramelize.*

2. Add the drained potato to the sauté pan and cook, stirring occasionally, for 2 minutes. Add the onion and fresh chiles and cook for 2 minutes, until they are slightly browned. Add the tomato and cook for 2 minutes. *At this point, you'll have created a base for the dish.*

3. Add the eggplant, salt, *Garam Masala,* coriander, and red chile powder to the sauté pan and cook, stirring occasionally, for 2 minutes.

4. Reduce the heat to low, partially cover the pan, and cook for 13 minutes. About halfway through the cooking time, add the water to help the ingredients pull together and to avoid sticking. Stir well. Remove from the heat, cover, and set aside for 5 minutes, to allow the flavors to blend completely.

5. Transfer to a serving bowl, garnish with the cilantro, and serve immediately with the *Roti* or *Naan.*

Baingan Bhartha Roasted Eggplant

YIELD: 5 CUPS / 1.2 L

I typically serve this with a side of crackers at my cooking demos, and it's always the first dish to disappear. Eat it as a snack or traditionally with Indian bread. The roasted eggplant is downright addictive and oh, so easy to make at home.

TOOLS: You'll need a baking sheet; a fork; a sharp knife; a deep spoon or ice cream scoop; a large mixing bowl; a heavy-bottomed, 4-quart / 4-L sauté pan; and a traditional or immersion (stick) blender.

3 medium eggplants with skin (the large, round, purple variety)
2 tablespoons vegetable oil
1 heaping teaspoon cumin seeds
1 teaspoon ground coriander
1 teaspoon turmeric powder
1 large yellow or red onion, diced
1 (2-inch / 5-cm) piece ginger, peeled and grated or minced
8 cloves garlic, peeled and grated or minced
2 medium tomatoes, peeled (optional) and diced
1–4 fresh Thai, serrano, or cayenne chiles, stems removed, chopped
1 teaspoon red chile powder or cayenne pepper
1 tablespoon salt
Roti (see recipe on p. 230), lentils, and *Kheera Raita* (see recipe on p. 50), or *Naan* slices (see recipe on p. 238), crackers, or tortilla chips, for serving

1. Set the oven rack at the second-highest position and preheat the broiler to 500°F / 260°C. Line a baking sheet with aluminum foil to avoid a mess later.

2. Poke holes in the eggplants with a fork and place them on the baking sheet. Broil for 30 minutes, turning once. *The skin will be charred and burnt in some areas when they are done.* Remove from the oven and set aside to cool for at least 15 minutes.

3. Using a sharp knife, cut a slit lengthwise from 1 end of each eggplant to the other, and pull open slightly. Scoop out the roasted flesh, being careful to avoid the steam and to salvage as much of the juice as possible. Place the roasted eggplant flesh in a large mixing bowl—you'll have about 4 cups / 950 mL of it.

4. In a heavy-bottomed, 4-quart / 4-L sauté pan over medium–high heat, warm the oil. Add the cumin seeds and cook for 40 seconds, until the cumin seeds sizzle and turn reddish-brown. Add the coriander and turmeric, stir, and cook for 30 seconds.

5. Add the onion to the sauté pan and cook for 2 minutes, until slightly browned. Add the ginger and garlic and cook for 2 minutes.

6. Add the tomatoes and fresh chiles to the sauté pan and cook for 3 minutes, until the mixture softens. Add the eggplant flesh and cook, stirring occasionally to avoid sticking, for 5 minutes. Add the red chile powder and salt and stir to combine. Remove from the heat. *At this point, you should also fish out and discard any stray pieces of charred eggplant skin.*

7. Using an immersion (stick) blender or a traditional blender, process the mixture. *Don't overdo it—there should still be some texture.*

8. Transfer to a serving bowl and serve traditionally as an Indian meal with the *Roti,* lentils, and *Kheera Raita* or as a dip with the toasted *Naan* slices, crackers, or tortilla chips.

Baked *Tandoori* Cauliflower

YIELD: 6 CUPS / 1.4 L

TOOLS: You'll need a large mixing bowl, a whisk, and a baking sheet.

VEGANIZE IT! Substitute plain, unsweetened soy or coconut yogurt for the dairy yogurt.

PICTURED ON P. 96

It's become trendy on various food blogs to prep a whole cauliflower with Indian spices and then bake it, but I find that this process actually dries it out. I'd rather cut the cauliflower into florets first and then bake it for a new twist to this very versatile veggie. This dish is great as an appetizer and/or part of a meal.

½ cup / 120 mL plain, unsweetened yogurt (whole, lowfat, or nonfat)
1 tablespoon *Tandoori Masala* (see recipe on p. 33), plus more for sprinkling
2 teaspoons salt
1 (1-inch / 3-cm) piece ginger, peeled and grated
Juice of 1 lemon or lime, divided
1 large head cauliflower, trimmed and cut in bite-sized pieces

1 small yellow or red onion, finely sliced
1–3 fresh Thai, serrano, or cayenne chiles, stems removed and finely chopped
2 tablespoons chopped fresh cilantro
Naan (see recipe on p. 238) and *Pudina ki* Chutney (see recipe on p. 41), for serving

1. In a large mixing bowl, combine the yogurt, the *Tandoori Masala,* the salt, the ginger, and ½ the lemon or lime juice and whisk until combined.

2. Carefully fold the cauliflower into the mixture, ensuring all the pieces are coated. Refrigerate the mixture for 2 hours or (ideally) overnight.

3. Set the oven rack at the highest position and preheat the oven to 400°F / 260°C.

4. Arrange the cauliflower in a single layer on a lightly greased baking sheet. Bake for 30 minutes, turning over the pieces once halfway through the cooking time to ensure all pieces are lightly browned on both sides. Remove from the oven.

5. Transfer the cauliflower to a serving bowl or tray. Sprinkle the remaininng lemon or lime juice over the dish. Smother the cauliflower with the onions, fresh chiles, and cilantro. For added punch, sprinkle on a bit more of the *Tandoori Masala* just before serving.

6. Serve immediately with the *Naan* and a side of the *Pudina ki* Chutney.

Gobi Manchurian

YIELD: 4–6 SERVINGS

TOOLS: You'll need a small mixing bowl; a food processor; a medium mixing bowl; a *kadhai,* wok, or saucepan; a plate lined with a paper towel; and a heavy-bottomed, 6-quart / 6-L sauté pan.

My fondest food memories in India involve Chinese food, believe it or not. There, Indo-Chinese cuisine has a loyal following—a combination of Chinese cooking techniques with Indian spices. This dish is a favorite of mine whenever visiting Delhi.

6 whole dried red chiles
⅓ cup / 80 mL boiling water
1 (2-inch / 5-cm) piece ginger, peeled and divided
5 cloves garlic, peeled and divided
¾ cup / 90 g all-purpose flour
1 tablespoon plus 2 teaspoons cornstarch or arrowroot, divided
1 teaspoon red chile powder or cayenne pepper
1 teaspoon ground black pepper
1 teaspoon ground white pepper
1½ teaspoons *Garam Masala* (see recipe on p. 35), divided
3 teaspoons salt, divided
¾ cup / 180 mL plus 1 teaspoon room-temperature water, divided
2 cups / 470 mL plus 2 tablespoons vegetable oil, divided

1 medium head cauliflower, cut into about 20 large florets
2 tablespoons soy sauce
2 teaspoons white distilled vinegar
1 teaspoon tomato ketchup
½ teaspoon light brown sugar
1 medium yellow onion, roughly chopped
1 large green bell pepper, roughly chopped
1–3 fresh Thai, serrano, or cayenne chiles, stems removed and thinly sliced lengthwise
3 scallions, thinly sliced with greens
Brown or white basmati rice, for serving

1. In a small mixing bowl, combine the dried chiles and the boiling water. Set aside to soften while you prep the remaining ingredients.

2. In the bowl of a food processor, grind together ½ the ginger and 2 of the garlic cloves into a smooth paste.

3. Transfer the paste from Step 2 to a medium mixing bowl. Add the flour, the 1 tablespoon of cornstarch, the red chile powder, the black and white pepper, 1 teaspoon of the *Garam Masala,* and 1 teaspoon of the salt and stir well. Slowly add the ¾ cup / 180 mL of room-temperature water, ¼ cup / 60 mL at a time, to the mixing bowl. Continue stirring until all the ingredients blend together, forming a batter. Set aside.

4. In a heavy-bottomed *kadhai* or wok over medium–high heat, warm the 2 cups / 470 mL of oil. *Test the oil by adding 1 cumin seed. If it sizzles and immediately comes to the top, the oil is ready.*

5. Add 8 florets of the cauliflower at a time to the batter. Using your hand, stir gently until the florets are evenly coated. Allow the excess batter to drip off, and gently drop the florets into the oil and cook for 2 to 3 minutes, until lightly browned, turning once halfway through the cooking time. Transfer to a plate lined with a paper towel to absorb the excess oil.

6. Repeat with the remaining florets until all have been battered and cooked. Set aside.

7. In the bowl of the food processor, grind the chiles and their soaking water from Step 1. Return the chile paste to the small mixing bowl and add the soy sauce, the vinegar, the ketchup, the brown sugar, the remaining 2 teaspoons of cornstarch, the remaining 2 teaspoons of salt, and the remaining 1 teaspoon of room-temperature water. Stir well and set aside.

8. Slice the remaining ginger into into 2-inch / 5-cm matchsticks and thinly slice the remaining 3 cloves of garlic.

9. In a heavy-bottomed, 6-quart / 6-L sauté pan over medium heat, warm the remaining 2 tablespoons of oil. Carefully add the onion and cook for 4 minutes, until slightly browned. Add the sliced ginger and garlic from the previous step and cook for 1 minute. Add the bell pepper and fresh chiles to the sauté pan and cook for 2 minutes.

10. Raise the heat to medium–high, add the sauce from Step 7, and bring to a boil. Reduce the heat to medium–low and simmer for 2 minutes, until the mixture thickens.

11. Carefully add the cauliflower to the sauté pan and simmer, uncovered and stirring gently, for 4 minutes. Remove from the heat. Add the scallions, sprinkle with the remaining ½ teaspoon of *Garam Masala,* cover, and set aside for 5 minutes, allowing the cauliflower to absorb the flavors.

12. Transfer to a serving bowl and serve with the brown or white basmati rice.

Green Bean *Thoran*

YIELD: 5 CUPS / 1.2 L

TOOLS: You'll need a large mixing bowl and a heavy-bottomed, 4-quart / 4-L sauté pan with a lid.

TIP: Using fresh coconut is key here, but it's very hard to find. If you have an Indian grocery store nearby, ask if they sell frozen, grated coconut, which I find has the closest consistency and flavor to the fresh stuff. If I am feeling really ambitious, I'll get a fresh coconut, have the store split it, and use the grater I brought back from Kerala and hand grate it myself. But be warned: This option is *definitely* a project.

The western coastal state of Kerala has a unique and wonderful food history unlike that found elsewhere in India. This dish gets its delicious appeal from the small dice of the vegetables and the subtle flavor of coconut. I ate a version of this dish practically every day on my visit in 2012 and have been making it at home ever since.

1½ pounds / 680 g Asian long beans or green beans, finely sliced (will yield 5 cups / 1.2 L)
3 small shallots, minced
3–4 fresh Thai, serrano, or cayenne chiles, stems removed and thinly sliced
1 teaspoon turmeric powder
1½ tablespoons coconut oil, divided
½ teaspoon mustard seeds
5 whole dried red chiles

10–15 curry leaves
1 tablespoon water
1 cup / 90 g dried, unsweetened grated coconut
1½ teaspoons salt
½ teaspoon red chile powder or cayenne pepper
Brown or white basmati rice or *Roti* (see recipe on p. 230), for serving

1. In a large mixing bowl, combine the long beans, shallots, fresh chiles, and turmeric and stir well. Set aside.

2. In a heavy-bottomed, 4-quart / 4-L sauté pan over medium–high heat, warm 1 tablespoon of the oil. Add the mustard seeds and cook for 40 seconds, until the mustard seeds pop. *They tend to pop out of the pan, so keep a lid handy.* Carefully add the dried chiles and curry leaves and cook, stirring constantly, for 10 seconds.

3. Add the bean mixture to the sauté pan. Reduce the heat to low and cook, uncovered and stirring occasionally, for 20 minutes, adding the water about 5 minutes before the end of the cooking time to prevent sticking.

4. Add the grated coconut, salt, red chile powder, and the remaining ½ tablespoon of oil to the sauté pan and cook, stirring constantly, for 3 minutes, until the mixture is cooked through. Remove from the heat, cover, and set aside for 3 to 5 minutes, allowing the flavors to blend.

5. Transfer to a serving bowl, stir well, and serve with the brown or white basmati rice or *Roti*.

Aria's Spiced Potato Mash

YIELD: 6 CUPS / 1.4 L

TOOLS: You'll need a food processor and a heavy-bottomed, 4-quart / 4-L sauté pan with a lid.

I had to include this recipe for my little one, Aria, who is hands down obsessed with mashed potatoes. She can eat them all day—every day. With this recipe, you and your family will be obsessed too.

1 (1-inch / 3-cm) piece ginger, peeled and coarsely chopped
6 cloves garlic, peeled
2 tablespoons vegetable oil
2 teaspoons cumin seeds
½ teaspoon mustard seeds
1 teaspoon turmeric powder
1 medium yellow onion, minced
1–4 fresh Thai, serrano, or cayenne chiles, stems removed and thinly sliced
4 large russet potatoes, boiled, peeled, and mashed
2 tablespoons water
1 teaspoon *Garam Masala* (see recipe on p. 35)
1 teaspoon *amchur* (dried mango powder)
1 teaspoon red chile powder or cayenne pepper
2 teaspoons salt
2 tablespoons *kasoori methi* (dried fenugreek leaves), lightly hand crushed to release flavor
Roti or *Dosa* (see recipes on pp. 230 and 253), for serving

1. In the bowl of a food processor, grind the ginger and garlic into a smooth paste. Set aside.

2. In a heavy-bottomed, 4-quart / 4-L sauté pan over medium–high heat, warm the oil. Add the cumin and mustard seeds and the turmeric and cook for 40 seconds, until the cumin seeds sizzle and turn reddish-brown. *The mustard seeds will pop a bit—keep a lid handy.*

3. Add the onion to the sauté pan and cook, stirring occasionally, for 3 minutes, until the onion is slightly brown. Add the ginger paste from Step 1 and the fresh chiles and cook, stirring constantly, for 1 minute.

4. Add the potatoes and water to the sauté pan and stir well. Add the *Garam Masala, amchur,* red chile powder, and salt and cook, uncovered and stirring occasionally to prevent sticking, for 4 minutes.

5. Add the *kasoori methi* to the sauté pan and cook for 1 minute. Remove from the heat.

6. Transfer to a serving bowl and serve with the *Roti* or rolled in a *Dosa.*

Baked Brussels Sprout Chips

YIELD: 4 CUPS / 950 ML COOKED LEAVES

TOOLS: You'll need a large, deep mixing bowl; a baking sheet; and tongs.

PICTURED ON P. 114

This dish uses the large outer leaves from Brussels sprouts that many cooks pick off and discard. Save the inner sprouts for another recipe. I'm proud to say that it was highlighted in my article on Diwali in the *Chicago Tribune* newspaper in 2013.

Outer leaves from about 2½ pounds / 1.13 kg of Brussels sprouts, loosely packed
2 tablespoons vegetable oil

½ teaspoon salt
½ teaspoon turmeric powder
1 tablespoon *Garam Masala* (see recipe on p. 35)

1. Set the oven rack at the second-highest position and preheat the oven to 350°F / 180°C.

2. In a large, deep mixing bowl, combine all the ingredients. Get your hands in there and mix everything together, making sure that all the leaves are coated with the oil and spices.

3. Spread the spiced leaves out on a baking sheet and bake for 15 minutes.

4. Carefully remove the sheet from the oven. Using tongs, lightly mix the leaves and turn the sheet around to ensure even cooking. Return to the oven and cook for 5 minutes. Remove from the oven. (If you prefer them to be really crispy, return to the oven for another 5 minutes.)

5. Transfer to a serving bowl and serve immediately. *They will be toasted on the sides, curled up, and melt-in-your-mouth delicious.*

Dal

Lentil and Bean Soups

**SABUT URAD/WHOLE
BLACK DAL**

**URAD DAL CHILKA/
SPLIT BLACK DAL**

URAD DAL DUHLI

**SABUT MOONG DAL/
WHOLE GREEN DAL**

**MOONG DAL CHILKA/
SPLIT GREEN DAL**

MOONG DAL DUHLI

**SABUT MASOOR DAL/
WHOLE MASOOR LENTILS**

**MASOOR DAL DUHLI/
RED SPLIT LENTIL**

**SABUT TOOR DAL/
WHOLE TOOR DAL**

**DUHLI TOOR DAL/
SPLIT TOOR DAL**

**KALA CHANA/
BLACK CHICKPEAS**

**CHANA DAL/SPLIT
BLACK CHICKPEAS**

**KABULI CHANA/
CHICKPEAS**

RED KIDNEY BEANS

What is considered common in most cuisines just might be royalty on the Indian dinner table. When cooked to perfection and spiced just so, basic lentils and beans are simply addictive. They are also incredibly healthy—high in fiber and protein—and a perfect addition to an Indian meal, where meat is often relegated to the chorus, rather than the lead.

Dal means different things in different parts of India, and it's the name of the ingredient and as well sometimes the name of the dish. In Punjab, where I was born, it refers to soupy and spiced lentils. In other regions of India, it can also refer to beans and peas—which, along with lentils, are also legumes (seeds that grow in pods). Getting to properly know all the beans and lentils out there will take some time, as there are so many. But know that there is a method to the madness.

In the spice tours I host in Chicago's Little India, Devon Avenue in the West Rogers Park neighborhood, I always remind folks that a single variety of bean and lentil can be found in up to four different forms. You can buy them whole, with the skin on *(sabut* or *sabud);* whole without the skin; split with the skin on *(chilka),* and split without the skin on *(duhli).* Confused yet?

It sounds bizarre, but it makes sense when you think about it. Each form has its own prep time and taste profile. For example, a whole *mung* (green) bean with its skin will take longer to cook (about 1 hour), use more water, and taste heartier than its split and skinned counterpart (yellow), which takes only 20 minutes to cook.

Folks always want to know if they should soak their beans and lentils. It has been shown that soaking does get rid of some of their antinutrients and complex starches, which can lead to gassiness and bloating for some. When in doubt, just soak your legumes (especially kidney beans and other beans in that category) overnight or for a few hours, drain them, and discard the water. Typically, split and skinned beans and lentils don't need to soak as long, and some need no soaking at all. Use your judgment when prepping beans, lentils, and peas to figure out what works best for you and your lifestyle.

Once you've read this section, you'll know exactly which type and form of bean and lentil to choose no matter what your cooking day looks like. The variety of beans and lentils out there is almost mindblowing, but most fall into a few key categories. Feel free to swap these category buddies out in the recipes that follow in this section.

Urad or **urud dal** (**black dal,** black gram, *matpe* beans, *Vigna mungo*): This bean is one of the best known throughout India, especially because it is a key part of many special Hindu ceremonies. Easily recognized from its tiny, jet-black, and oval appearance, it takes longer to cook because of its tough outer skin and really shines when cooked in a slow cooker.

Moong or *mung dal* (**green** *dal,* **green gram,** *Vigna radiata):* These beans look like their black counterparts, *urad dal,* in shape and size, but they are green in color. This is the most commonly cooked *dal* in North India, between its whole form with skin (green), its split form with skin, and its split form without skin (yellow).

Masoor, masar, or *mussoor dal* (**brown, red, or green lentils,** *lens culinaris):* These light brown, round lentils are usually sold in Western grocers in both split and skinned varieties, when they are almost salmon in color. In the West, they are often referred to as red lentils—which is ironic, because they turn yellow when cooked.

Toor, toovar, arhar, or *tur dal* (**pigeon peas,** *Cajanus cajun):* This bean is used quite often in South and West India. When whole, it is small, round, and tan in color and found in a lot of West Indian dishes. When split and skinned, it has a yellowish beige color; it's the primary base for *sambhar,* a spicy soup eaten in South India with a savory gluten-free crepe called *dosa* (plural *dosai).*

Chana (**chickpeas, garbanzo beans,** *Cicer arietinum):* In Indian cuisine, chickpeas rule. They are used in many dishes and are eaten often whole or even ground into flour *(besan).* In the West, this flour has become well known as a wonderful gluten-free substitute for all-purpose flour. In India, we eat two different types of *chana.* The lighter is known as *kabuli chana* and is what we refer to as chickpeas or garbanzo beans in the West. A lesser-known variety of the chickpea is the black chickpea, or *kala chana.* As its name suggests, this bean looks like a chickpea, but it's about half the usual size and blackish-brown (and sometimes green) in color. It's high in protein and needs to be cooked longer than its lighter counterpart. It's fantastic soaked overnight and then sprouted as an addition to soups or salads.

Chana dal (**split gram**): These are derived from splitting and skinning the black chickpea. When raw, it looks like the split and skinned version of *toor dal,* so be sure to label your containers.

Rajmah (**kidney beans,** *Phaseolus vulgaris):* One of the most popular dishes in North India is made from the red kidney bean. Many types are available: dark and light red and *Jammu* and *Kashmiri rajmah.* Some prefer the smaller and sweeter *Kashmiri rajmah,* but I love the light red because it breaks down better when cooking. The key to using kidney beans is to boil them for 10 minutes or soak them at least 2 hours and discard the water before cooking to eliminate any antinutrients.

Lobhia, rongi (cowpeas, black-eyed peas/beans, *Vigna unguiculata*), and ***sabut chowli*** (red cowpeas, *Vigna unguiculata*): Black-eyed peas are white or beige in color with a black spot in the middle. Red cowpeas are reddish-brown in color. Use the two interchangeably—they both make a fabulously creamy Indian curry.

One rule of thumb when using legumes is to sift them by hand before you use them or transfer them to another container. Often, bits of debris, small rocks, and other particles get mixed in, and you'd never want a guest to chomp down on a piece of gravel. Never wash legumes until you are ready to cook them, as storing them with moisture can spoil the whole batch. If you get a bag with a layer of powder on the bottom, inspect the legumes for insects. It does happen occasionally, and if it does, either discard the batch or take it back to the store and notify the manager.

I am always asked about my take on canned beans and lentils. My kids have become so spoiled that they won't eat canned legumes anymore. I avoid them for two reasons. One, they usually have added salt and other preservatives. Two, they have a mushy consistency, just don't cook up as well, and are less able to absorb the flavor of the sauce in which they are cooked. If you want a quick option for cooking whole legumes ahead of time, I suggest using a slow cooker so that you can cook them in plain water. I typically make a batch of dried legumes in water this way in a 5-quart / 5-L slow cooker; then, I can use half immediately in a recipe and freeze the other half in either 1-cup / 250-mL or 3-cup / 700-mL portions for later. There is a whole section on how to effectively do this along with cooking times and water portions in my second book, *Vegan Indian Cooking*.

If you truly don't have time and need to use canned, as life can get hectic, then keep in mind that a 15-ounce / 430-g can of a bean or lentil is roughly equivalent to ½ cup / 110 g of the dried variety. *(Experiment, as this is not a hard and fast rule.)* Be sure you drain and rinse the canned beans thoroughly before using.

Keep in mind that all legumes are rich sources of protein, which are composed of amino acids. A complete protein includes all the nine essential amino acids. All animal proteins are complete proteins, but legumes are incomplete proteins that can be made complete by pairing them with a grain—either in the same or in subsequent meals. That's why in Indian cuisine, legumes are typically served with rice or bread.

Feel free to also use all of these recipes as soups. I'll often make a *dal* one night and serve the leftovers for lunch the next day with some added chopped veggies, cooked quinoa or rice, a sprinkle of grated cheese, and tortilla chips on the side.

Dal Makhani Buttered Black Lentils

YIELD: 8 CUPS / 1.9 L

TOOLS: You'll need a large, deep mixing bowl; a deep, heavy-bottomed, 6-quart / 6-L stockpot or Dutch oven; a food processor; and an 8-inch / 20-cm sauté pan with a lid.

VEGANIZE IT! Substitute vegan margarine for the *ghee* and Cashew Cream (see recipe on p. 47) or coconut or soy creamer for the dairy cream.

PICTURED ON P. 116

In Hindi, *makhan* means butter. Probably the most frequently ordered *dal* in Indian restaurants, this Punjabi version is a combination of *urad dal*, kidney beans, and butter, and is at once hearty and comforting. Make it in its traditional celebratory style with layers of butter and cream, or lighten it up for daily fare.

1¾ cups / 360 g *sabut urad* (whole, dried black *dal* with skin), picked over and washed
½ cup / 90 g *rajmah* (dried red kidney beans), picked over and washed
1 teaspoon turmeric powder
2 cassia or bay leaves
1 (3-inch / 8-cm) stick cinnamon
3 whole cloves
12 cups / 2.8 L water, plus more if needed
1 medium yellow or red onion, coarsely chopped
1 (1-inch / 3-cm) piece ginger, peeled and coarsely chopped
4 cloves garlic, peeled
4 tablespoons / 60 mL *ghee* or vegetable oil
1 teaspoon cumin seeds
1 teaspoon cumin powder
1 teaspoon ground coriander

1 teaspoon red chile powder or cayenne pepper
1–3 fresh Thai, serrano, or cayenne chiles, stems removed and chopped
1 (6-ounce / 170-g) can tomato paste, unsalted
¼ cup / 60 mL water, plus more if needed
1 tablespoon plus 1 teaspoon salt
¼ teaspoon cardamom seeds, ground
1 teaspoon *kasoori methi* (dried fenugreek leaves), lightly hand crushed to release flavor
¼ cup / 60 mL half & half or heavy cream
2 heaping tablespoons minced fresh cilantro, for garnish
Brown or white basmati rice, *Roti*, or *Naan* (see recipes on pp. 230 and 238), for serving

1. In a large, deep mixing bowl, soak the *sabut urad* and *rajmah* in at least 8 cups / 1.9 L of water overnight. *If you're pressed for time, place them in boiling water and allow them to soak them for at least 4 hours. If you do, you should increase the cooking time by 30 to 45 minutes.* Drain and discard the water when finished soaking. *This will seem like a lot of water, but the beans absorb a lot.*

2. Combine the 2 beans, the turmeric, the cassia leaves, the cinnamon, the cloves, and the 12 cups / 2.8 L water in a deep, heavy-bottomed, 6-quart / 6-L stockpot or Dutch oven over medium–high heat and bring to a boil.

3. Reduce the heat to medium–low and simmer, partially covered, for 1½ hours. Remove from the heat, cover, and set aside to cool slightly while you prep the remaining ingredients. *If a light film forms at the start of cooking, simply skim it off, discard, and continue to cook.*

4. In the bowl of a food processor, grind together the onion, ginger, and garlic into a watery paste. Set aside.

5. In a separate 8-inch / 20-cm sauté pan over medium–high heat, warm the *ghee.* Add the cumin seeds and cook for 40 seconds, until the cumin seeds sizzle and turn reddish-brown.

6. Carefully add the paste from Step 4 to the sauté pan. *It will splatter as the moisture from the onion hits the hot oil, so keep a lid handy.* Stir well and cook for 4 minutes, until the mixture is slightly browned. Add the cumin powder, coriander, red chile powder, and fresh chiles, stir well, and cook for 40 seconds.

7. Carefully add the tomato paste, the ¼ cup / 60 mL water, and the salt to the sauté pan. *This mixture can also splatter, so keep the lid handy.* Cook, stirring occasionally, for 2 minutes. *Use a little more water if needed to make sure the mixture doesn't dry out.* Remove from the heat.

8. Transfer the contents of the sauté pan to the stockpot containing the cooked beans and stir well until combined. Add the cardamom and *kasoori methi,* stir, and return the stockpot to medium heat. Allow the mixture to reach a simmer and simmer for 15 minutes.

9. Add the cream to the stockpot and cook for 1 to 2 minutes. Remove from the heat and remove and discard the whole spices.

10. Transfer to a serving bowl. Garnish with the cilantro and serve with the brown or white basmati rice, *Roti,* or *Naan.*

Rajmah Punjabi Kidney Beans

YIELD: 10 CUPS / 2.4 L

Ask anyone who hails from North India and I guarantee they will tell you a nostalgic childhood story about *rajmah,* a dish eaten just about every weekend in Punjabi homes. Know that this recipe has been tested and approved by the toughest critics in our home—my two girls, Neha and Aria. Whenever we have *rajmah* in the house, my little one will insist on taking a Thermos full of it for the car trip to school, another for lunch, and a plateful after school as well.

TOOLS: You'll need a food processor; a heavy-bottomed, 6-quart / 6-L or larger stockpot; and an 8-inch / 20-cm skillet.

1 large yellow or red onion, divided
1 (2-inch / 5-cm) piece ginger, peeled and coarsely chopped
6 cloves garlic, peeled
1 large tomato, coarsely chopped
1–3 fresh Thai, serrano, or cayenne chiles, stems removed
3 cups / 530 g *rajmah* (dried red kidney beans), picked over, washed, soaked overnight, and drained
3 whole cloves
1 black cardamom pod
1 (3-inch / 8-cm) stick cinnamon
2 cassia or bay leaves

11 cups / 2.6 L water
2 tablespoons vegetable oil
½ teaspoon *hing* (asafetida)
1 teaspoon turmeric powder
2 teaspoons cumin seeds
2 teaspoons *Garam Masala* (see recipe on p. 35)
2 teaspoons ground coriander
2 teaspoons red chile powder or cayenne pepper
1 tablespoon plus 2 teaspoons salt
¼ cup / 5 g chopped fresh cilantro
Brown or white basmati rice and *Kheera Raita* (see recipe on p. 50), for serving

1. In the bowl of a food processor, grind together ½ of the onion (mince the other half and reserve for use in Step 4), the ginger, the garlic, the tomato, and the fresh chiles until the mixture forms a watery paste.

2. Combine the *rajmah,* the paste from Step 1, the cloves, the cardamom, the cinnamon, the cassia leaves, and the water in a heavy-bottomed, 6-quart / 6-L or larger stockpot over medium–high heat. *This will seem like a lot of water, but the beans absorb a lot.* Bring to a boil.

3. Reduce the heat to medium–low and simmer, partially covered and stirring occasionally, for 2 hours, until the beans soften and break down slightly. Remove from the heat, cover, and set aside to cool slightly while you prep the remaining ingredients.

4. In an 8-inch / 20-cm skillet over medium–high heat, warm the oil. Add the *hing,* turmeric, and cumin seeds and cook for 40 seconds, until the cumin seeds sizzle and turn reddish-brown. Add the reserved onion (minced) from Step 1 and cook for 4 minutes, until the onion is browned. Remove from the heat and transfer the contents of the skillet to the stockpot containing the *rajmah.*

5. Add the *Garam Masala,* coriander, red chile powder, and salt to the stockpot and cook, uncovered, for 30 minutes. Remove from the heat. Remove and discard the whole spices (you can leave the cloves if they are tough to find).

6. Transfer to a serving bowl and garnish with the cilantro. Serve immediately with the brown or white basmati rice and *Kheera Raita.*

Moong Sabut Whole Green *Dal*

YIELD: 13 CUPS / 3.1 L

This is an everyday sort of *dal* in Punjabi households. My mother would make it for us at least once a week, if not more. It was never exciting back then when she'd announce she was making it, but once we had it on our plates, we'd gobble it up.

TOOLS: You'll need a heavy-bottomed, 6-quart / 6-L stockpot or Dutch oven with a lid; a food processor; medium and small mixing bowls; and an 8-inch / 20-cm frying pan.

3 cups / 660 g dried *sabut moong dal* (whole green *dal* with skin), picked over, washed, soaked overnight, and drained
12 cups / 2.8 L water
1 (1-inch /3-cm) piece ginger, peeled and coarsely chopped
6 cloves garlic, peeled
1–3 fresh Thai, serrano, or cayenne chiles, stems removed
1 medium tomato, coarsely chopped
3 tablespoons /45 mL *ghee* or vegetable oil, divided
½ teaspoon *hing* (asafetida)
2 teaspoons cumin seeds
1 teaspoon turmeric powder
1 small yellow onion, finely diced
1 teaspoon crushed red chile flakes
1 tablespoon *Garam Masala* (see recipe on p. 35)
1 tablespoon ground coriander
1 tablespoon plus 2 teaspoons salt
2 tablespoons chopped fresh cilantro
Brown or white basmati rice, *Roti,* or *Naan* (see recipes on pp. 230 and 238), for serving

1. Combine the *sabut moong dal* and water in a heavy-bottomed, 6-quart / 6-L stockpot or Dutch oven over medium–high heat and bring to a boil.

2. Reduce the heat to medium–low and simmer, partially covered, for 40 minutes, until the *dal* breaks down and resembles a porridge consistency. Remove from the heat, cover, and set aside to cool slightly while you prep the remaining ingredients.

3. In the bowl of a food processor, grind together the ginger, garlic, and fresh chiles into a paste. Transfer the ginger–garlic–chile paste to a medium mixing bowl. Add the tomato to the bowl of the food processor and grind into a watery paste. *No need to wash the food processor bowl in between.* Transfer the ground tomato to a separate small mixing bowl and set aside.

4. In an 8-inch / 20-cm frying pan over medium–high heat, warm 2 tablespoons of the *ghee.* Add the *hing,* cumin seeds, and turmeric and cook for 40 seconds, until the cumin seeds sizzle and turn reddish-brown.

5. Add the onion to the frying pan and cook, stirring occasionally to prevent sticking, for 3 minutes, until the onion is slightly browned. Transfer the contents of the frying pan to the stockpot containing the *sabut moong dal.* Stir well.

6. Return the frying pan to medium–high heat and warm the remaining 1 tablespoon of *ghee.* Add the ginger paste from Step 3 and the red chile flakes. Cook, stirring constantly, for 1 minute. Carefully fold in the ground tomato from Step 3 and cook, stirring constantly, for 1 to 2 minutes. Remove from the heat and transfer the contents of the frying pan to the stockpot containing the *sabut moong dal.* Stir well.

7. Return the stockpot to medium heat and add the *Garam Masala,* coriander, and salt. Stir well and cook for 2 to 3 minutes, until heated through. Remove from the heat.

8. Transfer to a serving bowl. Garnish with the cilantro and serve immediately with the brown or white basmati rice, *Roti,* or *Naan.*

Sambhar
Spiced South Indian Stew

YIELD: 12 CUPS / 2.8 L

TOOLS: You'll need a heavy-bottomed, 6-quart / 6-L stockpot or Dutch oven with a lid; a blender; and a 4-quart / 4-L sauté pan with a lid.

Although I grew up eating (and loving) Punjabi cuisine, this South Indian dish is what I lived for when we visited close friends who hailed from South India. My Malathi, Parvathi, Jayanthi, and Saroja aunties are just a few who would happily feed me whenever I asked. Thanks to all of you for helping me create a palate and appreciation for authentic South Indian food.

2 cups / 460 g *duhli toor dal* (dried, split, and skinned pigeon peas), picked over, washed, and soaked for 1 hour in 6 cups / 1.4 L of boiling water, and drained

7 cups / 1.7 L room-temperature water

1 teaspoon turmeric powder

6 cups / 1.4 L boiling water, divided

2 cloves garlic, peeled and minced

2 teaspoons tamarind paste

2 teaspoons red chile powder or cayenne pepper

1 tablespoon plus 2 teaspoons salt

1 tablespoon *Sambhar* Powder (see recipe on p. 38)

3 tablespoons / 45 mL vegetable oil, divided

5 cups / 750 g chopped vegetables (I use a mix of onion, carrots, potato, daikon, tomato, okra, eggplant, and cauliflower)

¼ teaspoon *hing* (asafetida)

½ heaping teaspoon mustard seeds

15 whole dried red chiles

15–20 fresh curry leaves

3–8 fresh Thai, serrano, or cayenne chiles, stems removed and sliced in half lengthwise

Brown or white basmati rice, *Dosa,* or *Idli* (see recipes on pp. 253 and 258), for serving

1. Combine the *duhli toor dal,* the room-temperature water, and the turmeric in a heavy-bottomed, 6-quart / 6-L stockpot or Dutch oven over medium–high heat and bring to a boil.

2. Reduce the heat to medium–low and simmer, partially covered, for 1 hour. *At this point, the* dal *will break down.* Remove from the heat.

3. Transfer the *duhli toor dal* to a blender and add 4 cups / 950 mL of the boiling water. Blend until smooth.

4. Return the stockpot to medium–high heat and add the *duhli toor dal,* the garlic, the tamarind paste, the red chile powder, the salt, and the *Sambhar* Powder. Bring to a boil. Remove from the heat, cover, and set aside to cool slightly while you prep the remaining ingredients.

5. In a heavy-bottomed, 4-quart / 4-L sauté pan over medium–high heat, warm 1 tablespoon of the oil. Add the chopped vegetables and cook for 2 minutes, until they are just wilted. *Feel free to use any vegetables—this is a dish where winter vegetables like parsnips and turnips shine.* Add the cooked vegetables to the stockpot containing the *duhli toor dal* and stir well.

6. Return the sauté pan to medium–high heat and warm the remaining 2 tablespoons of oil. Add the *hing,* mustard seeds, dried chiles, curry leaves, and fresh chiles. *Be careful to keep a lid handy, as this can splatter.* Cook for 1 minute, until the red chiles are slightly browned. Transfer the mixture to the stockpot containing the *duhli toor dal.*

7. Add the remaining 2 cups / 470 mL of boiling water to the stockpot and return it to medium–high heat. Bring the mixture to a boil. Reduce the heat to medium–low and simmer, uncovered, for 10 minutes. Remove from the heat and stir well.

8. Transfer to a serving bowl and serve immediately with the brown or white basmati rice or, more traditionally, with *Dosa* or *Idli.*

Toor Dal
Spiced Split Pigeon Peas

YIELD: 8 CUPS / 1.9 L

TOOLS: You'll need a heavy-bottomed, 6-quart / 6-L stockpot or Dutch oven with a lid; an 8-inch / 20-cm frying pan; a plate; a mortar and pestle or spice grinder; a food processor; and a small mixing bowl.

At once hearty and earthy, *toor dal* is the base for the South Indian stew *sambhar*, but is just as delicious in its own right. I love this combination of savory and spicy with a touch of sweet. It's perfect over a scoop of basmati rice.

3 cups / 680 g *duhli toor dal* (dried, split, and skinned pigeon peas), picked over, washed, and soaked for 2–4 hours, and drained
10 cups / 2.4 L water
4–5 pieces dried *kokum*
2 tablespoons coriander seeds
2 tablespoons cumin seeds
1 small yellow onion, coarsely chopped
2 medium tomatoes, coarsely chopped
1–4 fresh Thai, serrano, or cayenne chiles, stems removed

2 tablespoons vegetable oil
6–8 whole dried red chiles
1 teaspoon turmeric powder
½ teaspoon mustard seeds
3 whole cloves
1 (2-inch / 5-cm) stick cinnamon
15–20 curry leaves
1 (1-inch / 3-cm) piece *gur* (jaggery) or 1 tablespoon light brown sugar
½ teaspoon tamarind paste
1 tablespoon salt
Brown or white basmati rice, for serving

1. Combine the *duhli toor dal,* water, and *kokum* in a heavy-bottomed, 6-quart / 6-L stockpot or Dutch oven over medium–high heat and bring to a boil.

2. Reduce the heat to medium–low and simmer, partially covered, for 1 hour. Remove from the heat, cover, and set aside to cool while you prep the remaining ingredients. Remove and discard the *kokum* pieces before adding other ingredients.

3. Combine the coriander and cumin seeds in an 8-inch / 20-cm frying pan over medium–high heat and cook for 5 minutes, until the seeds turn reddish-brown and become aromatic. During the entire cooking time, shake the pan every 15 to 20 seconds to prevent the spices from burning. *When roasting spices, never leave the pan unattended—they burn easily.* Remove from the heat, transfer to a plate, and set aside to cool for 15 minutes.

4. Transfer the roasted spices to a mortar and pestle or spice grinder and grind them into a powder.

5. In the bowl of a food processor, grind the onion until smooth. Transfer to a plate. Add the tomatoes and fresh chiles to the bowl of the food processor and grind into a watery paste. *No need to wash the food processor bowl in between.* Transfer the tomato–chile paste to a small mixing bowl and set aside.

Continued

PICTURED AT LEFT

1 *Toor Dal*
2 *Palak Dal* (p. 140)

6. Return the same frying pan to medium–high heat and warm the oil. Add the dried chiles, turmeric, mustard seeds, cloves, cinnamon, and curry leaves and cook for 1 minute, until the mustard seeds pop and the leaves are curled and browned. *Keep a lid handy—the seeds pop out when hot.*

7. Very, very carefully, fold the ground onion from Step 5 into the mixture in the frying pan. *It's a wet mixture, and it will splatter once it hits the hot oil.* Stir well and cook for 3 minutes, until the onion is browned and slightly caramelized.

8. Add the puréed tomato from Step 5, the *gur,* and the tamarind paste to the frying pan. Stir well and cook for 8 minutes, until the mixture is thickened. Remove from the heat and transfer the contents of the frying pan to the stock-pot containing the *duhli toor dal.*

9. Return the stockpot to medium heat and add the salt and the roasted cori-ander and cumin seeds from Step 4. Stir well and cook for 3 to 5 minutes, until heated through. Remove from the heat.

10. Transfer to a serving bowl. Serve immediately ladled over the brown or white basmati rice.

South Indian *Parippu*

YIELD: 11 CUPS / 2.6 L

Parippu means lentils or *dal* in several South Indian languages. This version includes curry leaves (in South India what cilantro is to North Indian cuisine) and creamy coconut milk. Combined with the split and skinned lentils, this dish is the perfect mix of sustenance and spice.

TOOLS: You will need a food processor; a heavy-bottomed, 6-quart / 6-L stockpot or Dutch oven with a lid; and an 8-inch / 20-cm frying pan.

1 medium yellow or red onion, roughly chopped
1 (1-inch / 3-cm) piece ginger, peeled and roughly chopped
2 cloves garlic, peeled
1–6 fresh Thai, serrano, or cayenne chiles, stems removed and roughly chopped
3 cups / 520 g *duhli masoor dal* (dried, split, and skinned red lentils), picked over and washed (no need to soak)
1 medium tomato, finely diced
2 teaspoons cumin powder
2 teaspoons coriander power
1 teaspoon turmeric powder

1 teaspoon red chile powder or cayenne pepper
6 cups / 1.4 L water (room temperature or boiling)
2 tablespoons vegetable oil (I use coconut or peanut)
1 teaspoon cumin seeds
½ teaspoon mustard seeds
10 whole dried red chiles
20–25 curry leaves, fresh or dried
1 medium yellow or red onion, finely minced
1 cup / 240 mL coconut milk (regular or light)
1 tablespoon salt
Brown or white basmati rice, for serving

1. In the bowl of a food processor, grind together the chopped onion, ginger, garlic, and fresh chiles until a smooth paste forms.

2. Combine the paste from Step 1, the *duhli masoor dal,* the tomato, the cumin powder, the coriander, the turmeric, the red chile powder, and the water in a heavy-bottomed, 6-quart / 6-L stockpot or Dutch oven over medium–high heat and bring to a boil.

3. Reduce the heat to medium–low and simmer, partially covered, for 12 minutes. Remove the cover and cook for 3 to 4 minutes. *Doing so leads to a drier end product—you don't want it to be too watery.* Remove from the heat, cover, and set aside to cool slightly while you prep the remaining ingredients. *It will have the consistency of porridge and will be yellow*—masoor dal *turns yellow after it is cooked.*

4. In an 8-inch / 20-cm sauté pan over medium–high heat, warm the oil. Add the cumin and mustard seeds and cook for 40 seconds, until the cumin seeds sizzle and turn reddish-brown. Add the dried chiles, curry leaves, and minced onion and cook for 3 minutes, until the onion is slightly browned and the curry leaves have curled. Remove from the heat and fold the contents of the sauté pan into the stockpot containing the *duhli masoor dal.*

5. Return the stockpot to medium heat and add the coconut milk and salt. Cook the mixture for 5 minutes, until all the ingredients come together.

6. Transfer to a serving bowl and serve with the brown or white basmati rice.

Mixed *Dal Tarka*

YIELD: 10 CUPS / 2.4 L

TOOLS: You'll need a large bowl to soak the *dal* and split gram; a heavy-bottomed, 6-quart / 6-L stockpot or Dutch oven with a lid; a food processor; and an 8-inch / 20-cm frying pan.

This is my parents' go-to *dal* that they order when they eat in Indian restaurants. *Tarka* refers to the finishing touch when you heat and spice oil or *ghee* and add it to the cooked *dal*. Indians don't typically eat *dal* cooked with a lot of cream and oil, so this is a perfect way to make the homestyle version a little fancier without overpowering it. It usually comes to the table sizzling.

¾ cup / 160 g *duhli moong dal* (dried, split, and skinned green *dal),* picked over and washed (they look yellow)

¾ cup / 130 g *duhli masoor dal* (dried, split, and skinned red lentils), picked over and washed

¾ cup / 150 g *chana dal* (dried, split, and skinned gram or black chickpeas), picked over and washed

¾ cup / 160 g *duhli urad* (dried, split, and skinned black *dal),* picked over and washed

7 cups / 1.7 L water (room temperature or boiling)

1 medium tomato, roughly chopped

4 tablespoons / 60 mL *ghee* or vegetable oil, divided

½ teaspoon *hing* (asafetida)

2 teaspoons cumin seeds

½ teaspoon mustard seeds

1 medium yellow or red onion, finely minced

1 teaspoon turmeric powder

1 (2-inch / 5-cm) piece ginger, peeled and grated or minced

6 cloves garlic, peeled and grated or minced

1–4 fresh Thai, serrano, or cayenne chiles, stems removed and finely sliced

1 teaspoon *Garam Masala* (see recipe on p. 35)

2 teaspoons red chile powder or cayenne pepper

1 tablespoon salt

1 small yellow or red onion, finely minced, for garnish

Brown or white basmati rice, *Roti,* or *Naan* (see recipes on pp. 230 and 238), for serving

1. Combine the 4 legumes in a deep bowl. Cover with water and set aside to soak for 3 to 6 hours. *Because the legumes in this recipe are split, they take less time to soak and cook than their whole versions.*

2. Drain the legumes. Combine the 7 cups / 1.7 L of water and the legumes in a heavy-bottomed, 6-quart / 6-L stockpot or Dutch oven over medium–high heat and bring to a boil.

3. Reduce the heat to medium–low and simmer, partially covered, for 25 minutes, until the legumes are soft and have a porridge-like consistency. *A film may form as they cook. Just skim it off the top and discard.* Remove from the heat, cover, and set aside to cool slightly as you prep the remaining ingredients.

Continued

4. In the bowl of a food processor, grind the tomato into a watery paste. *You can also finely dice it, but my kids prefer not to bite into cooked tomatoes.* Set aside.

5. In an 8-inch /20-cm frying pan over medium–high heat, warm 2 tablespoons of the *ghee*. Add the *hing,* cumin and mustard seeds and cook for 40 seconds, until the seeds sizzle and turn reddish-brown. *Keep the lid handy, as the mustard seeds will pop.* Add the onion and cook for 6 to 8 minutes, until the onion is browned and caramelized. Stir well.

6. Add the turmeric, ginger, and garlic to the frying pan and cook for 3 minutes. Add the ground tomato from Step 4 and the fresh chiles and cook for 3 to 5 minutes, until the oil starts to pull away from the sides. Add the *Garam Masala* and cook for 1 minute, until cooked through. Stir well, remove from the heat, and transfer the contents of the frying pan to the stockpot containing the legumes.

7. Return the stockpot to medium–high heat. Add the red chile powder and salt, stir well, and cook for 5 minutes, until warmed through. Remove from the heat.

8. Return the frying pan to medium–high heat and warm the remaining 2 tablespoons of *ghee.* Make a *tarka* by adding the minced onion to the pan and cooking for 8 minutes, until the onion is crispy and browned. Remove from the heat.

9. Transfer the legumes to a large serving bowl. Pour the *tarka* over the legumes. Serve with the brown or white basmati rice, *Roti,* or *Naan.*

Urad-Chana Dal

YIELD: 11 CUPS / 2.6 L

TOOLS: You'll need a deep mixing bowl; a heavy-bottomed, 6-quart / 6-L stockpot or Dutch oven with a lid; and an 8-inch / 20-cm sauté pan.

For some reason, my young girls are obsessed with this *dal.* My mother-in-law makes it all the time for them; they gobble it up and literally lick their bowls when they are done. I think what they like most is the smooth texture of the legumes and the grated ginger and garlic. The end result is more like a soup.

1¾ cups / 360 g *sabut urad* (whole, dried black *dal* with skin), picked over and washed
¼ cup / 50 g *chana dal* (split and skinned gram or black chickpeas), picked over and washed
20 cups / 4.7 L water, divided
1 (2-inch / 5-cm) piece ginger, peeled and grated or minced
6 cloves garlic, peeled and minced

½ teaspoon *hing* (asafetida)
1 tablespoon salt
1 teaspoon red chile powder or cayenne pepper
2 tablespoons *ghee* or vegetable oil
1 small yellow or red onion, finely minced
Brown or white basmati rice, *Roti,* or *Naan* (see recipes on pp. 230 and 238), for serving

1. Combine the *sabut urad* and *chana dal* in a deep mixing bowl with 8 cups / 1.9 L of the water. Set aside to soak for at least 6 hours (preferably overnight). If you are in a rush, soak them in hot, boiled water for 4 hours. Urad dal, *also known as* kaali *(black)* dal, *is a tough* dal *that takes a long time to soften and cook. You have to either soak it or cook it in a slow cooker.*

2. Drain the legumes, discarding the water, and place them in a heavy-bottomed, 6-quart / 6-L stockpot or Dutch oven over medium–high heat. Add the remaining 12 cups / 2.8 L water, the ginger, the garlic, the *hing,* the salt, and the red chile powder and bring to a boil.

3. Reduce the heat to medium–low and simmer, partially covered, for 1 hour and 15 minutes. Remove from the heat, cover, and set aside while you prep the remaining ingredients.

4. In an 8-inch / 20-cm sauté pan over medium–high heat, warm the *ghee.* Add the onion and cook, stirring occasionally to prevent sticking, for 3 minutes, until it is slightly browned. Remove from the heat.

5. Transfer the contents of the sauté pan to the stockpot containing the legumes and stir well.

6. Transfer to a serving bowl and serve ladled over the brown or white basmati rice or with the *Roti* or *Naan. This is also perfect served with a little butter or vegan margarine, or with a small spoonful of chopped fresh onion for crunch.*

Chana Dal with *Ghiya*
Split Gram Lentils with Winter Melon

YIELD: 8 CUPS / 1.9 L

TOOLS: You'll need an 8-inch / 20-cm frying pan, a plate, a mortar and pestle or spice grinder, a food processor, and a heavy-bottomed, 6-quart / 6-L stockpot or Dutch oven with a lid.

Ghiya is a very common vegetable in Punjabi home cooking. I still remember eating it when I was a little girl—it was stir-fried with spices, ginger, and tomato over rice. Mixing it with *chana dal* and roasted ground coriander makes for pure comfort food and is perfect for a cold night. You can easily find it in most Indian grocery stores.

¼ cup / 20 g coriander seeds
1 (2-inch / 5-cm) piece ginger, peeled and grated or minced
6 cloves garlic, peeled and grated or minced
1–3 fresh Thai, serrano, or cayenne chiles, stems removed and finely sliced
1 medium tomato, coarsely chopped
3 cups / 600 g *chana dal* (dried, split, and skinned gram or black chickpeas), picked over, washed, soaked for 2–4 hours in 7 cups / 1.7 L of water, and drained
1 medium *ghiya* (winter melon/calabash) or fresh pumpkin, peeled and diced

8 cups / 1.9 L water
2 tablespoons *ghee* or vegetable oil
1 teaspoon cumin seeds
½ teaspoon turmeric powder
1 medium yellow onion, minced
1 teaspoon *Garam Masala* (see recipe on p. 35)
2 teaspoons red chile powder or cayenne pepper
1 tablespoon salt
1 tablespoon chopped fresh cilantro
Brown or white basmati rice, for serving

1. Place the coriander seeds in an 8-inch / 20-cm frying pan over medium–high heat and dry roast for 5 minutes, until the seeds turn reddish-brown and become aromatic. During the entire cooking time, shake the pan every 15 to 20 seconds to prevent the spices from burning. *When roasting spices never leave the pan unattended—they burn easily.* Remove from the heat, transfer to a plate, and set aside to cool for 15 minutes.

2. Transfer the roasted coriander seeds to a mortar and pestle or spice grinder and grind them into a powder.

3. In the bowl of a food processor, grind together the ginger, garlic, fresh chiles, and tomato until a smooth, watery paste forms.

4. Combine the paste from Step 3, the *chana dal,* the *ghiya,* and the water in a heavy-bottomed, 6-quart / 6-L stockpot or Dutch oven over medium–high heat and bring to a boil.

5. Reduce the heat to medium–low and simmer, partially covered, for 1 hour. Remove from the heat, cover, and set aside to cool slightly while you prep the remaining ingredients.

6. Return the frying pan used in Step 1 to medium–high heat and warm the *ghee.* Add the cumin seeds and turmeric and cook for 40 seconds, until the cumin seeds sizzle and turn reddish-brown. Add the onion and cook for 6 minutes, until the onion is browned. Stir well.

7. Add the roasted coriander that was set aside in Step 1, the *Garam Masala,* and the red chile powder to the frying pan and stir until fully combined. Remove from the heat and transfer the contents of the frying pan to the stockpot.

8. Add the salt and cilantro to the stockpot and stir well. Cook, stirring occasionally, for 5 minutes, until the mixture is warmed through and well blended.

9. Transfer to a serving bowl and serve with the brown or white basmati rice.

Palak Dal Yellow *Dal* with Spinach

YIELD: 12 CUPS / 2.8 L

TOOLS: You'll need a heavy-bottomed, 6-quart / 6-L stockpot or Dutch oven with a lid and an 8-inch / 20-cm sauté pan.

NOTE: If you love tomatoes, add 1 diced tomato with the spices in Step 5. This is a very basic recipe for *dal*; really, you can substitute any fast-cooking bean or lentil for the *duhli moong dal,* including *masoor dal* (split and skinned red lentils).

PICTURED ON P. 130

This is one of the simplest *dals* in Punjabi cuisine and is eaten almost weekly (sometimes daily) in our households. It cooks up fast and is easy to digest. It's especially delicious topped with fresh, spiced onions; sliced fresh green chiles; and a dollop of *achaar* (Indian pickle). Here, I include spinach, which is how it's typically made in Indian restaurants. Feel free to make it without the greens, like most households do.

3 cups / 640 g *duhli moong dal* (dried, split, and skinned green *dal),* picked over and washed (they look yellow)

9 cups / 2.1 L water

3 tablespoons / 45 mL *ghee* or vegetable oil

½ teaspoon *hing* (asafetida)

1 tablespoon cumin seeds

1 teaspoon turmeric powder

1 medium white or red onion, finely diced

2–3 teaspoons plus 1 pinch salt, divided

1½-inch / 4-cm piece ginger, peeled and minced or grated

2 cloves garlic, peeled and minced

2–3 fresh Thai, serrano, or cayenne chiles, stems removed and finely chopped

1 tablespoon *Garam Masala* (see recipe on p. 35)

1 tablespoon ground coriander

1–2 teaspoons red chile powder or cayenne pepper

6 ounces / 170 g fresh spinach, roughly chopped

1 heaping tablespoon chopped fresh cilantro

Brown or white basmati rice, *Roti,* or *Naan* (see recipes on pp. 230 and 238), for serving

1. Combine the *duhli moong dal* and water in a heavy-bottomed, 6-quart / 6-L stockpot or Dutch oven over medium–high heat and bring to a boil.

2. Reduce the heat to medium and simmer, uncovered, for 20 minutes. *I cook mine uncovered and keep an eye on it to make sure it does not overflow. At first, you'll see a white film form over the* duhli moong dal. *Just skim it off and discard, and continue to boil until the* dal *is soft.* Remove from the heat, cover, and set aside to cool slightly while you prep the remaining ingredients. *This will end up a little thick, but will loosen up after the following steps. If you want to thin it out a bit, just add a little more water until it's at the preferred consistency.*

3. In an 8-inch / 20-cm sauté pan over medium–high heat, warm the *ghee.* Add the *hing,* cumin seeds, and turmeric and cook for 40 seconds, until the cumin seeds sizzle and turn reddish-brown.

4. Add the onion and the pinch of salt to the sauté pan and cook, stirring occasionally, for 2 to 3 minutes, until the onion is slightly browned. Add the ginger, garlic, and fresh chiles and cook for 2 minutes.

5. Add the *Garam Masala*, coriander, and red chile powder to the sauté pan and cook, stirring well, for 20 seconds or so. *Be careful not to burn the spices.* Add the spinach and cook for 1 minute, until just wilted. Remove from the heat and transfer the contents of the sauté pan to the stockpot containing the *duhli moong dal.*

6. Add the remaining 2 teaspoons of salt and the cilantro to the stockpot and stir well.

7. Transfer to a serving bowl and serve ladled over the brown or white basmati rice or with the *Roti* or *Naan. This is delicious as a soup as well.*

Sookhi Dal Dry, Spiced Lentils

YIELD: 7 CUPS / 1.7 L

TOOLS: You'll need a heavy-bottomed, 6-quart / 6-L (or larger) stockpot or Dutch oven with a lid and an 8-inch / 20-cm frying pan.

In the Punjabi home, this dried version of soupy lentils is eaten with unleavened bread and a curry on the side. I tend to use it as my favorite filling for a wrap or pita on days when we just can't think of anything else to make for dinner. I often buy mini pitas and stuff them with this dry lentil dish for my kids' lunches.

2 cups / 420 g *duhli moong dal* (dried, split, and skinned green *dal)*, picked over and washed (they look yellow)

3 cassia or bay leaves

2 whole cloves

1 (3-inch/ 8-cm) stick cinnamon

3 whole dried red chiles

½ teaspoon turmeric powder

3 cups / 710 mL water

3 tablespoons / 45 mL *ghee* or vegetable oil

1 pinch *hing* (asafetida)

1 teaspoon cumin seeds

1 medium yellow or red onion, diced

2 teaspoons plus 1 pinch salt, divided

1 tablespoon grated or minced ginger

3 cloves garlic, peeled and minced or grated

4 fresh Thai, serrano, or cayenne chiles, stems removed and chopped

1 teaspoon *amchur* (dried mango powder)

1 teaspoon *Garam Masala* (see recipe on p. 35)

1 teaspoon ground coriander

1 teaspoon red chile powder or cayenne pepper

Juice of ½ lemon

½ cup / 10 g fresh cilantro, minced

Roti or *Naan* (see recipes on pp. 230 and 238), for serving (optional)

Tortilla wrap or pita, for serving (optional)

Hummus, for serving (optional)

Chopped onion, tomatoes, lettuce, and avocado, for garnish (optional)

1. Combine the *dal,* cassia leaves, cloves, cinnamon, dried chiles, turmeric, and water in a heavy-bottomed, 6-quart / 6-L (or larger) stockpot or Dutch oven over medium–high heat and bring to a boil. *Typically, a frothy film will form over the* dal *as they boil—just skim off and discard it.*

2. Reduce the heat to medium–low and simmer, partially covered, for 11 minutes. Remove from the heat, cover completely, and set aside for 5 minutes, allowing the *dal* to absorb the extra moisture.

3. Carefully remove and discard the whole spices. Stir gently. *The dal should be al dente—firm, but cooked through.* Cover and set aside to cool slightly while you prep the remaining ingredients.

Continued

4. In an 8-inch / 20-cm frying pan over medium–high heat, warm the *ghee.* Add the *hing* and cumin seeds and cook for 40 seconds, until the cumin seeds sizzle and turn reddish-brown.

5. Add the onion and the pinch of salt to the frying pan. Cook for 2 minutes, until slightly browned. Add the ginger and garlic and cook, stirring constantly, for 1 minute.

6. Add the fresh chiles, *amchur*, *Garam Masala*, coriander, and red chile powder. Cook for 5 to 10 seconds and remove from the heat.

7. Transfer the contents of the frying pan to the stockpot containing the *dal.* Add the remaining 2 teaspoons of salt, the lemon juice, and the cilantro and stir carefully, taking care not to break down the *dal* too much.

8. Serve traditionally, with the *Roti* or *Naan,* or as a wrap in a tortilla or stuffed in a pita smeared with a little hummus and garnished with the onion, tomatoes, lettuce, and avocado.

Duhli Moong Dal Kitchari

YIELD: 8 CUPS / 1.9 L

TOOLS: You'll need a heavy-bottomed, 6-quart / 6-L (or larger) stockpot or Dutch oven with a lid and an 8-inch / 20-cm sauté pan.

TIP: If this dish gets cold, it tends to thicken because of the starchiness of the rice and lentils. The best way to reheat it is slowly, in a saucepan over medium–low heat. Add a little water to return it to the perfect consistency—and add a little salt if needed.

The Hindi–English translation of *kitchari* is "all mixed up." This, the Punjabi version of chicken noodle soup, is perfect for treating a bellyache or for anyone who's a little under the weather. Why? Because *dal* and rice are very easy on the digestive system. Spicing it up like I do below gives you a gourmet version of porridge that can be served to company as well.

2 cups / 420 g *duhli moong dal* (dried, split, and skinned green *dal),* picked over and washed (they will look yellow)
1 cup / 190 g white basmati rice
8 cups / 1.9 L water
3 tablespoons / 45 mL *ghee* or vegetable oil
1 teaspoon cumin seeds
1 teaspoon *ajwain* (carom seeds)
1 teaspoon turmeric powder
2 black cardamom pods (use green if you don't have black)
1 small yellow or red onion, finely diced

1 (2-inch / 5-cm) piece ginger, peeled and grated or minced
1–2 cloves garlic, peeled and grated or minced
1–3 fresh Thai, serrano, or cayenne chiles, stems removed and chopped
2 teaspoons salt
½ teaspoon red chile powder or cayenne pepper
1 tablespoon each chopped fresh onion and cilantro, for garnish
1 tablespoon butter or vegan margarine, for garnish

1. Combine the *duhli moong dal,* rice, and water in a heavy-bottomed, 6-quart / 6-L (or larger) stockpot or Dutch oven over medium–high heat and bring to a boil. *Brown rice is a good substitute for white; if using, add another ½ cup water.*

2. Reduce the heat to medium–low and simmer, partially covered, for 25 to 30 minutes, until all the ingredients soften and blend together and the mixture has a porridge-like consistency. *A light film may form during the cooking process—just skim it off the top and discard.* Remove from the heat, cover, and set aside to cool slightly while you prep the remaining ingredients.

3. In an 8-inch / 20-cm sauté pan over medium–high heat, warm the *ghee.* Add the cumin seeds, *ajwain,* turmeric, and cardamom and cook for 40 seconds, until the cumin seeds sizzle and turn reddish-brown.

4. Add the onion, ginger, garlic, and fresh chiles. Cook for 2 minutes, until the mixture is slightly browned. Remove from the heat. *Add more chopped veggies, including corn, carrots, or tomatoes, at this point, if you like.*

5. Transfer the contents of the sauté pan to the stockpot containing the *dal,* add the salt and red chile powder, and stir well. Remove and discard the cardamom pods.

6. Transfer the mixture into individual serving bowls. Garnish with the onion, cilantro, and butter and serve immediately, piping hot.

Vegetable Curries

The word "curry" is widely misunderstood. In the West, especially in the United States, it refers to a spice blend that is added to water, vegetables, and/or meat to lend a distinctly Indian flavor profile.

In the South Asian mind, curry refers less to spice and more to the consistency of a dish. We rarely—if ever—cook with the spice blend known as curry. To us, curry means "gravy." A typical Indian meal is made up of stir-fries and a curry or two, along with rice and/or bread.

So if we don't use the spice curry, what do we use to spice our food? Answer: either whole spices, like cumin seeds, turmeric powder, and ground coriander, or spice blends, like *Garam Masala* and *Chana Masala* (see recipes on pp. 35 and 36), which are created from whole spices and tailored to provide a precise flavor profile for a specific dish.

Indian food gets its layers of flavors by roasting and pan-frying spices in hot oils and *ghee,* which you can only do well if you cook with whole spices. By that, I mean spices in the form of seeds, sticks, and leaves. You can't get the same layers of flavor with just a single blended powder, like Western curry powder. When we do add powdered spice blends, we typically do so in addition to heating whole spices in hot oil.

One exception to this rule is when you're making dishes in a slow cooker, where the longer cooking

times help draw out the essential oils from spices much as putting spices in hot oil can create.

Most folks who come to my demos and say "I don't like the taste of curry" end up tasting my food and loving it—largely because it tastes like food, rather than chalky powder. I do use curry powder in some dishes, just for a change of pace, but not all curry powders are made the same. Some have more complex flavors than others. The only way you will know what works for you is to experiment.

Imlee Lobhia
Black-Eyed Peas in Tamarind– Coconut Curry

YIELD: 9 CUPS / 2.1 L

TOOLS: You will need a heavy-bottomed, 6-quart / 6-L stockpot or Dutch oven with a lid; a food processor; and an 8-inch / 20-cm frying pan.

Decadent is the only accurate way to describe this dish. It is at once creamy—with no dairy—fulfilling, and comforting. The unique combination of tamarind, coconut milk, and black-eyed peas really makes this dish shine.

- 3 cups / 546 g *lobhia* (dried black-eyed peas), picked over, washed, soaked overnight, and drained
- 1 teaspoon turmeric powder
- 8 cups / 1.9 L boiling water, divided
- 1 (2-inch / 5-cm) cube dried tamarind pulp or 1 teaspoon tamarind paste
- 1 large tomato, peeled and diced*
- 2 tablespoons coconut oil
- 1 medium yellow or red onion, finely diced
- 1 (1-inch / 3-cm) piece ginger, peeled and grated or minced
- 2 cloves garlic, peeled and grated or minced
- 1–3 fresh Thai, serrano, or cayenne chiles, stems removed and finely sliced
- 1 tablespoon dark brown sugar
- 2 teaspoons ground coriander
- 2 teaspoons red chile powder or cayenne pepper
- 1 tablespoon salt
- 1 cup / 240 mL regular or light coconut milk
- 1 heaping tablespoon chopped fresh cilantro, for garnish
- Brown or white basmati rice, *Roti*, or *Naan* (see recipes on pp. 230 and 238), for serving

1. Combine the *lobhia,* turmeric, and 7 cups / 1.7 L of the water in a heavy-bottomed, 6-quart / 6-L or larger stockpot or Dutch oven over medium–high heat and bring to a boil.

2. Reduce the heat to medium–low, partially cover, and simmer for 30 to 40 minutes, until the *lobhia* soften. Remove from the heat, cover, and set aside to cool slightly while you prep the remaining ingredients. *There is no need to drain the beans, as the liquid will make a nice base for the curry later.*

3. While the beans are cooking, soak the tamarind pulp in the remaining 1 cup / 240 mL of water for at least 30 minutes. *Once finished, use the back of a fork to break down the pulp and squeeze the liquid out by hand. Discard the pulp, seeds, and fiber, and using a fine strainer, strain the juice. Reserve the juice for the curry.*

4. In the bowl of a food processor, grind the reserved tamarind juice from Step 3 and the tomato into a watery paste. Set aside.

5. In an 8-inch / 20-cm frying pan over medium–high heat, warm the oil. Add the onion and cook for 6 to 7 minutes, until browned and caramelized. Add the ginger and garlic and cook for 1 minute.

6. Slowly and carefully add the tamarind paste from Step 4, the fresh chiles, and the brown sugar to the frying pan. Stir well and cook for 4 minutes. Remove from the heat and transfer the mixture to the stockpot containing the *lobhia*.

7. Return the stockpot to medium–high heat and add the coriander, red chile powder, and salt. Simmer, uncovered, for 10 minutes.

8. Add the coconut milk and cook for 1 minute, until warmed through. Remove from the heat.

9. Transfer the mixture to a serving bowl. Garnish with the cilantro and serve with the brown or white basmati rice, *Roti,* or *Naan.*

*See notes for peeling tomatoes on page 28. A serrated peeler is the easiest way.

Chana Masala
Curried Chickpeas

YIELD: 9 CUPS / 2.1 L

TOOLS: You'll need a heavy-bottomed, 6-quart / 6-L stockpot or Dutch oven with a lid and a 6-quart / 6-L sauté pan.

Need I say more? This is one of the most-loved Indian vegetarian dishes beyond India's borders. The key spice that goes into it has the same name as the dish, which is a little confusing. But there's nothing confusing about the outcome—it is deliciously addictive. My family needs a good, spicy *Chana Masala* at least once a week.

3 cups / 570 g *kabuli chana* (dried white chickpeas), picked over, washed, soaked overnight, and drained
8 cups / 1.9 L water
3 tablespoons / 45 mL vegetable oil, plus more if needed
½ teaspoon *hing* (asafetida)
½ teaspoon turmeric powder
1 heaping teaspoon cumin seeds
2 tablespoons *Chana Masala* (see recipe on p. 36)
1 medium yellow onion, finely minced
1 tablespoon water, plus more if needed (optional)

1 (2-inch / 5-cm) piece ginger, peeled and grated or minced
6 cloves garlic, peeled and grated or finely minced
1 large tomato, finely diced
1–6 fresh Thai, serrano, or cayenne chiles, stems removed and diced
1 teaspoon *Garam Masala* (see recipe on p. 35)
1 tablespoon salt
1 tablespoon red chile powder or cayenne pepper
Brown or white basmati rice, *Roti, Naan,* or *Bhatura* (see recipes on pp. 230, 238, and 241), for serving

1. Combine the *kabuli chana* and the 8 cups / 1.9 L of water in a heavy-bottomed, 6-quart / 6-L or larger stockpot or Dutch oven over medium–high heat and bring to a boil.

2. Reduce the heat to medium–low and simmer, partially covered, for 45 minutes to 1 hour, until the chickpeas soften. Remove from the heat, cover, and set aside to cool slightly while you prep the remaining ingredients. *You can also cook the chickpeas in a 3½-quart / 3.5-L slow cooker. Use 3 cups / 570 g dried* kabuli chana *and 5 cups / 1.2 L water and cook on high for 4 hours.*

3. Drain the *kabuli chana* and reserve the chickpeas and cooking liquid in separate bowls. Keep about 4 cups / 950 mL of cooking liquid and discard the rest; if there's not quite that much, make up the difference with water. Set aside.

4. In a 6-quart / 6-L sauté pan over medium–high heat, warm the oil. Add the *hing,* turmeric, and cumin seeds and cook for 40 seconds, until the cumin seeds sizzle and turn reddish-brown. Stir well, add the *Chana Masala,* and cook for 30 seconds.

5. Add the onion to the sauté pan and cook, stirring constantly, for 2 minutes. *If the mixture gets dry at this point, add 1 tablespoon of oil or water.* Add the ginger and garlic and cook for 1 minute.

6. Add the tomato and fresh chiles to the sauté pan and cook, stirring constantly, for 2 minutes. *You'll start to see the oil pull out of the mixture at the edges.* Add the *Garam Masala,* salt, and red chile powder and stir until combined.

7. Slowly add the reserved liquid from cooking the *kabuli chana* to the sauté pan. Bring to a boil. Reduce the heat to medium–low and simmer for 5 minutes, until the mixture starts to thicken slightly.

8. Add the chickpeas and simmer, stirring occasionally, for 10 minutes. There should be some liquid to this dish; if it is too dry, just add a little more water and simmer for 2 to 3 minutes.

9. Transfer to a serving bowl and serve immediately with the brown or white basmati rice, *Roti, Naan,* or *Bhatura.*

Khata Chana
Tangy Chickpeas

YIELD: 9 CUPS / 2.1 L

TOOLS: You'll need a heavy-bottomed, 6-quart / 6-L stockpot or Dutch oven with a lid; a small mixing bowl; a fine strainer; a food processor; and a 6-quart / 6-L sauté pan.

NOTE: If you don't have tamarind pulp, substitute 1 tablespoon of tamarind paste diluted in ¼ cup / 60 mL of water. You can also substitute canned and drained chickpeas, but the flavor and consistency of dried chickpeas is hard to beat. You can purchase *chaat masala* from most Indian grocery stores or my website, indianasapplepie.com.

This dish reminds me of the chickpeas I used to eat as a little girl by the lake in Chandigarh. Hot, spicy, and tangy, it was even better served in a little cone of newspaper. Be aware: This dish has quite the kick to it. Feel free to tone the chiles down, but if you like spicy food, this will most definitely hit the spot.

3 cups / 570 g *kabuli chana* (dried white chickpeas), picked over, washed, soaked overnight, and drained
8 cups / 1.9 L water
1 (2-inch / 5-cm) cube dried tamarind pulp
1 cup / 240 mL boiling water
1 medium yellow onion, coarsely chopped
1 (2-inch / 5-cm) piece ginger, peeled and coarsely chopped
6 cloves garlic, peeled
1–3 whole fresh Thai, serrano, or cayenne chiles, stems removed
3 tablespoons / 45 mL vegetable oil
½ teaspoon *hing* (asafetida)
1 teaspoon turmeric powder
2 teaspoons cumin seeds
1 tablespoon ground coriander

2 teaspoons red chile powder or cayenne pepper
2 tablespoons *Garam Masala* (see recipe on p. 35)
¼ cup / 60 mL plain, unsweetened yogurt (dairy, soy, or coconut)
Juice of 1 medium lemon
2–3 fresh Thai, serrano, or cayenne chiles, stems removed and sliced lengthwise
½ teaspoon ground black pepper
1 tablespoon *Chaat Masala* (see recipe on p. 37)
1 (1-inch / 3-cm) piece ginger, peeled and cut in matchsticks
1 tablespoon plus 1 teaspoon salt
1 medium red onion, sliced into thin rings, divided
¼ cup / 5 g chopped fresh cilantro
Naan or *Bhatura* (see recipes on pp. 238 and 241), for serving

1. Combine the *kabuli chana* and the 8 cups / 1.9 L water in a heavy-bottomed, 6-quart / 6-L or larger stockpot or Dutch oven over medium–high heat and bring to a boil.

2. Reduce the heat to medium–low and simmer, partially covered, for 45 minutes to 1 hour, until the chickpeas soften. Remove from the heat, cover, and set aside to cool slightly while you prep the remaining ingredients. *You can also cook the chickpeas in a 3½-quart / 3.5-L slow cooker. Use 3 cups / 570 g dried* kabuli chana *and 5 cups / 1.2 L water and cook on high for 4 hours.*

3. While the chickpeas are cooking, place the tamarind pulp in a small mixing bowl, pour the boiling water over it, and set aside to soak for at least 30 minutes.

Continued

4. Once the soaking time is up, use the back of a fork to break down the pulp and squeeze the liquid out of it. Discard the pulp, seeds, and fiber and, using a fine strainer, strain the juice. Set aside the juice.

5. Drain the *kabuli chana* and reserve the chickpeas and cooking liquid in separate bowls. Keep about 4 cups / 950 mL of cooking liquid and discard the rest; if there's not quite that much, make up the difference with water. Set aside.

6. In the bowl of a food processor, grind the onion, the coarsely chopped ginger, the garlic, and the whole fresh chiles into a smooth paste. *Take your time: Process, scrape down the sides, and process again, until the mixture forms a watery paste.* Set aside.

7. In a heavy-bottomed, 6-quart / 6-L sauté pan over medium–high heat, warm the oil. Add the *hing,* turmeric, and cumin seeds and cook for 40 seconds, until the cumin seeds sizzle and turn reddish-brown.

8. Carefully add the onion paste from Step 6 to the sauté pan and cook, stirring constantly, for 3 minutes, until slightly browned. Remove from the heat and add the coriander, the red chile powder, the *Garam Masala,* the yogurt, and the reserved tamarind juice. Stir to combine.

9. Return the sauté pan to medium–high heat. Bring to a boil and boil for 1 minute. Add the reserved cooking liquid from the *kabuli chana* and simmer for 8 to 10 minutes, until the sauce thickens and the oil starts to separate and collect at the top. Stir occasionally to avoid sticking.

10. Add the lemon juice, the sliced fresh chiles, the black pepper, the *Chaat Masala,* the ginger chopped into matchsticks, and the salt and stir well. Add the reserved *kabuli chana* and ½ of the ringed onions and cook, stirring occasionally, for 8 minutes, until cooked through. Remove from the heat. *This is an amazing sauce all by itself. Experiment by swapping out chickpeas for other main ingredients, from veggies to meat.*

11. Transfer to a serving bowl and garnish with the remaining onion and cilantro. Serve immediately with the *Naan* or *Bhatura.*

Mattar Paneer
Peas and Homemade Cheese

YIELD: 7 CUPS / 1.7 L

In our house, this dish rules—especially on Tuesday, when my husband's family avoids eating meat and eggs. For many Hindus, *paneer* is the key protein on days of religious observance.

TOOLS: You'll need a food processor; 2 small mixing bowls; and a heavy-bottomed, 4-quart / 4-L sauté pan or Dutch oven.

VEGANIZE IT! Use 1 (14-ounce / 400-g) container of tofu, baked (see recipe for Baked Tofu on p. 46) instead of the *Paneer*—you may not even notice the difference.

1 medium yellow or red onion, roughly chopped
1 (1-inch / 3-cm) piece ginger, peeled and roughly chopped
6 cloves garlic, peeled
1 medium tomato, coarsely chopped
2 tablespoons vegetable oil
1 teaspoon cumin seeds
1 black cardamom pod
1 (3-inch / 8-cm) stick cinnamon
2 tablespoons tomato paste
1–2 fresh Thai, serrano, or cayenne chiles, stems removed and thinly sliced
1 teaspoon turmeric powder
1 teaspoon *Garam Masala* (see recipe on p. 35)
1 teaspoon ground coriander
¼ teaspoon red chile powder or cayenne pepper
3 cups / 710 mL plus 1–2 tablespoons water, divided
2 cups / 270 g frozen peas
2–3 teaspoons salt
1 pound / 450 g cubed *Paneer* (1½ cups / 350 mL; see recipe on p. 44)
1 heaping tablespoon chopped fresh cilantro, for garnish
Brown or white basmati rice, *Roti*, or *Naan* (see recipes on pp. 230 and 238), for serving

1. In the bowl of a food processor, grind the onion, ginger, and garlic into a coarse paste. Transfer to a small mixing bowl and set aside. *No need to clean the food processor bowl in between.* Add the tomato to the food processor bowl and grind into a watery paste. Transfer to a second small mixing bowl and set aside.

2. In a heavy-bottomed, 4-quart / 4-L sauté pan or Dutch oven over medium–high heat, warm the oil. Add the cumin seeds, cardamom, and cinnamon and cook for 40 seconds, until the cumin seeds sizzle and turn reddish-brown.

3. Add the onion paste from Step 1 to the sauté pan and cook, stirring intermittently, for 10 minutes, until the mixture is slightly browned. *You must stir often to prevent sticking. If the mixture dries out, add a little water, 1 tablespoon at a time.*

4. Add the ground tomato from Step 1, the tomato paste, the fresh chiles, the turmeric, the *Garam Masala*, the coriander, and the red chile powder to the sauté pan and cook, stirring constantly, for 5 minutes, adding the 1 to 2 tablespoons of water as you stir to make sure the mixture does not burn. Add the peas and cook for 5 minutes. Add the remaining 3 cups / 710 mL of water and the salt to the sauté pan and bring to a boil.

5. Reduce the heat to medium and simmer, partially covered, for 8 to 10 minutes.

6. Raise the heat to medium–high and gently add the *Paneer* to the sauté pan. Bring to a boil and cook at a steady boil for 1 to 2 minutes. Remove from the heat, cover, and set aside for 30 minutes. *It's important that you don't let the dish boil too long, or the* paneer *(if homemade) will start to crumble and fall apart. Letting the dish sit also enables the* paneer *to swell and absorb flavors.*

7. Transfer to a serving bowl and garnish with the cilantro. Serve over the brown or white basmati rice *(my way)* or with the *Roti* or *Naan (the way my husband prefers it).*

Palak Paneer
Spiced Spinach and Cheese

YIELD: 4–5 CUPS / 1–1.2 L BEFORE ADDING *PANEER*

TOOLS: You'll need a 6-quart / 6-L sauté pan and an immersion (stick) blender, food processor, or blender.

VEGANIZE IT! Replace the *ghee* with the vegetable oil, the dairy cream with Cashew Cream (see recipe on p. 47) or soy, almond, or coconut milk. Replace the *Paneer* with Baked Tofu (see recipe on p. 46).

NOTE: If using canned tomatoes, cut the water in half.

PICTURED ON P. 96

This is a mainstay on the Punjabi dinner table. No matter the occasion, there is always a place for deliciously spiced spinach and homemade cheese. I've been subbing the *paneer* with baked tofu lately without missing a beat. Try it either way.

2 tablespoons *ghee* or vegetable oil
½ teaspoon *hing* (asafetida)
1 tablespoon cumin seeds
1 teaspoon turmeric powder
1 large yellow or red onion, roughly chopped
2 teaspoons plus 1 pinch salt, divided
1 (3-inch / 8-cm) piece ginger, peeled and diced small
10 cloves garlic, peeled and diced
2 teaspoons *Garam Masala* (see recipe on p. 35)
2 teaspoons ground coriander
1 teaspoon red chile powder or cayenne pepper
2 large tomatoes, roughly diced
1 cup / 240 mL water, divided

1 heaping tablespoon tomato paste
1 heaping tablespoon *kasoori methi* (dried fenugreek leaves), lightly hand crushed to release flavor
2–5 fresh Thai, serrano, or cayenne chiles, stems removed and chopped
12 packed cups / 550 g fresh spinach, washed
½–1 cup / 120–240 mL cream or half & half
2 heaping cups / 620 g diced *Paneer,* fresh or pan-fried (see recipe on p. 44)
Brown or white basmati rice, *Roti,* or *Naan* (see recipes on pp. 230 and 238), for serving

1. In a 6-quart / 6-L sauté pan over medium–high heat, warm the *ghee.* Add the *hing,* cumin seeds, and turmeric and cook for 40 seconds, until the cumin seeds sizzle and turn reddish-brown. Stir well to ensure the seeds are coated with oil and to avoid burning and sticking.

2. Add the onion and the pinch of salt to the sauté pan and cook for 3 minutes, stirring occasionally, until the onion is slightly browned. Add the ginger and garlic and cook for 1 minute.

3. Add the *Garam Masala,* coriander, and red chile powder to the sauté pan and cook for 40 seconds, watching carefully to ensure the spices do not burn.

4. Add the tomatoes and ½ cup /60 mL of the water to the sauté pan and cook for 2 minutes. Add the remaining ½ cup / 60 mL of water, the tomato paste, the *kasoori methi,* the fresh chiles, and the remaining 2 teaspoons of salt. Cook, stirring occasionally, for 3 minutes, until blended.

5. Slowly add the spinach to the sauté pan, allowing it to wilt down so the pan will be able to accommodate all the spinach. Stir occasionally and cook, uncovered, for 8 minutes, until the spinach cooks down completely. Remove from the heat and set the mixture aside to cool for 2 to 3 minutes.

6. Using an immersion blender, food processor, or blender, pulse the mixture until all the ingredients have broken down and blended together. *Here, you should use your best judgment. If you like it smooth, process it more. If you like more texture, just pulse it a bit.*

7. Return the mixture to the sauté pan over medium heat and simmer for 5 to 6 minutes, until all the ingredients, including the spices, come together. Add the cream and *Paneer* and cook for 2 minutes, until warmed through. *If using home-made paneer, be careful not to cook it too much because the cubes will break down. You want it to stay cubed when you serve it.* Stir gently until combined. Remove from the heat.

8. Serve immediately with the brown or white basmati rice, *Roti,* or *Naan.*

Sarson ka Saag
Spiced Mustard Greens

YIELD: 5 CUPS / 1.2 L

TOOLS: You'll need a heavy-bottomed, 6-quart / 6-L sauté pan or Dutch oven with a lid; a blender; a food processor; and a small sauté pan.

PICTURED ON P. 250

When you drive into the heart of Punjab, the first thing you'll be struck by are all of the green mustard fields dotted with tiny yellow flowers. I see it every time I travel to my father's childhood village. It's a sight you keep in your heart, and no surprise that this crop is the inspiration for many a Bollywood movie dance scene. If you wanted to take the state of Punjab and neatly wrap it up in one dish, it would be this one, served with a side of stacked *makki ki roti* (corn flatbread). Need I say more?

4 tablespoons / 60 mL *ghee* or vegetable oil, divided
2 teaspoons cumin seeds
1 medium yellow or red onion, finely diced
1 tablespoon plus 2 pinches salt, divided
2 large bunches mustard greens (about 1½ pounds / 680 g), trimmed and finely chopped
1 small bunch spinach (about 6 ounces / 180 g), cleaned and chopped
3 tablespoons / 30 g cornmeal
2½ cups / 590 mL water
1 small red or yellow onion, coarsely chopped

1 (2-inch / 5-cm) piece ginger, peeled and coarsely chopped
8 cloves garlic, peeled
1–6 fresh Thai, serrano, or cayenne chiles, stems removed
2 teaspoons *Garam Masala* (see recipe on p. 35)
2 teaspoons ground coriander
2 teaspoons red chile powder or cayenne pepper
1 teaspoon turmeric powder
1 tablespoon butter or vegan margarine
Makki ki Roti (corn bread), *Roti, Naan* (see recipes on pp. 251, 230, and 238), or brown or white basmati rice, for serving

1. In a heavy-bottomed, 6-quart / 6-L sauté pan or Dutch oven over medium–high heat, warm 2 tablespoons of the *ghee*. Add the cumin seeds, the diced onion, and 1 pinch of the salt and cook for 2 minutes, until the mixture is opaque and slightly brown.

2. Add the mustard greens, spinach, cornmeal, and water to the sauté pan. Reduce the heat and cook, uncovered, for 15 minutes. *The greens will break down and the water will dry up a bit.* Remove from the heat.

3. Once cool enough to handle, transfer the ingredients to a blender and process the ingredients until smooth. Return the ingredients to the sauté pan, cover, and set aside as you prep the remaining ingredients.

4. In the bowl of a food processor, grind together the chopped onion, ginger, garlic, and fresh chiles until the mixture forms a rough paste.

5. In a small sauté pan over medium–high heat, warm the remaining 2 table-spoons of *ghee*. Add the paste from Step 4 and the remaining pinch of salt. Cook for 4 minutes, until the mixture is slightly browned. Remove from the heat.

6. Transfer this mixture to the sauté pan containing the greens. Add the *Garam Masala*, the coriander, the red chile powder, the turmeric, and the remaining 1 tablespoon of salt and stir until combined. Return the sauté pan to medium–high heat and cook for 5 minutes, until the moisture evaporates just a little. *The ingredients may bubble and splash. If so, just cover with a lid.*

7. Transfer to a serving bowl and place the butter on top of the greens. Serve immediately with *Makki ki Roti*, or with *Roti, Naan,* or rice. *You can be a little decadent with this recipe—it's culturally acceptable!*

Chana Aloo
Curried Chickpeas and Potatoes

YIELD: 11 CUPS / 2.6 L

TOOLS: You'll need a heavy-bottomed, 6-quart / 6-L stockpot or Dutch oven with a lid; a food processor; 3 small mixing bowls; and a 6-quart / 6-L sauté pan.

Chickpeas. Potatoes. Put them together and you'll have a comforting, whole-some dish that is also an easy dinner option. No matter how often I serve it, my kids always ask me to make it again.

3 cups / 570 g *kabuli chana* (dried white chickpeas), picked over, washed, soaked overnight, and drained
14 cups / 3.3 L plus 3 tablespoons / 45 mL water, divided
1 large yellow onion, roughly chopped
1 (4-inch / 10-cm) piece ginger, peeled and roughly chopped
¼ cup / 35 g garlic cloves, peeled
1–4 fresh Thai, serrano, or cayenne chiles, stems removed
2 large tomatoes, coarsely chopped
2 tablespoons *ghee* or vegetable oil
2 (3-inch / 8-cm) sticks cinnamon

3 whole cloves
6 green cardamom pods
1 tablespoon cumin seeds
1 teaspoon turmeric powder
2 tablespoons *Garam Masala* (see recipe on p. 35)
2 tablespoons *Chana Masala* (see recipe on p. 36)
1 tablespoon red chile powder or cayenne pepper
2 large russet potatoes, boiled, peeled, and cut in 8 pieces
1 tablespoon salt
Brown or white basmati rice, *Roti*, or *Naan* (see recipes on pp. 230 and 238), for serving

1. Combine the *kabuli chana* and 8 cups of the water in a heavy-bottomed, 6-quart / 6-L or larger stockpot or Dutch oven over medium–high heat and bring to a boil.

2. Reduce the heat to medium–low and simmer, partially covered, for 45 minutes to 1 hour, until the chickpeas soften. Remove from the heat, cover, and set aside to cool slightly while you prep the remaining ingredients. *You can also cook the chickpeas in a 3½-quart / 3.5-L slow cooker. Use 3 cups / 680 g dried* kabuli chana *and 5 cups / 1.2 L water and cook on high for 4 hours.* Drain and discard the water.

3. In the bowl of a food processor, grind the onion into a watery paste. Transfer to a small mixing bowl and set aside. *No need to clean the food processor bowl in between.* Add the ginger, garlic, and fresh chiles to the food processor bowl and grind into a paste. Transfer to a second small mixing bowl and set aside. *Again, no need to clean.* Add the tomatoes to the food processor bowl and grind into a watery paste. Transfer to a third small mixing bowl and set aside.

4. In a heavy-bottomed, 6-quart / 6-L sauté pan over medium–high heat, warm the *ghee*. Add the cinnamon, cloves, and cardamom and cook for 40 seconds, until the spices sizzle.

5. Add the cumin seeds and turmeric to the sauté pan and cook for 40 seconds, until the cumin seeds sizzle and turn reddish-brown.

6. Very carefully, add the onion paste from Step 3 to the sauté pan. *Keep the lid handy—the liquid can splatter.* Cook for 4 minutes, until slightly browned. Stir well. Add the ginger paste from Step 3 and 1 tablespoon of the water and cook, stirring constantly, for 2 minutes.

7. Add the *Garam Masala*, *Chana Masala*, red chile powder, and 2 tablespoons of the water to the sauté pan. Stir well and cook for 1 minute. Carefully add the ground tomato from Step 3 and bring the mixture to a boil.

8. Reduce the heat to medium and simmer for 5 minutes, until the mixture is slightly thickened.

9. Add the chickpeas, the potatoes, the remaining 6 cups / 1.4 L of water, and the salt and raise the heat to medium–high. Bring to a boil.

10. Reduce the heat to medium and simmer, stirring occasionally, for 15 minutes. Remove the whole spices and remove from the heat.

11. Transfer the mixture to a serving bowl. Serve with the brown or white basmati rice, *Roti,* or *Naan.*

Shahi Paneer
Creamy Spiced Homemade Cheese

YIELD: 7 CUPS / 1.7 L INCLUDING THE *PANEER*

TOOLS: You'll need a food processor; 4 small mixing bowls; a heavy-bottomed, 4-quart / 4-L sauté pan; and a blender.

VEGANIZE IT! Easily make this recipe vegan by substituting Baked Tofu (see recipe on p. 46) for the *Paneer* and plain, unsweetened soy or coconut yogurt for the dairy.

When I think of making a vegetarian treat for the whole family—this dish is a must. It's a classic example of Mughlai cuisine—rich from the cashews, spices, and homemade cheese—a real treat, and one that fits the name. *Shahi* means royalty, which your guests will feel like when you serve them this dish.

1 medium yellow or red onion, coarsely chopped
1 (2-inch / 5-cm) piece ginger, peeled and coarsely chopped
10 cloves garlic, peeled
1 large tomato, coarsely chopped
2 heaping tablespoons raw, unsalted cashews
½ cup / 120 mL plus 2 tablespoons water (plus more, if needed), divided
3 tablespoons / 45 mL *ghee* or vegetable oil
½ teaspoon *hing* (asafetida)
½ teaspoon cumin seeds
3 whole cloves
3 cassia or bay leaves
3 whole black peppercorns
2 green cardamom pods
1 (3-inch / 8-cm) stick cinnamon

1 tablespoon *Garam Masala* (see recipe on p. 35)
1 tablespoon ground coriander
1 teaspoon turmeric powder
1 teaspoon red chile powder or cayenne pepper
2 teaspoons unsmoked paprika
¾ cup / 180 mL plain, unsweetened yogurt
2 teaspoons salt
1–3 fresh Thai, serrano, or cayenne chiles, stems removed and finely chopped
2 cups / 600 g *Paneer* (see recipe on p. 44)
1 heaping tablespoon chopped fresh cilantro, for garnish
Brown or white basmati rice, *Roti*, or *Naan* (see recipes on pp. 230 and 238), for serving

1. In the bowl of a food processor, grind the onion into a watery paste. Transfer to a small mixing bowl and set aside. *No need to clean the food processor bowl in between.* Add the ginger and garlic to the food processor bowl and grind into a paste. Transfer to a second small mixing bowl and set aside. *Again, no need to clean.* Add the tomato to the food processor bowl and grind into a watery paste. Transfer to a third small mixing bowl and set aside. *Again, no need to clean.* Add the cashews and 2 tablespoons of the water to the food processor bowl and grind into a paste. Transfer to a fourth small mixing bowl and set aside.

2. In a heavy-bottomed, 4-quart / 4-L sauté pan over medium–high heat, warm the *ghee.* Add the *hing,* cumin seeds, cloves, cassia leaves, peppercorns, cardamom, and cinnamon and cook for 40 seconds, until the cumin seeds sizzle and turn reddish-brown and the mixture becomes aromatic. *Be careful not to cook the spices too long, as they will burn.*

3. Add the onion paste from Step 1 to the sauté pan and cook, stirring occasionally, for 4 minutes, until the onion is slightly browned. Add the ginger paste from Step 1 and cook for 1 minute. Add the ground tomato from Step 1 and cook, stirring constantly, for 2 minutes. Add the cashew paste from Step 1 and cook for 1 minute.

4. Add the *Garam Masala,* coriander, turmeric, red chile powder, and paprika to the sauté pan and cook, stirring constantly, for 3 minutes.

5. Reduce the heat to low and add the remaining ½ cup / 120 mL of the water, the yogurt, the salt, and the fresh chiles to the sauté pan. Simmer, uncovered and stirring occasionally, for 10 minutes, until the ingredients come together and separate slightly from the oil. *You can always add a little more water if the mixture seems too thick, but you don't want it to be too watery either. Exercise caution.*

6. Remove the whole spices. *I typically pull out all the big stuff and leave the little spices like cloves and peppercorns in to be ground down.* Remove from the heat and set aside to cool.

7. Transfer the contents of the sauté pan to a blender. Blend until smooth. Return to the sauté pan and return the pan to medium–high heat.

8. Add the *Paneer* to the sauté pan and cook for 4 minutes, until just heated through. Garnish with the cilantro and serve immediately with the brown or white basmati rice, *Roti,* or *Naan.*

North Indian Tempeh Curry

YIELD: 6 CUPS / 1.4 L

TOOLS: You'll need a food processor, a large mixing bowl, a whisk, and a 6-quart / 6-L sauté pan or Dutch oven with a lid.

This is my vegan version of chicken curry. I've made it for my Whole Foods classes and many a meat eater has begrudgingly admitted loving it.

1 medium yellow or red onion, roughly chopped

1 (4-inch / 10-cm) piece ginger, peeled and roughly chopped

10 cloves garlic, peeled

2 cups / 470 mL plain, unsweetened soy or coconut yogurt

1 tablespoon plus 1 teaspoon plus 1 pinch salt, divided

1 tablespoon turmeric powder

1 tablespoon *Garam Masala* (see recipe on p. 35)

1 tablespoon red chile powder or cayenne pepper

2 teaspoons ground coriander

2 teaspoons roasted cumin, ground

⅓ cup / 10 g *kasoori methi* (dried fenugreek leaves), lightly hand crushed to release flavor

24–28 ounces / 680–790 g tempeh, Baked Tofu (see recipe on p. 46), or seitan, cut into slices or cubes

3 tablespoons / 45 mL *ghee* or vegetable oil

1 teaspoon cumin seeds

2 (3-inch / 8-cm) sticks cinnamon

5 whole cloves

5 green cardamom pods, lightly crushed

2 black cardamom pods

1 large yellow or red onion, thinly sliced

3 large tomatoes, diced

3–4 fresh Thai, serrano, or cayenne chiles, stems removed and thinly sliced

2 heaping tablespoons chopped fresh cilantro, for garnish

Brown or white basmati rice, *Roti,* or *Naan* (see recipes on pp. 230 and 238), for serving

1. In the bowl of a food processor, grind the chopped onion, ginger, and garlic into a smooth paste.

2. Transfer the onion paste from Step 1 to a large mixing bowl and add the yogurt, the 1 tablespoon and 1 teaspoon of salt, the turmeric, the *Garam Masala,* the red chile powder, the coriander, the roasted cumin, and the *kasoori methi.* Whisk together all the ingredients until well combined. *Dried kasoori methi can be found in an Indian grocery store. Omit it if you cannot find it. Do not substitute fresh leaves or fenugreek seeds, as they will alter the dish's taste.*

3. Slowly add the tempeh to the mixing bowl, stirring gently, until every piece is evenly coated with the marinade. Cover and refrigerate for 2 hours to overnight. *If using tempeh, you may wish to steam or pan-fry it before marinating.*

Continued

4. In a 6-quart / 6-L sauté pan or Dutch oven over medium–high heat, warm the *ghee*. Add the cumin seeds, cinnamon, cloves, and green and black cardamom and cook for 40 seconds, until the cumin seeds sizzle, turn reddish-brown, and become aromatic.

5. Add the sliced onion and the remaining pinch of salt to the sauté pan. Cook, scraping the bottom of the pan to prevent burning, for 3 minutes, until the onion is slightly browned. *Don't worry, scraping the pan will only add flavor.*

6. Add the tomatoes to the sauté pan and, cook, uncovered and stirring occasionally, for 11 minutes, until the tomatoes break down. Use the back of the spoon to help break them down.

7. Add the marinated mixture from Step 3 and the fresh chiles to the sauté pan and cook, uncovered and stirring occasionally, for 10 minutes. Remove from the heat, cover, and set aside for 5 minutes, until the flavors come together.

8. Transfer to a serving bowl. Garnish with the cilantro and serve with the brown or white basmati rice, *Roti,* or *Naan.*

Malai Kofta
Spicy Vegetarian Dumplings

YIELD: 6–8 SERVINGS (16 *KOFTAS* AND 4 CUPS / 950 ML CURRY)

TOOLS: For the *koftas*, you'll need a sheet of cheesecloth or muslin; a large mixing bowl; a *kadhai,* wok, or heavy-bottomed pan; a slotted spoon; and a tray lined with paper towels or a dish cloth. For the curry, you'll need a food processor; 3 small mixing bowls; a heavy-bottomed, 4-quart / 4-L sauté pan; a slotted spoon; and a high-powered blender or immersion blender.

In Punjab, where there are so many vegetarians, *koftas* are like meatballs, but made with minced vegetables and spices. Though most Indian restaurants use potatoes, my mother remembers freshly fried *koftas* made with grated *ghiya,* or winter melon, from her childhood. You can also use grated green cabbage.

FOR THE *KOFTAS:*
1 pound / 450 g *ghiya* (winter melon), peeled and grated (will yield 3 cups / 710 mL)
¼ cup / 40 g finely diced yellow or red onion
1 heaping tablespoon grated ginger
½ teaspoon salt
½ teaspoon ground coriander
½ teaspoon *Garam Masala* (see recipe on p. 35)
½ teaspoon red chile powder or cayenne pepper
⅓ cup / 40 g plus 1 tablespoon *besan* (gram or chickpea flour)
2 cups / 470 mL vegetable oil, for frying

FOR THE CURRY:
1 large yellow or red onion, roughly chopped
1 (1-inch / 3-cm) piece ginger, peeled and roughly chopped

5 large cloves garlic, peeled
2 large tomatoes, roughly chopped
3 tablespoons / 45 mL vegetable oil
1 (3-inch/ 8-cm) stick cinnamon
2 cassia or bay leaves
4 green cardamom pods
2 black cardamom pods
2 teaspoons plus 1 pinch salt, divided
1 tablespoon *Garam Masala* (see recipe on p. 35)
1 teaspoon red chile powder or cayenne pepper
1 teaspoon turmeric powder
2 tablespoons Cashew Cream (see recipe on p. 47)
4 cups / 950 mL boiling water
Brown or white basmati rice, *Roti,* or *Naan* (see recipes on pp. 230 and 238), for serving

TO MAKE THE *KOFTAS:*

1. Place the *ghiya* in a sheet of cheesecloth or muslin and squeeze tightly with your hands, until the *ghiya* is as dry as possible. *Once you have squeezed out the liquid, you will have 2 cups / 470 mL of* ghiya. *Drink the water or add it to the curry recipe, as it has a lot of nutrients.*

2. Combine all the ingredients for the *koftas,* except the oil, in a large mixing bowl and stir until the mixture is evenly blended. *Move quickly to Steps 3 through 5—you do not want this mixture to become watery.*

Continued

3. In a small *kadhai,* wok, or heavy-bottomed pan over medium–high to high heat, warm the oil (about 1 inch / 3 cm deep) until it's hot—but just before it gets too hot. *Test the oil by putting in a drop of batter. If it sizzles and immediately comes to the top, the oil is ready. If it falls to the bottom, the oil is not hot enough.*

4. Drop tablespoon-sized balls of dough, 1 at a time, into the hot oil. Depending on the size of the pan, cook 4 to 6 *koftas* at a time, being careful not to overcrowd.

5. After 1 minute of cooking time, reduce the heat to medium. *Don't cook them in very, very hot oil, or they will sear on the outside and remain uncooked on the inside.* Cook, turning halfway through the cooking time, for a total of 5 to 7 minutes, until the *koftas* are golden brown on all sides. Remove from the heat.

6. Using a slotted spoon, remove the *koftas* to a tray lined with paper towels or a dish cloth to absorb the oil. Continue until you finish the batter. Remove from the heat.

TO MAKE THE CURRY:

1. In the bowl of a food processor, grind the onion into a watery paste. Transfer to a small mixing bowl and set aside. *No need to clean the food processor bowl in between.* Add the ginger and garlic to the food processor bowl and grind into a paste. Transfer to a second small mixing bowl and set aside. *Again, no need to clean.* Add the tomatoes to the food processor bowl and grind into a watery paste. Transfer to a third small mixing bowl and set aside.

2. In a heavy-bottomed, 4-quart / 4-L sauté pan over medium–high heat, warm the oil. Add the cinnamon, cassia leaves, and green and black cardamom and cook for 40 seconds, until the spices sizzle and release their essential oils.

3. Using a slotted spoon, add the ground onion from Step 1 to the sauté pan, leaving the onion water behind but reserving it for later use in Step 5. Add the pinch of the salt and cook, uncovered, for 6 minutes, until the onion is slightly browned and opaque.

4. Add the ginger paste from Step 1 to the sauté pan and cook for 1 minute. Add the ground tomato from Step 1 and cook for 6 minutes. *The paste will start to thicken and come together, and the oil will start to separate slightly.*

5. Add the onion water from Step 3, the *Garam Masala,* the red chile powder, the turmeric, the remaining 2 teaspoons of salt, and the Cashew Cream to the sauté pan. Cook, uncovered, for 6 minutes, until the ingredients come together. Add the water and allow the mixture to come to a boil.

6. Reduce the heat to medium and simmer, uncovered and stirring occasionally to prevent sticking, for 20 to 25 minutes. Remove and discard the cardamom pods. Remove from the heat.

7. When finished cooking, transfer the curry to a blender or use an immersion blender in the sauté pan and process on high for 1 to 2 minutes. *This last step really pulls the curry together.*

8. Return the curry to the sauté pan over medium heat. Fold the *koftas* into the curry and cook for 5 minutes, until warmed through. Remove from the heat, cover, and set aside for 10 minutes, until the *koftas* soften and absorb the flavors of the curry.

9. Transfer the curry and *koftas* to a serving bowl. Serve immediately with the brown or white basmati rice, *Roti,* or *Naan.*

TRY THIS! Instead of frying, try baking the *koftas.* Set the oven rack at the middle position and preheat the oven to 350°F / 180°C. Arrange the *koftas* on a well-greased baking sheet about 1 inch / 3 cm apart. Cook for 40 to 60 minutes, until they are browned and cooked through. *About halfway through the cooking time, remove the baking sheet from the oven and check to make sure they are not sticking. I use a spatula to loosen them up and then return them to the oven to finish cooking. You don't want the bottoms of the* koftas *to be hard and crusty when you add them to the curry.* Once cooked, remove the baking sheet from the oven and set aside to cool for 15 minutes before adding the *koftas* to the curry and serving.

Punjabi *Kadi Pakoras* Spiced Yogurt Gravy with Dumplings

YIELD: 9 CUPS / 2.1 L (BEFORE ADDING THE *PAKORAS*) AND 15 *PAKORAS*

TOOLS: You'll need a large mixing bowl; a *kadhai,* wok, or heavy-bottomed pan; a slotted spoon; a tray lined with paper towels or a dish cloth; a blender; and a deep, heavy-bottomed, 4-quart / 4-L stockpot.

VEGANIZE IT! Although the key to this dish is the tartness of the dairy yogurt, you can make it vegan by substituting the same amount of unsweetened soy or coconut yogurt. Add the juice of ½ a lemon or 1 to 2 teaspoons of *amchur* (dried mango powder) for additional tartness toward the end of the cooking time.

Once you taste this dish, you'll understand why North Indians go crazy for it. At once slightly tart, zesty, spicy, and filling, it's a perfect menu item for a lazy weekend lunch served over rice. Even though the word sounds like a curry, it's very different from the traditional Indian-style gravy. Every household has a different version, and that's why, no matter how many ways I make it, I always crave my mom's.

FOR THE *PAKORAS* (CHICKPEA DUMPLINGS):
2 cups / 220 g *besan* (gram or chickpea flour)
1 teaspoon salt
½ teaspoon red chile powder or cayenne pepper
½ teaspoon turmeric powder
½ teaspoon *ajwain* (carom seeds)
1 cup / 240 mL plus 1 tablespoon warm water
2 cups / 470 mL vegetable oil, for frying

FOR THE *KADI:*
3 cups / 710 mL plain, unsweetened yogurt
¾ cup / 80 g *besan* (gram or chickpea flour)
1 heaping tablespoon turmeric powder
6 cups / 1.4 L water, divided

2 tablespoons *ghee* or vegetable oil
½ teaspoon fenugreek seeds
1 medium yellow or red onion, thinly sliced
2 tablespoons plus 1 pinch salt, divided
1 (4-inch / 10-cm) piece ginger, peeled and grated
10 cloves garlic, peeled and grated or minced
1–3 fresh Thai, serrano, or cayenne chiles, stems removed and thinly sliced
2–6 whole dried red chiles
1 teaspoon red chile powder or cayenne pepper
½ teaspoon ground black pepper
2 tablespoons chopped fresh cilantro, for garnish
Brown or white basmati rice, for serving
Sliced onions, for serving

TO MAKE THE *PAKORAS:*

1. Combine all the ingredients for the *pakoras,* except the oil, in a large mixing bowl and stir until the mixture is evenly blended. *Move quickly to Steps 2 through 4—you do not want this mixture to become watery.*

2. In a small *kadhai,* wok, or heavy-bottomed pan over medium–high to high heat, warm the oil (about 1 inch / 3 cm deep) until it's hot—but just before it gets too hot. *Test the oil by putting in a drop of batter. If it sizzles and immediately comes to the top, the oil is ready. If it falls to the bottom, the oil is not hot enough.*

Continued

3. Drop tablespoon-sized balls of dough, 1 at a time, into the hot oil. Depending on the size of the pan, cook 4 to 6 *pakoras* at a time, being careful not to overcrowd the pan. Cook, turning halfway through the cooking time, for a total of 2 minutes, until the *pakoras* are golden brown on all sides. Remove from the heat. *Unlike* pakoras *for appetizers, you don't have to worry if these are a little raw in the middle. They will eventually go into the* kadi *and will cook through then.*

4. Using a slotted spoon, remove the *pakoras* to a tray lined with paper towels or a dish cloth to absorb the extra oil. Continue until you finish the batter. Remove from the heat.

TO MAKE THE *KADI:*

1. Combine the yogurt, the *besan,* the turmeric, and 4 cups / 950 mL of the water in a blender and process well. The result will look like a frothy yellow milkshake. Set aside.

2. In a deep, heavy-bottomed, 4-quart / 4-L stockpot over medium–high heat, warm the *ghee.* Add the fenugreek seeds and cook for 20 seconds, until the seeds are just browned. *Be careful not to overcook them—they turn bitter very quickly.*

3. Add the onion and the pinch of salt to the stockpot and cook for 2 to 3 minutes, until slightly browned. Add the ginger and garlic and cook, stirring occasionally to prevent sticking, for 2 to 3 minutes.

4. Add the fresh chiles, the dried chiles, the red chile powder, the black pepper, the remaining 2 tablespoons of salt, the yogurt mixture from Step 1, and the remaining 2 cups / 470 mL of water to the stockpot and bring the mixture to a boil.

5. Reduce the heat to medium–low and simmer, partially covered, for 45 minutes, until the mixture thickens.

6. Carefully fold the fried *pakoras* into the mixture in the stockpot and simmer for 5 minutes, until they soften. Remove from the heat, cover, and set aside for 10 minutes, until the *pakoras* absorb the flavors of the curry.

7. Transfer the mixture to a serving bowl. Garnish with the cilantro and serve with the basmati rice and the sliced onions.

NOTE: If you don't have the time to make the *pakoras,* just chop up about 6 cups / 900 g of vegetables (I use a mix of carrots, cauliflower, cabbage, eggplant, kale, and spinach). Add the vegetables with the fresh and dried chiles in Step 4 before adding the yogurt mixture. Then, proceed with the instructions above.

Navratan Korma

YIELD: 10 CUPS / 2.4 L

TOOLS: You'll need a 6-quart / 6-L stockpot; a large bowl filled with ice water; a food processor; a small mixing bowl; a spice grinder or mortar and pestle; a heavy-bottomed, 6-quart / 6-L sauté pan; and a blender or an immersion blender.

VEGANIZE IT! Substitute Baked Tofu (see recipe on p. 46) or pan-fried tofu for the *Paneer* and omit the heavy cream. This dish gets plenty of creaminess from the cashews alone.

Navratan means "nine jewels," and in this creamy curry, it refers to the recipe's various vegetables and dried fruit. This dish has roots in the imperial kitchens of the Mughal Empire, and is at once regal, decadent, and hearty.

8 cups / 1.2 kg fresh cauliflower florets, sliced carrots, green beans, sliced zucchini, cubed potato, red bell pepper; and frozen peas, corn, edamame
Water, to cover
1 small yellow or red onion, chopped
1 (2-inch / 5-cm) piece ginger, peeled and coarsely chopped
10 cloves garlic, peeled
1 teaspoon cardamom seeds
20 whole cloves
3 tablespoons / 45 mL *ghee* or vegetable oil
3 medium tomatoes, chopped
1 cup / 140 g raw cashews, soaked overnight in water and drained*
2 cups / 470 mL water

1 teaspoon turmeric powder
1 teaspoon ground coriander
1 teaspoon *Garam Masala* (see recipe on p. 35)
1 teaspoon red chile powder or cayenne pepper
1 tablespoon salt
½ cup / 80 g golden raisins or any dried fruit
7 ounces / 200 g *Paneer*, cubed and baked or pan-fried (will yield 2 cups / 470 mL; see recipe on p. 44)
½ cup / 120 mL half & half or heavy cream
Brown or white basmati rice, *Roti*, or *Naan* (see recipes on pp. 230 and 238), for serving

1. Cover the cauliflower, carrots, green beans, zucchini, and potato with the water in a 6-quart / 6-L stockpot over medium–high heat and bring to a boil. Cook at a steady boil for 4 minutes. Remove from the heat. *If using bell peppers, add them in Step 10 to prevent overcooking.*

2. Immediately remove the vegetables from the water and transfer them to a large bowl filled with ice water. Set aside. *The ice bath halts the cooking process, keeping the veggies al dente. You can skip Steps 1 and 2 and add the veggies directly to the curry, but I find that it helps to take the time to blanch them. Otherwise, you'll have to cook them later, and if so, the curry will likely get too thick.*

3. In the bowl of a food processor, grind the onion, ginger, and garlic into a watery paste. Transfer to a small mixing bowl and set aside.

4. Using a spice grinder or a mortar and pestle, grind the cardamom and cloves into a powder.

5. In a heavy-bottomed, 6-quart / 6-L sauté pan over medium–high heat, warm the *ghee*. Add the cardamom–clove powder and cook for 40 seconds, until it sizzles. *Be careful not to burn the powder.*

Continued

6. Add the paste from Step 3 to the sauté pan. *Be careful, as it may splatter as it goes into the hot oil.* Cook, stirring and scraping the bottom of the pan constantly, for 2 minutes, until slightly browned. *I sometimes add 1 tablespoon of oil at this point to help pull the ingredients together.*

7. Reduce the heat to medium and add the tomatoes and cashews to the sauté pan. Simmer, uncovered and stirring occasionally to avoid sticking, for 5 minutes. Add the 2 cups / 470 mL of water and cook for 5 minutes. Remove from the heat.

8. When finished cooking, transfer the mixture to a blender or use an immersion blender in the sauté pan and process on high for 1 to 2 minutes. *This last step really pulls the curry together.*

9. Return the curry to the sauté pan before placing it over the heat. *Keeping it off the heat will prevent splatter.* Place the sauté pan over medium–low heat and add the turmeric, coriander, *Garam Masala,* red chile powder, and salt. Stir well. Add the blanched vegetables from Steps 1 and 2 and the raisins and stir again. Simmer, uncovered and stirring occasionally, for 10 minutes.

10. Add the frozen vegetables and bell pepper to the sauté pan and cook for 3 minutes. *If the sauce becomes too thick, add a tiny bit of water to loosen it up.* Fold the *Paneer* and half & half into the mixture and cook for 1 minute. Remove from the heat.

11. Transfer to a serving bowl and serve immediately over the brown or white basmati rice or with the *Roti* or *Naan.*

*Cashews are always creamier if soaked overnight. No worries if you can't, however. Just soak them in warm water while you prep the remainder of the ingredients.

Gobi Mussallam Drowned Cauliflower

YIELD: 6–8 SERVINGS

TOOLS: You'll need 3 small mixing bowls; a food processor; a 4-quart / 4-L sauté pan; a blender or an immersion blender; a 10-quart / 9.5-L stockpot; a colander; and a 2-quart / 2-L ovenproof dish.

VEGANIZE IT! Replace the butter with Earth Balance spread and the half & half with coconut milk creamer. You can also leave the cream out entirely, as the cashews will make it creamy all by themselves.

There is nothing that says you're ready to party better than this dish. The cauliflower is so festive displayed on a platter along with a deep, rich sauce. Your guests will rave. Just don't tell them how truly easy it is to make.

- ¼ cup / 35 g raw, unsalted cashews
- ¼ cup / 40 g golden raisins
- 3 cups / 710 mL boiling water, divided
- 1 medium yellow or red onion, roughly chopped
- 1 (2-inch / 5-cm) piece ginger, peeled and roughly chopped
- 10 cloves garlic, peeled
- 2 tablespoons vegetable oil
- ½ teaspoon cumin seeds
- 4 green cardamom pods, slightly crushed
- 2 black cardamom pods
- 2 tablespoons butter
- 4 medium tomatoes, diced
- 1 teaspoon *Garam Masala* (see recipe on p. 35)
- 1 teaspoon ground coriander
- 3 teaspoons salt, divided
- 1 teaspoon red chile powder or cayenne pepper
- 2 tablespoons tomato paste
- 1 small fresh Thai, serrano, or cayenne chile, stem removed and finely sliced
- ¼ cup / 60 mL half & half or heavy cream
- 1 large head cauliflower (about 6 inches / 15 cm in diameter), keep the bottom base of greens and stalk intact
- 1 teaspoon turmeric powder
- 5 large cassia or bay leaves
- 10 whole black peppercorns, crushed
- 5 whole cloves, crushed
- 14 cups / 3.3 L room-temperature water
- 1 tablespoon minced fresh cilantro, for garnish

1. Place the cashews and raisins in separate small mixing bowls and add 1 cup / 240 mL of the boiling water to each. Set them aside to soak as you prep the remaining ingredients.

2. In the bowl of a food processor, grind the onion, ginger, and garlic into a watery paste. Transfer to a small mixing bowl and set aside.

3. In a 4-quart / 4-L sauté pan over medium–high heat, warm the oil. Add the cumin seeds and green and black cardamom pods and cook for 40 seconds, until the cumin seeds sizzle and turn reddish-brown.

4. Very carefully, add the paste from Step 2 to the sauté pan. *Keep a lid handy in case the mixture splatters.* Cook, stirring occasionally to prevent sticking, for 3 minutes, until the mixture is slightly browned. Add the butter and cook, stirring constantly, for 1 minute.

Continued

5. Add the tomatoes to the sauté pan and cook for 2 minutes, until the tomatoes start to break down. Add the remaining 1 cup / 240 mL of boiling water and cook for 1 minute.

6. Drain the cashews and add them, along with the *Garam Masala,* the coriander, 2 teaspoons of the salt, the red chile powder, and the tomato paste, to the sauté pan. Bring to a boil.

7. Reduce the heat to medium and simmer, uncovered, for 7 minutes, until the tomatoes break down completely and the mixture comes together. If the mixture thickens too much, add 1 teaspoon or so of water. *Be careful not to add too much, as the sauce must not be too watery later, during the baking time.*

8. Remove and discard the black cardamom pods and the skin of the green cardamom, if possible. *It's not a problem if you can't find all of the pods, as they will get blended down and just add flavor to the dish.*

9. When finished cooking, transfer the mixture to a blender or use an immersion blender in the sauté pan and process on high for 1 to 2 minutes. *I always use a little water to clean out the bottom of the blender and be sure I get every last bit of the curry.*

10. Drain the raisins. Return the curry to the sauté pan over medium–low heat and add the raisins, the fresh chile, and the half & half and cook for 3 minutes, until the mixture is warmed through. Remove from the heat and set aside.

11. Set the oven rack at the second-from-top position and preheat the oven to 300°F / 150°C.

12. Place the cauliflower upside down (stalk facing up) in a 10-quart / 9.5-L stockpot over medium–high heat. *Turning the cauliflower upside down allows the edible parts to all get cooked perfectly.* Add the turmeric, the remaining 1 teaspoon of salt, the cassia leaves, the peppercorns, the cloves, and the room-temperature water and bring to a boil.

13. Reduce the heat to medium and simmer for 10 to 12 minutes. *I like my cauliflower al dente; if you prefer it to be softer, by all means, cook it a little longer. Test the cauliflower's softness with a fork before removing it from the pot.* Remove from the heat.

14. Carefully remove the cauliflower from the stockpot. Set it in a colander to drain thoroughly and transfer it to a 2-quart / 2-L ovenproof dish. *The key is to put it in a dish just big enough to just hold it. If the dish is too large, then the topping will eventually dry out while baking.*

15. Pour all but 1 cup / 240 mL of the curry in the sauté pan over the cauliflower. *Be sure to coat the entire head.* Bake for 25 minutes, until the flavors really have a chance to soak into the cauliflower. Remove from the oven and gather the sauce that has pooled on the sides of the cauliflower head. Pour the sauce over the cauliflower head again and return to the oven for 5 minutes. Remove from the oven.

16. Pour the reserved 1 cup / 240 mL of the curry *(you may wish to warm it a bit beforehand)* over the dish to spruce it up a bit. Garnish with the cilantro and serve immediately. *I like to place the whole cauliflower on a platter surrounded by basmati rice so that everyone can help himself or herself.* You can also serve with Roti *or* Naan *and cut it into wedges.*

Tofu *Biryani*

YIELD: 6 SERVINGS

TOOLS: You'll need a small mixing bowl; a food processor; a large mixing bowl; a heavy-bottomed, 4-quart / 4-L sauté pan with a lid; a slotted spoon; a plate; a medium stockpot; and a 2-quart / 2-L ovensafe casserole dish with a tight lid (use aluminum foil if you don't have a lid).

NOTE: For the best flavor, the tofu needs to be baked first. Be sure to give yourself enough time to prepare ahead of time.

This is the ultimate one-pot meal—a bed of rice and a spiced curry that are baked together until the flavors blend to perfection. It's an easy dish to assemble ahead of time; just pop it into the oven about 1 hour before dinnertime.

¼ cup / 60 mL warmed milk or milk alternative
1 teaspoon saffron strands
1 (2-inch / 5-cm) piece ginger, peeled and roughly chopped
4 cloves garlic, peeled
1–4 fresh Thai, serrano, or cayenne chiles, stems removed
1 cup / 20 g fresh cilantro
½ cup / 10 g fresh mint leaves
2 tablespoons *Garam Masala* (see recipe on p. 35)
1 teaspoon red chile powder or cayenne pepper
1 teaspoon turmeric powder
1 cup / 240 mL plain, unsweetened soy or coconut yogurt

1 (14-ounce/ 400-g) package of extra-firm tofu, baked and diced (see the Baked Tofu recipe on p. 46)
¼ cup / 60 mL plus 2 tablespoons vegetable oil, divided
2 large yellow onions, cut in thin rings
1 tablespoon plus 2 pinches salt, divided
2 medium tomatoes, diced
1 cup / 185 g uncooked white or brown basmati rice, washed
¼ cup / 40 g golden raisins
Water, to cover

1. In a small mixing bowl, combine the warmed milk and saffron strands and set aside to soak for at least 30 minutes while you prep the remaining ingredients.

2. In the bowl of a food processor, grind the ginger, garlic, fresh chiles, cilantro, and mint leaves into a paste. Transfer to a large mixing bowl. Add the *Garam Masala,* red chile powder, turmeric, and yogurt and stir until well combined.

3. Slowly fold the tofu into the yogurt mixture and stir gently until all the pieces are evenly coated. *Baked tofu works best here, because it holds up better during cooking. I've tried this recipe without baking the tofu and it worked, but the texture was a little too soft for my family's taste. You be the judge.* Cover and refrigerate for 2 hours to overnight.

4. In a heavy-bottomed, 4-quart / 4-L sauté pan over medium–high heat, warm ¼ cup / 60 mL of the oil. Add the onions and 2 pinches of the salt. Cook, stirring occasionally, for 15 minutes, until the onions are browned. Using a slotted spoon, transfer the onions to a plate and leave the oil behind in the sauté pan.

5. Return the sauté pan to medium–high heat and warm the remaining 2 tablespoons of oil. Add the tomatoes and 1 tablespoon of salt, and cook 1 to 2 minutes, until softened. Add the tofu with the marinade and ¾ of the onions cooked in Step 4 (reserving the rest for later use) and cook for 4 minutes, until warmed through. Turn the heat off and cover the pan.

6. Set the oven rack at the second-from-top position and preheat the oven to 400°F / 204°C.

7. In a separate medium stockpot over medium–high heat, combine the rice, the raisins, and water to cover the rice by 2 inches / 5 cm and bring to a boil. Reduce the heat to medium and cook, uncovered, for 7 minutes. If using brown rice, cook about 12 minutes. Remove from the heat, cover, and set aside. *If too much water remains in the pot after the cooking time, just drain and discard.*

8. Transfer the tofu mixture from Step 5 to a 2-quart / 2-L ovensafe casserole dish. Layer the rice over the tofu in the dish. Tightly pack the rice in the dish and garnish with the browned onions reserved from Step 4. Pour the bowl of saffron and milk from Step 1 over the casserole.

9. Tightly cover the casserole dish and bake for 40 minutes. Remove from the oven.

10. Serve immediately as a delicious one-pot meal.

TRY THIS! Substitute my Brown Rice–Quinoa *Palau* (see recipe on p. 49) for the rice. If you want to try this recipe using *Paneer* instead of the Baked Tofu, use about 2 pounds / 910 g of it diced into 1-inch / 3-cm cubes. If you are making this recipe with vegetables, use hardier ones that will hold up to cooking like cauliflower, bell peppers, and carrots. If you are making this recipe using both *Paneer* and vegetables, follow the same instructions and cooking times. And, as always, you can also substitute an equal amount of seitan or tempeh for the tofu.

Poultry, Meat, and Seafood

Contrary to popular belief, folks in certain parts of India follow a diet based on poultry, meat, and seafood. In Kerala, a state in the southwest region of India, for example, no dinner is complete without a healthy supply of prawns, freshly caught fish, or green-lipped mussels. In West Bengal, situated on the Bay of Bengal, fish is understandably a staple.

The cuisine in parts of Delhi and Kashmir is influenced by the Mughals, whose rule, beginning in the 16th century, left a deep and lasting effect. The Moghul emperors arrived from Central Asia, bringing with them, amongst many other things, a Persian style of cooking that included cream, butter, nuts, dried fruit, and meats. These elements combined beautifully with Indian spices to create dishes you enjoy today in many Indian restaurants in the West.

In a country as large and as diverse as India, you really can't make a single statement about the cuisine that's true for everyone. That's precisely why Indian food has options that can accommodate everyone. Some Hindus don't eat beef but will eat lamb. Some Muslims shun pork but eat beef, and others, especially from regions like Goa, have a cultural affiliation for pork. Some families have a mix of all of the above, along with members who adhere to a strict vegetarian diet—including not eating food cooked in pots which have held meat.

Imagine preparing dinner for such a crowd. We often do. In our home, I prefer a plant-based diet, while my husband eats everything. My mother and mother-in-law are vegetarians who eat dairy but no eggs or meat. Our fathers also eat everything. I call it organized chaos.

Although I love following a plant-based diet—and everything it stands for—I also believe that food should bring us all together, rather than setting us apart. I always say that everyone—regardless of food choices or dietary restrictions—should feel welcome at my dinner table. I cook meat dishes for my family if they request it, and for this section, I relied on my husband as my key taste tester.

Here, meat eaters will find all the favorites, but those who prefer a meat-free diet will also find tips on how to replace the meat with vegetarian or vegan options.

Tandoori Chicken

YIELD: 6–8 SERVINGS

TOOLS: You'll need a food processor, a large mixing bowl, a whisk, a fork, and a grill.

VEGANIZE IT! Replace the chicken with 2 (14-ounce / 400-g) containers of cubed, extra-firm organic tofu, tempeh, or seitan. Instead of dairy yogurt, use soy or coconut yogurt. Cook for 25 minutes, turning once to ensure even cooking.

PICTURED ON P. 190

Like *samosas, tandoori* chicken has become a symbol for Indian food in the United States. Most Americans know this dish just as a sizzling plate of bright red, grilled chicken. Traditionally, *tandoori* chicken is marinated in a spicy yogurt sauce and cooked in a *tandoor* oven with temperatures that range from 500°F / 260°C to 900°F / 480°C. But I've got good news: It can also be made at home, on the grill, with the right spice combination. The only difference is in the color, which, I'm afraid, usually comes from the use of red food dye. Cook without it, and you'll have a much healthier dish that's just as delicious.

1 cup / 100 g ginger, peeled and coarsely chopped
1 cup / 140 g peeled garlic cloves
1½ cups / 350 mL plain, unsweetened yogurt
3 tablespoons / 20 g *Tandoori Masala* (see recipe on p. 33)
2 tablespoons salt
1 tablespoon red chile powder or cayenne pepper
1 teaspoon *Garam Masala* (see recipe on p. 35), plus more for sprinkling

4 pounds / 1.81 g skinless whole bone-in chicken, cut into 8–10 pieces (including cutting each breast in ½), or 2 pounds / 910 g boneless chicken
½ lemon, for squeezing
Thinly sliced onion, for garnish
Chopped fresh cilantro, for garnish
Brown or white basmati rice, *Roti,* or *Naan* (see recipes on pp. 230 and 238), for serving

1. In the bowl of a food processor, grind the ginger and garlic into a smooth, watery paste.

2. Transfer the paste into a large mixing bowl. Add the yogurt, *Tandoori Masala,* salt, red chile powder, and *Garam Masala* and whisk until fully combined.

3. Prepare the chicken by poking holes in it with a fork to help it absorb the yogurt marinade. Carefully add the pieces of chicken and gently stir until all the pieces are evenly coated. Cover and refrigerate for 6 hours to overnight.

4. Preheat the grill to medium–high (350°F / 180°C to 400°F / 200°C), making sure the grill has been well oiled or sprayed with a nonstick cooking or grilling spray.

5. Place the marinated pieces of chicken on the grill and cook, turning once to ensure even cooking, for up to 1 hour, until cooked through and the chicken reaches an internal temperature of 165°F / 74°C. *Your cooking time may differ, depending on your grill and how well done you prefer the chicken to be. We prefer it well done.* Remove from the grill and transfer to a serving platter.

6. Squeeze the 1/2 lemon over the cooked chicken. Sprinkle with some of the *Garam Masala.* Garnish with the onion and cilantro and serve hot over the brown or white basmati rice or with the *Roti* or *Naan.*

Chicken *Tikka Masala*

YIELD: 5 CUPS / 1.2 L *MASALA*
(BEFORE ADDING CHICKEN)

This dish, which is ubiquitous on Indian restaurant menus, likely had origins outside of India. According to one story, a restaurateur in England created it by combining grilled chicken, tomatoes, cream, and spices. Some say its origin was in Glasgow or Birmingham, while others (including my cousins Rahul, Vikram, and Puja) insist the recipe comes from Newcastle, their childhood home. No matter how or where it came about, we're all so glad it did.

TOOLS: You'll need a heavy-bottomed, 4-quart / 4-L sauté pan and a blender or immersion (stick) blender.

VEGANIZE IT! Instead of chicken, you can use 24 to 28 ounces / 680 to 790 g of Baked Tofu (see recipe on p. 46), seitan, or tempeh and substitute Cashew Cream (see recipe on p. 47) or coconut creamer for the half & half. You can even leave the cream out entirely, as the almonds should add all the richness you'll need. If you choose to do so, the cook time for Step 4 should increase to 20 minutes, and you may need to add a little water if the sauce starts to dry out.

- 1 tablespoon / 45 mL *ghee* or vegetable oil
- 2 teaspoons cumin seeds
- 1 teaspoon turmeric powder
- 1 large yellow or red onion, diced
- 1 tablespoon plus 1 pinch salt, divided
- 1 (2-inch / 5-cm) piece ginger, peeled and minced or grated
- 10 cloves garlic, peeled and minced or grated
- 4 large tomatoes, peeled and diced*
- 1 heaping tablespoon tomato paste
- 1–3 fresh Thai, serrano, or cayenne chiles, stems removed and chopped
- 6 green cardamom pods, slightly crushed
- 1 teaspoon ground cinnamon
- 1 tablespoon light brown sugar
- 1 teaspoon ground black pepper
- 1 teaspoon red chile powder or cayenne pepper
- 1 cup / 240 mL boiling water
- ¼ cup / 25 g blanched sliced almonds, toasted
- ¼ cup / 60 mL half & half or heavy cream
- 3 cups / 420 g diced *Tandoori* Chicken (see recipe on p. 189)
- 2 teaspoons unsmoked paprika
- Brown or white basmati rice, *Roti*, or *Naan* (see recipes on pp. 230 and 238), for serving

1. In a heavy-bottomed, 4-quart / 4-L sauté pan over medium–high heat, warm the *ghee*. Add the cumin seeds and turmeric and cook for 40 seconds, until the cumin seeds sizzle and turn reddish-brown.

2. Add the onion and the pinch of the salt to the sauté pan and cook, stirring occasionally, for 4 minutes, until the onion is slightly browned. Add the ginger and garlic and cook for 1 minute.

3. Add the tomatoes, the tomato paste, the fresh chiles, the cardamom, the cinnamon, the brown sugar, the remaining 1 tablespoon of salt, the black pepper, and the red chile powder to the sauté pan and bring the mixture to a boil.

4. Reduce the heat to medium and simmer, stirring occasionally, for 10 minutes, until the tomatoes break down and all the ingredients start to pull together except the oil, which will start to separate. Add the water and almonds and cook for 5 minutes. Remove from the heat.

5. Transfer the mixture to a blender or use an immersion (stick) blender in the sauté pan and process until smooth.

6. Return the sauté pan containing the mixture to medium heat and add the half & half. Fold in the chicken and paprika and cook for 5 minutes, until warmed through. Serve immediately with the brown or white basmati rice, *Roti,* or *Naan.*

*You can easily peel tomatoes with a serrated peeler. For more detailed instructions, see my notes on page 28.

Chicken *Makhani*

YIELD: 4–6 SERVINGS

TOOLS: You'll need a food processor; a large mixing bowl; a whisk; 4 small mixing bowls; heavy-bottomed 4-quart / 4-L and 6-quart / 6-L sauté pans with lids; and a blender or an immersion (stick) blender.

VEGANIZE IT! You can easily replace the chicken with 24 to 28 ounces / 680 to 790 g of cubed Baked Tofu (see recipe on p. 46), seitan, or tempeh. Follow all of the steps above, except that in Steps 8 and 9, the cooking time can be reduced to 4 minutes. Swap out the dairy by using nondairy alternatives like vegan margarine and soy or coconut cream.

Buttery, smooth, and decadent are the characteristics of this dish. It's not one we typically make in Indian households, but has become a household name in homes outside of India.

FOR THE MARINADE:
1 (4-inch / 10-cm) piece ginger, peeled and coarsely chopped
10 cloves garlic, peeled
2 cups / 470 mL plain, unsweetened yogurt
1 heaping tablespoon *Tandoori Masala* (see recipe on p. 33)
2 teaspoons *amchur* (dried mango powder)
1 tablespoon ground black pepper
1 tablespoon salt
½ cup / 10 g *kasoori methi* (dried fenugreek leaves), lightly hand crushed to release flavor
Juice of ½ lemon
2 pounds / 910 g boneless, skinned chicken, cut in strips

FOR THE CURRY:
½ cup / 70 g raw, unsalted cashews
5 cups / 1.2 L boiling water, divided
1 medium yellow or red onion, coarsely chopped
1 (4-inch / 10-cm) piece ginger, peeled and coarsely chopped
10 cloves garlic, peeled
4 large tomatoes, roughly chopped
3–6 fresh Thai, serrano, or cayenne chiles, stems removed and thinly sliced
¼ cup / 60 mL plus 3 tablespoons / 45 mL *ghee,* butter, or vegetable oil, divided
2 (3-inch / 8-cm) sticks cinnamon
4 black cardamom pods
4 green cardamom pods
1 teaspoon fenugreek seeds
1 tablespoon *Garam Masala* (see recipe on p. 35)
2 teaspoons red chile powder or cayenne pepper
1 tablespoon salt
¼ cup / 5 g *kasoori methi* (dried fenugreek leaves), lightly hand crushed to release flavor
¼ cup / 60 mL heavy cream
Brown or white basmati rice, *Roti,* or *Naan* (see recipes on pp. 230 and 238), for serving

TO MAKE THE MARINADE:

1. In the bowl of a food processor, grind the ginger and garlic until a smooth paste forms. *You'll use the food processor again when making the curry. No need to wash it before moving on to Step 2 in the curry recipe.*

2. Transfer the paste into a large mixing bowl. Add the yogurt, *Tandoori Masala, amchur,* black pepper, salt, *kasoori methi,* and lemon juice and whisk until fully combined.

3. Fold the chicken into the yogurt marinade. Stir gently, cover, and refrigerate for 2 to 4 hours.

4. Allow the marinated chicken to rise to room temperature for 20 minutes before making the curry.

Continued

TO MAKE THE CURRY:

1. In a small mixing bowl, combine the cashews and 2 cups / 470 mL of the boiling water and allow them to soak while you prep the remaining ingredients.

2. In the bowl of the food processor, grind the onion until smooth. Transfer to a small mixing bowl and set aside. *No need to clean the food processor bowl in between.* Add the ginger and garlic to the food processor bowl and grind into a smooth paste. Transfer to a second small mixing bowl and set aside. *Again, no need to clean.* Add the tomatoes and fresh chiles to the food processor bowl and grind into a watery paste. Transfer to a third small mixing bowl and set aside.

3. In a heavy-bottomed, 6-quart / 6-L sauté pan over medium heat, warm the ¼ cup / 60 mL of *ghee.* Add the cinnamon, black and green cardamom pods, and fenugreek seeds and cook for 40 seconds, until the seeds are browned. *Don't overcook the fenugreek seeds—they will turn bitter.*

4. Carefully add the ground onion from Step 2 to the sauté pan. Raise the heat to medium–high and cook for 4 minutes, stirring constantly.

5. Add the ginger paste from Step 2 to the sauté pan and cook, stirring constantly, for 2 minutes, until cooked through. Add the ground tomato from Step 2 and cook for 20 minutes, until the moisture becomes dry and the *ghee* starts to pull away from the sides.

6. Add 2 cups / 470 mL of the boiling water, the *Garam Masala,* the red chile powder, the salt, and the *kasoori methi* to the sauté pan and cook for 15 minutes. Remove from the heat and carefully remove the whole spices.

7. Transfer the curry to a blender or use an immersion blender in the sauté pan. Drain the cashews, discarding the water, and add them to the mixture. Process on high for 1 to 2 minutes.

8. Return the curry to the sauté pan over medium heat. Add the remaining 1 cup / 240 mL of the water *(if you used a blender, you might want to run that cup / 240 mL of water through the blender in order to get every last drop of the curry),* 1 tablespoon of the *ghee,* and the cream and cook, covered, for 5 minutes, until warmed through. Remove from the heat and set aside.

9. In a heavy-bottomed, 4-quart / 4-L sauté pan over medium–high heat, warm the remaining 2 tablespoons of the *ghee*. Carefully add ½ of the marinated chicken and cook, turning once to ensure even cooking, for 8 minutes, until cooked through. Remove the chicken from the pan and set aside on a serving platter.

10. Repeat with the remaining ½ of the chicken and discard the marinade. Remove from the heat.

11. Add all the cooked chicken to the sauté pan containing the curry and return the pan to medium–high heat. Cook for 4 minutes, until warmed through.

12. Transfer the chicken and curry to a large serving bowl and serve immediately with the brown or white basmati rice, *Roti,* or *Naan.*

Lamb *Biryani*

YIELD: SERVES 4–6

TOOLS: You'll need a small mixing bowl; a food processor; a large mixing bowl; a heavy-bottomed, 4-quart / 4-L sauté pan; a slotted spoon; a plate; tongs; a medium stockpot; and a 2-quart / 2-L ovenproof casserole dish with a tight lid (use aluminum foil if you don't have a lid).

TIP: Assemble this dish ahead of time and pop it into the oven 1 hour before dinner. It's a delicious and easy meal, and you'll have time to entertain your guests.

VEGANIZE IT! See my recipe for Tofu *Biryani* on page 180.

Think one-pot South Asian meal, and typically a good *biryani* will come to mind. The idea is that while the main protein and rice are partially cooked separately, the culinary magic happens when they come together in the oven. The juices from the meat below blend with the rice layered on top to create something uniquely delicious.

¼ cup / 60 mL warmed milk
1 teaspoon saffron strands
1 (2-inch / 5-cm) piece ginger, peeled and roughly chopped
4 cloves garlic, peeled
1–4 fresh Thai, serrano, or cayenne chiles, stems removed
1 cup / 20 g fresh cilantro
¼ cup / 5 g fresh mint leaves
2 tablespoons *Garam Masala* (see recipe on p. 35)
1 teaspoon red chile powder or cayenne pepper
1 teaspoon turmeric powder
1 cup / 240 mL plain, unsweetened yogurt

2 pounds / 910 g boneless lamb shoulder or leg, cut into 1-inch / 3-cm cubes
¼ cup / 60 mL plus 2 tablespoons vegetable oil, divided
3 large yellow onions, thinly sliced in rings
½ teaspoon plus 3 pinches salt, divided
2 cups / 370 g uncooked white or brown basmati rice, washed
¼ cup / 40 g golden raisins
Water, to cover
4–6 fried eggs, for serving

1. In a small mixing bowl, combine the warmed milk and saffron strands and set aside to soak for at least 30 minutes while you prep the remaining ingredients.

2. In the bowl of a food processor, grind the ginger, garlic, fresh chiles, cilantro, and mint leaves into a smooth paste. Transfer to a large mixing bowl. Add the *Garam Masala,* red chile powder, turmeric, and yogurt, and stir until well combined.

3. Slowly fold the lamb into the yogurt mixture and stir gently until all the pieces are evenly coated. Cover and refrigerate for 2 hours to overnight.

4. In a heavy-bottomed, 4-quart / 4-L sauté pan over medium–high heat, warm ¼ cup / 60 mL of the oil. Add the onions and 3 pinches of the salt. Cook, stirring occasionally, for 15 minutes, until the onions are browned. Using a slotted spoon, transfer the onions to a plate and leave the oil behind in the sauté pan.

Continued

5. Return the sauté pan to medium–high heat and warm the remaining 2 tablespoons of oil. Using tongs, carefully add the marinated lamb to the sauté pan, leaving the marinade behind in the bowl. *Reserve it—you'll need it later.* Cook for 2 minutes on each side.

6. Reduce the heat to low and add the reserved marinade and all but 2 tablespoons of the onions reserved from Step 4 to the sauté pan. Sprinkle with the remaining ½ teaspoon of the salt. Cook, partially covered and stirring occasionally, for 30 minutes. *This mixture will stick slightly to the bottom of the pan, but the lamb will also release enough fat to keep it from sticking too much. Just be sure to stir occasionally and add a little water if you need it.* Remove from the heat and set aside.

7. Set the oven rack at the second-from-top position and preheat the oven to 450°F / 230°C.

8. In a separate medium stockpot over medium–high heat, combine the rice, the raisins, and water to cover the rice by 2 inches / 5 cm and bring to a boil. Reduce the heat to medium and cook, uncovered, for 7 minutes. If using brown rice, cook for 12 minutes. Remove from the heat, cover, and set aside. *If too much water remains in the pot after the cooking time, just drain and discard.*

9. Transfer the lamb mixture to a 2-quart / 2-L ovenproof casserole dish and layer the rice over the lamb. Tightly pack the rice in the dish and garnish with the browned onions reserved from Step 4. Pour the bowl of saffron and milk from Step 1 over the casserole. Cover the dish with its lid or tightly with aluminum foil. Bake for 40 minutes. Remove from the oven. *You can also make individual servings of biryani in smaller ovenproof dishes—you may need to slightly reduce the cooking time.*

10. Serve immediately as a delicious one-pot meal with a fried egg on top of each serving.

Indo-Chinese Chile Chicken

YIELD: 4–6 SERVINGS

TOOLS: You'll need a small and a large mixing bowl; a whisk; a food processor; a heavy-bottomed, 6-quart / 6-L sauté pan; and a large plate lined with paper towels.

VEGANIZE IT! Substitute 24 to 28 ounces / 680 to 790 g of tempeh, extra-firm tofu, or seitan for the chicken. Cut into 1-inch / 3-cm cubes and follow the recipe. Bake your tofu for an extra-firm texture using the Baked Tofu recipe on page 46.

One cuisine I love as much as Indian is Chinese. My favorite spin is using Indian spices in Chinese dishes. Whenever I visit Delhi, my Alka *bhabhi* (sister-in-law) and I always hit my favorite restaurants in the business district, Connaught Place, again and again (she's a trouper, but let's face it—she usually has no choice). I usually go for the vegetarian dishes, but this chicken is often on the menu. Try baking the chicken if you want to avoid pan-frying it.

6 whole dried red chiles
⅓ cup / 80 mL boiling water
¾ cup / 180 mL all-purpose flour
1 tablespoon plus 2 teaspoons cornstarch or arrowroot, divided
1 teaspoon dried ginger powder
1 teaspoon garlic powder
1 teaspoon red chile powder or cayenne pepper
1 teaspoon ground black pepper
1 teaspoon ground white pepper
1½ teaspoons *Garam Masala* (see recipe on p. 35), divided
2 teaspoons salt, divided
2 pounds / 910 g boneless chicken breast, cut into 1-inch / 3-cm cubes
2 tablespoons soy sauce
2 teaspoons white distilled vinegar
1 teaspoon ketchup
½ teaspoon light brown sugar
1 cup / 240 mL room-temperature water
¼ cup / 60 mL plus 2 tablespoons vegetable oil, divided
1 medium yellow onion, roughly chopped
1 (1-inch/ 3-cm) piece ginger, peeled and sliced into long matchsticks
3 cloves garlic, peeled and thinly sliced
1 large green bell pepper, roughly chopped
1–3 fresh Thai, serrano, or cayenne chiles, stems removed and thinly sliced lengthwise
3 scallions, thinly sliced, with greens attached, for garnish
Brown or white basmati rice, for serving

1. In a small mixing bowl, combine the dried chiles and the boiling water. Set them aside to soak and soften for at least 30 minutes while you prep the remaining ingredients.

2. In a large mixing bowl, combine the flour, 1 tablespoon of the cornstarch, the ginger and garlic powders, the red chile powder, the black and white pepper, 1 teaspoon of the *Garam Masala,* and 1 teaspoon of the salt. Whisk until combined.

3. Add the chicken to the large mixing bowl. Stir gently until all the pieces are coated with the spiced flour mixture. Set aside.

4. In the bowl of a food processor, grind the dried chiles and their soaking water from Step 1 into a smooth paste.

5. Return the chile paste from Step 4 to the small mixing bowl and add the soy sauce, the vinegar, the ketchup, the brown sugar, the remaining 2 teaspoons of cornstarch, the remaining 1 teaspoon of salt, and the room-temperature water. Stir until fully combined and set aside.

6. In a heavy-bottomed, 6-quart / 6-L sauté pan over medium heat, warm ¼ cup / 60 mL of the oil. Carefully add ⅓ of the chicken pieces to the sauté pan and pan fry, turning once to ensure even cooking, for 8 minutes total, until they are golden brown on each side. Remove the chicken pieces from the sauté pan and set aside on a large plate lined with paper towels to absorb the extra oil.

7. Repeat until you finish cooking all of the chicken. Scrape out and discard all remnants of the chicken and its breading from the sauté pan, but leave the oil in the pan.

8. Raise the heat to medium–high and add the remaining 2 tablespoons of oil and the onion to the sauté pan. Cook for 4 minutes, until the onion is slightly browned. Add the ginger and garlic and cook for 1 minute.

9. Add the bell pepper and fresh chiles to the sauté pan and cook for 2 minutes. Add the sauce from Step 5 and bring to a boil.

10. Reduce the heat to medium and simmer for 2 minutes, until the mixture thickens. Carefully return the chicken pieces to the sauté pan and simmer, uncovered and stirring occasionally, for 4 minutes, until the chicken is warmed through. Remove from the heat.

11. Sprinkle the scallions and the remaining ½ teaspoon of *Garam Masala* over the dish. Cover and set aside for 5 minutes, to allow the chicken to absorb all the flavors.

12. Uncover and serve immediately with the brown or white basmati rice.

Kerala Fish Curry

YIELD: 6–8 SERVINGS

TOOLS: You'll need a large mixing bowl; an 8-inch / 20-cm frying pan; 2 plates; a spice grinder or mortar and pestle; a small mixing bowl; a fork; and a heavy-bottomed, 6-quart / 6-L sauté pan with a lid.

VEGANIZE IT! Substitute 24 to 28 ounces / 680 to 790 g of tempeh, extra-firm tofu, or seitan for the fish. Cut into 2-inch / 5-cm cubes and follow the instructions.

PICTURED ON P. 182

I was inspired to recreate this recipe after a visit to the beautiful, unique Indian state of Kerala. The food there was utterly addictive, with dishes that my Punjabi palate had never experienced before. I was visiting along with a camera crew who devoured this version of fish curry while I got up close and personal with local chefs.

2 pounds / 910 g firm, white fish, such as halibut, skin removed and cut into 2-inch / 5-cm cubes
2½ teaspoons salt, divided
½ teaspoon ground black pepper
½ teaspoon turmeric powder
1 teaspoon cumin seeds
1 tablespoon coriander seeds
1 (2-inch / 5-cm) cube dried tamarind pulp*
1 cup / 240 mL boiling water
4 tablespoons / 60 mL coconut oil, divided
½ teaspoon black mustard seeds
20 curry leaves

1 medium onion, finely minced
1 (2-inch / 5-cm) piece ginger, peeled and grated or minced
6 cloves garlic, peeled and grated or minced
1 medium tomato, finely diced
3–6 fresh Thai, serrano, or cayenne chiles, stems removed and thinly sliced lengthwise
1 teaspoon red chile powder or cayenne pepper
1 (14-ounce / 400-g) can coconut milk (regular or light)
Brown or white basmati rice, for serving

1. Place the fish cubes in a large mixing bowl and sprinkle them with ½ teaspoon of the salt, the black pepper, and the turmeric. Rub the spices into the fish. Cover and set aside to marinate at room temperature for at least 30 minutes while you prep the remaining ingredients.

2. Combine the cumin and coriander seeds in an 8-inch / 20-cm frying pan over medium–high heat and dry roast for 5 minutes, until the seeds turn reddish-brown and become aromatic. During the entire cooking time, shake the pan every 15 to 20 seconds to prevent the spices from burning. *When roasting spices, never leave the pan unattended—they burn easily.* Remove from the heat, transfer to a plate, and set aside to cool for 15 minutes.

3. Transfer the roasted seeds to a mortar and pestle or spice grinder and grind them into a powder. Set aside.

4. In a small mixing bowl, combine the tamarind pulp and the boiling water. Set them aside to soak and soften for at least 30 minutes.

5. Once the soaking time is up, use the back of a fork to break down the pulp and squeeze the liquid out of it. Discard the pulp, seeds, and fiber and strain the juice. Set aside the juice.

6. In a heavy-bottomed, 6-quart / 6-L sauté pan over medium–high heat, warm 2 tablespoons of the oil. Add the mustard seeds and curry leaves and cook for 30 seconds. *Keep a lid handy—the seeds do pop when hot.* Carefully add the fish and sear for no more than 1 minute on each side. Carefully remove the fish, curry leaves, mustard seeds, and excess oil to a clean plate. Scrape the bottom of the pan to remove and discard any remnants.

7. To the same sauté pan, add the remaining 2 tablespoons of oil and the onion. Cook, stirring occasionally, for 3 minutes, until slightly browned. Add the ginger and garlic to the sauté pan and cook for 1 minute. Add the tomato and fresh chiles and cook, stirring constantly, for 1 minute.

8. Reduce the heat to medium–low and add the tamarind juice from Step 5, the roasted coriander and cumin seeds, the red chile powder, and the remaining 2 teaspoons of salt to the sauté pan. Stir well and simmer, uncovered, for 5 minutes, until the mixture thickens and the oil starts to pull away from the curry.

9. Add the coconut milk to the sauté pan and cook, uncovered and stirring constantly, for 3 minutes. *Regular coconut milk will give you a richer curry, but both regular and light will do the trick.*

10. Return the fish, curry leaves, mustard seeds, and oil to the sauté pan and cook, turning once to ensure even cooking, for a total of 5 minutes, being careful to keep the fish pieces whole. Remove from the heat, cover, and set aside for 3 minutes before serving.

11. Transfer to a serving bowl and serve with the brown or white basmati rice.

*If you don't have dried tamarind pulp, you can substitute 1 teaspoon of tamarind paste. If using paste, there is no need to soak it in boiling water first. Just add it to the dish.

Lamb Kabobs

YIELD: 20–25 (5- TO 6-INCH / 13- TO 15-CM) KABOBS

TOOLS: You'll need a grill, a food processor (small if you have one), a large mixing bowl, a small mixing bowl filled with water, and about 25 skewers (bamboo, wooden, or metal).

TRY THIS! Instead of grilling these on skewers, you can make small burgers on the stovetop. If doing so, cook for 3 minutes on each side over medium heat.

VEGANIZE IT! See my recipe for Veggie Kabobs on page 87. I got the inspiration for it after making this recipe for my husband and craving something similar that was just for me.

No one does a barbecue better than my Sheela *bua* and her family in Hounslow, England. My aunt and uncle, along with their three children Sangita, Angie, and Bob, are dedicated to the art of the perfect lamb kabob. This recipe is inspired by their dedication to the grill, rain or shine!

1 (6-inch / 15-cm) piece ginger, peeled and roughly chopped
2 pounds / 910 g ground or minced lamb
1 medium yellow or red onion, finely minced
2–4 fresh Thai, serrano, or cayenne chiles, stems removed and thinly sliced
¼ cup / 5 g minced fresh cilantro
¼ cup / 5 g *kasoori methi* (dried fenugreek leaves), lightly hand crushed to release flavor

1 tablespoon *Garam Masala* (see recipe on p. 35)
1 tablespoon ground coriander
2 teaspoons red chile powder or cayenne pepper
1 tablespoon salt
Pudina ki Chutney, *Imlee ki* Chutney (see recipes on pp. 41 and 42), or ketchup, for serving

1. Preheat the grill to medium–high (350°F / 180°C to 400°F / 200°C), making sure the grill has been well oiled or sprayed with a nonstick cooking or grilling spray.

2. In the bowl of a food processor, grind the ginger into a smooth paste.

3. Place the lamb in a large mixing bowl. Add the ground ginger from Step 2, the onion, the fresh chiles, the cilantro, the *kasoori methi,* the *Garam Masala,* the coriander, the red chile powder, and the salt. Using your hands or a large spoon, mix until all the ingredients are evenly blended.

4. Dip your hands in a bowl of warm water. Using 1 hand, gather ⅓ cup / 80 mL of the lamb mixture and mold it around a skewer to about 5 to 6 inches / 13 to 15 cm in length—1 lamb ball per skewer. Continue until you use all of the lamb mixture and fill all 20 to 25 of the skewers, cleaning your hands in the bowl of water as needed.

5. Place the skewered kabobs on the grill and cook, turning at least once, for a total of 15 minutes. Remove from the grill and transfer to a foil-covered serving platter.

6. Serve with the *Pudina ki* or *Imlee ki* Chutney or ketchup.

Tamarind Shrimp Curry

YIELD: 6–8 SERVINGS

TOOLS: You'll need a small frying pan, a plate, a spice grinder or a mortar and pestle, 2 large mixing bowls, and a 6-quart / 6-L sauté pan.

VEGANIZE IT! Substitute 24 to 28 ounces / 680 to 790 g of tempeh, extra-firm organic tofu, or seitan for the shrimp. Cut into 1-inch / 3-cm cubes and follow the instructions. Bake the tofu according to instructions on page 46 for added texture.

I learned how to make this curry during a stay at Ayisha Manzil Homestay in Thalassery (Tellicherry), Kerala. Our hostess, Mrs. Moosa, used turmeric powder to marinate the shrimp and freshly roasted and ground coriander to round out the flavors in this uniquely spiced curry. For a fun twist, serve your guests a small plate of this recipe—1 cooked shrimp nestled in 1 tablespoon of curry.

¼ cup / 20 g coriander seeds
1 pound / 450 g medium shrimp, peeled and deveined (28–32 pieces)
2 teaspoons turmeric powder, divided
1½ teaspoons red chile powder or cayenne pepper, divided
1 tablespoon plus ½ teaspoon plus 1 pinch salt, divided
4 tablespoons / 60 mL coconut oil, divided
½ teaspoon mustard seeds
20 fresh curry leaves
1 large yellow or red onion, finely diced
1–2 fresh Thai, serrano, or cayenne chiles, stems removed and finely diced
1 (2-inch / 5-cm) piece ginger, peeled and grated
10 cloves garlic, peeled and minced or grated
5 medium tomatoes, peeled and diced*
1 teaspoon tamarind paste
1 tablespoon light brown sugar
2 cups / 470 mL water
¼ cup / 60 mL coconut milk (regular or light)
Brown or white basmati rice, for serving

1. Place the coriander seeds in a small frying pan over medium–high heat and dry roast for 5 minutes, until the seeds turn reddish-brown. *When roasting spices, never leave the pan unattended—they burn easily.* Transfer to a plate and set aside to cool completely.

2. Using a spice grinder or mortar and pestle, grind the coriander seeds into a fine powder. Set aside.

3. In a large mixing bowl, combine the shrimp, 1 teaspoon of the turmeric, ½ teaspoon of the red chile powder, and ½ teaspoon of the salt. Mix well, cover, and set aside to marinate at room temperature for at least 20 minutes while you prep the remaining ingredients.

4. In a 6-quart / 6-L sauté pan over medium–high heat, warm 2 tablespoons of the oil. Add the shrimp and sear, turning once to ensure even cooking, for a total of 2 minutes. *Be careful not to cook the shrimp through, or they will be overcooked later.* Remove from the heat. Carefully remove the shrimp from the pan and transfer to a clean bowl. Set aside.

Continued

5. Return the sauté pan to medium–high heat and add the remaining 2 tablespoons of oil. Once the oil is hot, add the mustard seeds and cook for 30 seconds, until the seeds pop. *Keep a lid handy, as the seeds can pop out of the pan.* Carefully add the curry leaves and cook for 20 to 40 seconds, until the leaves wilt slightly. *If you don't have fresh leaves on hand, use dried or frozen ones. If you can't find curry leaves, don't worry—just omit them.*

6. Add the onion, the pinch of salt, the remaining 1 teaspoon of turmeric, the remaining 1 teaspoon of red chile powder, and the fresh chiles to the sauté pan. Cook, stirring occasionally to prevent sticking, for 3 to 5 minutes, until slightly browned.

7. Add the ginger and garlic to the sauté pan and cook for 1 minute. Add the ground coriander and stir well.

8. Reduce the heat to medium and add the tomatoes, the tamarind paste, the remaining 1 tablespoon of salt, and the brown sugar to the sauté pan. Simmer for 6 minutes, until the tomatoes start to break down.

9. Slowly add the water, ¼ cup / 60 mL at a time, to the sauté pan and simmer for 10 to 12 minutes, until the oil starts to separate slightly and the ingredients start to pull together. Add the coconut milk and cook for 3 minutes, until warmed through.

10. Add the shrimp to the sauté pan and cook for 2 minutes, until they are cooked through and slightly opaque. Remove from the heat.

11. Transfer to a serving bowl. Serve immediately over a bed of the brown or white basmati rice.

*See notes for peeling tomatoes on page 28. A serrated peeler is the easiest way.

Punjabi Chile Chicken

YIELD: 4–6 SERVINGS

TOOLS: You'll need an 8-inch / 20-cm frying pan; 2 plates; a mortar and pestle or spice grinder; a food processor; 3 small mixing bowls; and a heavy-bottomed, 6-quart / 6-L sauté pan with a lid.

VEGANIZE IT! Substitute 24 to 28 ounces / 680 to 790 g of tempeh, extra-firm organic tofu, or seitan, cut in 2-inch / 5-cm cubes, for the chicken. Follow the above steps, but reduce the cooking times in Steps 9 and 10 to about 15 minutes total. Bake your tofu to achieve extra texture—the recipe is on p. 46.

This is the real Punjabi deal: spicy, complex, and delicious. It's one of my husband's favorite dishes and one that you'll make a staple in your home as well.

- 2 heaping tablespoons coriander seeds
- 1 small yellow onion, coarsely chopped
- 1 cup / 100 g ginger, peeled and coarsely chopped
- 1 cup / 140 g peeled garlic cloves
- 2½ cups / 590 mL plus 1 tablespoon water, divided
- 1 medium tomato, coarsely chopped
- 5 tablespoons / 75 mL vegetable oil, divided
- 4 pounds / 1.81 g skinless whole bone-in chicken, cut into 8–10 pieces (including cutting each breast in ½), or 2 pounds / 910 g boneless chicken
- 2 (3-inch / 8-cm) sticks cinnamon
- 6 green cardamom pods, slightly crushed
- 2 tablespoons *Garam Masala* (see recipe on p. 35)
- 1 tablespoon plus 2 teaspoons salt
- 2 teaspoons red chile powder or cayenne pepper
- 6–15 fresh Thai, serrano, or cayenne chiles, stems removed and sliced in half lengthwise
- Brown or white basmati rice, *Roti,* or *Naan* (see recipes on pp. 230 and 238), for serving

1. Place the coriander seeds in an 8-inch / 20-cm frying pan over medium–high heat and dry roast for 5 minutes, until the seeds turn reddish-brown and become aromatic. During the entire cooking time, shake the pan every 15 to 20 seconds to prevent the spices from burning. *When roasting spices, never leave the pan unattended—they burn easily.* Remove from the heat, transfer to a plate, and set aside to cool for 15 minutes.

2. Transfer the roasted seeds to a mortar and pestle or spice grinder and grind them into a powder.

3. In the bowl of a food processor, grind the onion into a watery paste. Transfer to a small mixing bowl and set aside. *No need to clean the food processor bowl in between.* Add the ginger, garlic, and the 1 tablespoon of water to the food processor bowl and grind into a watery paste. Transfer to a second small mixing bowl and set aside. *Again, no need to clean.* Add the tomato to the food processor bowl and grind into a watery paste. Transfer to a third small mixing bowl and set aside.

4. In a heavy-bottomed, 6-quart / 6-L sauté pan over medium–high heat, warm 2 tablespoons of the oil. Add the chicken and sear, turning once to ensure even cooking, for a total of 4 minutes, until slightly browned. Transfer the chicken and any scrapings from the bottom of the pan to a plate and set aside.

5. Return the sauté pan to medium–high heat and warm the remaining 3 tablespoons / 45 mL of oil. Add the cinnamon and cardamom and cook for 1 minute, until slightly browned.

6. Carefully add the onion paste from Step 3 to the sauté pan. *The moisture from the onion can splatter, so keep the lid handy.* Cook, stirring and scraping the bottom of the pan constantly, for 3 minutes, until slightly browned.

7. Add the ginger paste from Step 3 to the sauté pan and cook, stirring constantly, for 2 minutes. Add the ground tomato from Step 3 and cook, stirring constantly, for 3 minutes. *At this point, the mixture will start to thicken and the oil will start to pull away from the edges.*

8. Reduce the heat to medium and add 1 cup / 240 mL of the water to the sauté pan. Simmer for 4 minutes. Add the ground coriander from Step 2, the *Garam Masala,* the salt, the red chile powder, the fresh chiles, and 1 cup / 240 mL of the water and cook for 4 minutes, until the sauce thickens a bit. *We love this dish spicy, and when we make it at home, I use 15 chiles. Tone it down as needed.*

9. Slowly, carefully return the chicken to the sauté pan. Add the remaining ½ cup / 120 mL of water and cook, uncovered and stirring occasionally, for 10 minutes, turning the chicken pieces once to ensure even cooking.

10. Reduce the heat to low, partially cover, and cook for 30 minutes, until the chicken has cooked through. Remove from the heat. Stir well and remove and discard the whole spices.

11. Transfer to a serving bowl and serve with the brown or white basmati rice, *Roti,* or *Naan.*

1 North Indian Chicken Curry (p. 212) 2 Egg Curry (p. 220)

North Indian Chicken Curry

YIELD: 8–10 SERVINGS

TOOLS: You'll need a food processor; a large and a small mixing bowl; a whisk; a fork; a heavy-bottomed, 6-quart / 6-L sauté pan with a lid; tongs; and a large plate.

VEGANIZE IT! You'll find the vegan version of this recipe on page 167.

PICTURED ON P. 210

This is like no other chicken curry you've ever had. It's at once thick, rich, and utterly comforting. The yogurt adds just the right amount of tartness balanced with the spices. Make extra for leftovers. Your family will thank you. It's my husband's top pick in this section, and a huge crowd pleaser when I conduct my cooking classes at our Lincoln Park Whole Foods in Chicago.

1 medium yellow or red onion, roughly chopped
1 (4-inch / 10-cm) piece ginger, peeled and roughly chopped
10 cloves garlic, peeled
2 cups / 470 mL plain, unsweetened yogurt (whole, lowfat, or nonfat)
1 tablespoon plus 1 teaspoon plus 1 pinch salt, divided
1 tablespoon turmeric powder
1 tablespoon *Garam Masala* (see recipe on p. 35)
1 tablespoon red chile powder or cayenne pepper
2 teaspoons ground coriander
2 teaspoons roasted cumin, ground
⅓ cup / 10 g *kasoori methi* (dried fenugreek leaves), lightly hand crushed to release flavor
4 pounds / 1.81 g skinless whole bone-in chicken, cut into 8–10 pieces (including cutting each breast in ½), or 2 pounds / 910 g boneless chicken

6 tablespoons / 90 mL *ghee* or vegetable oil, divided
1 teaspoon cumin seeds
2 (3-inch / 8-cm) sticks cinnamon
5 whole cloves
5 green cardamom pods, lightly crushed
2 black cardamom pods
1 large yellow or red onion, thinly sliced
3 large tomatoes, diced
2–4 fresh Thai, serrano, or cayenne chiles, stems removed and thinly sliced
2 heaping tablespoons chopped fresh cilantro, for garnish
Brown or white basmati rice, *Roti,* or *Naan* (see recipes on pp. 230 and 238), for serving

1. In the bowl of a food processor, grind the chopped onion, the ginger, and the garlic into a smooth paste. Transfer to a large mixing bowl and add the yogurt, the 1 tablespoon plus 1 teaspoon of the salt, the turmeric, the *Garam Masala,* the red chile powder, the coriander, the cumin, and the *kasoori methi.* Whisk until well blended. Kasoori methi *can be found in Indian grocery stores. Omit if you cannot find it. Do not use fresh leaves or fenugreek seeds, as they will alter the taste.*

2. Prepare the chicken by poking holes in it with a fork to help it absorb the yogurt marinade. Carefully add the pieces of chicken to the large mixing bowl and gently stir until all the pieces are evenly coated. Cover and refrigerate for 2 hours to overnight.

3. In a heavy-bottomed, 6-quart / 6-L sauté pan over medium–high heat, warm 3 tablespoons / 45 mL of the *ghee.* Using tongs, carefully transfer the pieces of chicken to the sauté pan, reserving the marinade for later use. Cook, turning once to ensure even cooking, for a total of 4 minutes. Transfer to a large plate, and transfer the remaining liquid in the pan to a small mixing bowl for later use.

4. Return the sauté pan to medium–high heat and warm the remaining 3 tablespoons / 45 mL of *ghee.* Add the cumin seeds, cinnamon, cloves, and green and black cardamom and cook for 2 minutes. Add the sliced onion and the remaining pinch of salt and cook, stirring constantly and scraping the pan to prevent burning, for 3 minutes, until the onion is slightly browned.

5. Add the tomatoes to the sauté pan and cook, uncovered and stirring occasionally (breaking down the tomatoes with the back of the spoon), for 11 minutes, until they are fairly smooth. Add the reserved marinade and cooking liquid from Step 3 and the fresh chiles to the sauté pan and cook for 2 minutes.

6. Reduce the heat to medium–low and slowly, carefully return the chicken to the sauté pan. Partially cover the pan and cook, stirring occasionally to ensure even cooking, for 35 to 40 minutes (20 minutes if using boneless chicken), until the chicken is cooked through. *Be sure not to overcook the chicken.* Remove from the heat.

7. Transfer to a serving bowl. Garnish with the cilantro and serve with the brown or white basmati rice, *Roti,* or *Naan.*

Grilled Ginger–Garlic Chicken

YIELD: 6–8 SERVINGS

TOOLS: You'll need a food processor, a large mixing bowl, a whisk, a fork, and a grill.

VEGANIZE IT! Substitute 24 to 28 ounces / 680 to 790 g of tempeh, extra-firm tofu, or seitan for the chicken. Slice the pieces so they're large enough to be manageable on the grill. Grill for 20 to 25 minutes, turning once in between, until cooked through.

My mother-in-law may be a vegetarian, but she is well known for her amazing grilled chicken. I could not write this section without showcasing her recipe. The key, according to her, is to use the yogurt sparingly, so the marinade "sticks."

1 large yellow onion, coarsely chopped
1 cup / 100 g ginger, peeled and diced
1 cup / 140 g peeled garlic cloves
1 tablespoon salt
2 teaspoons red chile powder or cayenne pepper
1 tablespoon lemon juice, plus more for serving
1 tablespoon ground black pepper
2 teaspoons unsmoked paprika

5 heaping / 85 mL tablespoons plain, unsweetened yogurt, (whole, lowfat, or nonfat)
4 pounds / 1.81 g skinless whole bone-in chicken, cut into 8–10 pieces (including cutting each breast in ½), or 2 pounds / 910 g boneless chicken
2 tablespoons finely minced fresh cilantro, for garnish

1. In the bowl of a food processor, grind the onion, ginger, and garlic into a watery paste. Transfer to a large mixing bowl and add the salt, the red chile powder, the 1 tablespoon of lemon juice, the black pepper, the paprika, and the yogurt. Whisk until well combined.

2. Prepare the chicken by poking holes in it with a fork to help it absorb the yogurt marinade. Carefully add the pieces of chicken to the large mixing bowl and gently stir until all the pieces are evenly coated. Cover and refrigerate for 2 to 6 hours.

3. Preheat the grill to medium–high (350°F / 180°C to 400°F / 200°C), making sure the grill has been well oiled or sprayed with a nonstick cooking or grilling spray.

4. Place the marinated pieces of chicken on the grill and cook, turning once to ensure even cooking, for 45 to 50 minutes, until cooked through and the chicken reaches an internal temperature of 165°F / 74°C. Remove from the grill and transfer to a serving platter. *We prefer our meat well done, so shorten the cook time if you prefer.*

5. Squeeze the remaining lemon juice over the cooked chicken. Garnish with the cilantro and serve immediately.

Keema

YIELD: 4 CUPS / 950 ML

Minced, spiced lamb is pure comfort food for Punjabis. There's just something about how the spices come together with the meat and a slight excess of oil. Even those who are watching their weight will splurge a little on this dish. I equate the experience to the New Yorker who just can't get enough thin-crust pizza, dripping with oil. But don't worry. You can always pull back on the oil—just don't tell my hubby I said that!

TOOLS: You'll need a food processor; 2 small mixing bowls; a spice grinder or mortar and pestle; and a heavy-bottomed, 6-quart / 6-L sauté pan.

VEGANIZE IT! This is so simple to make either vegan or vegetarian. You can substitute 2 (14-ounce / 400-g) packages of extra-firm organic tofu (crumbled), 2 frozen bags of meatless crumbles, or textured vegetable protein. Other ways to make this recipe fun is add spinach, bell pepper, and/or sliced mushrooms. The cooking times remain the same. You can fool the most discerning meat eater. (I even successfully fooled my husband!)

1 large yellow or red onion, roughly chopped
1 (3-inch / 8-cm) piece ginger, peeled and roughly chopped
10 cloves garlic, peeled
2–4 fresh Thai, serrano, or cayenne chiles, stems removed
1 heaping tablespoon tomato paste
2 tablespoons hot water
4 green cardamom pods
3 whole cloves
1 teaspoon black peppercorns
¼ cup / 60 mL vegetable oil
3 cassia or bay leaves
1 (3-inch / 8-cm) stick cinnamon
½–1 cup / 70–130 g frozen peas
1 pound / 450 g minced or ground lamb (chicken or turkey works too)
2 teaspoons *Garam Masala* (see recipe on p. 35)
2 teaspoons ground coriander
2 teaspoons ground cumin
1 tablespoon salt
1 teaspoon red chile powder or cayenne pepper
½ teaspoon turmeric powder
¼ cup / 5 g chopped fresh cilantro, for garnish
Brown or white basmati rice, for serving

1. In the bowl of a food processor, grind the onion, ginger, garlic, and fresh chiles into a smooth paste. Transfer to a small mixing bowl and set aside.

2. In another small mixing bowl, combine the tomato paste and hot water. Stir and set aside.

3. In a mortar and pestle, lightly crush together the cardamom, cloves, and peppercorns. *If you don't like to bite into whole spices, grind these in a spice grinder.* Set aside.

4. In a heavy-bottomed, 6-quart / 6-L sauté pan over medium–high heat, warm the oil. Add the cassia leaves and cinnamon and cook, stirring constantly, for 40 seconds, until the spices are slightly browned. Add the cardamom mixture and cook, stirring constantly, for 40 seconds.

5. Add the onion paste from Step 1 to the sauté pan and cook, stirring constantly to prevent sticking, for 3 minutes, until the mixture is slightly browned. Add the peas and cook for 1 minute.

6. Add the lamb, the water–tomato paste mixture from Step 2, the *Garam Masala,* the coriander, the cumin, the salt, the red chile powder, and the turmeric to the sauté pan. *This dish is all about comfort for North Indians, so I always like to drizzle in another 1 to 2 tablespoons of oil at this point.*

7. Cook, stirring occasionally, for 6 to 8 minutes, until the lamb is cooked through and the oil pulls away from the other ingredients. Remove and discard the whole spices. Remove from the heat.

8. Transfer to a serving bowl. Garnish with the cilantro and serve over the brown or white basmati rice.

Lamb *Korma*

YIELD: 8 CUPS / 1.9 L

TOOLS: You'll need 2 small mixing
bowls; a large, shallow dish; an 8-inch
/ 20-cm frying pan; 2 plates; a spice
grinder or mortar and pestle; a food
processor; and a heavy-bottomed,
6-quart / 6-L sauté pan.

SUBSTITUTIONS: You can substitute
beef for the lamb, but if you do,
lengthen the cooking time in Step 11
to 2 hours. For chicken, cook for 40
minutes for bone-in and 20 minutes
for boneless. For shrimp, cook for
10 to 15 minutes, until just cooked
through. For vegetables, cook about
10 minutes, or longer if you want
them softer.

VEGANIZE IT! Page over to my recipe
for *Navratan Korma* (see recipe on p.
175) and follow the notes for making
it vegan.

Korma is simply the name for a sauce that derives its richness from nuts and its
sweet notes from dried fruit like raisins. The main ingredient can be anything
at all. I used lamb because it's most often linked to a *korma* on Indian restaurant menus. Feel free to use vegetables, poultry, beef, or even shrimp. Just
know that cooking times will vary slightly according to the main ingredient.

¼ cup / 40 g golden raisins
2 cups / 470 mL boiling water
2 pounds / 910 g boneless lamb
 (leg or shoulder), cut into 1-inch /
 3-cm cubes
2½ teaspoons plus 1 pinch salt,
 divided
1 teaspoon turmeric powder
10 whole cloves
1 tablespoon cumin seeds
1 tablespoon coriander seeds
1 tablespoon black peppercorns
1 teaspoon cardamom seeds
1 (2-inch / 5-cm) piece ginger,
 peeled and coarsely chopped
10 cloves garlic, peeled
2–3 fresh Thai, serrano, or cayenne
 chiles, stems removed
6 tablespoons / 90 mL *ghee* or
 vegetable oil, divided

1 (4-inch / 10-cm) stick cinnamon
1 large onion (yellow or red), thinly
 sliced
2 cups / 470 mL room-temperature
 water, divided
3 large tomatoes, diced
2 tablespoons tomato paste
1 teaspoon red chile powder or
 cayenne pepper
½ cup / 120 mL heavy cream or
 half & half
12 raw, unsalted cashews, split in
 half and dry roasted, for garnish
2 tablespoons chopped fresh
 cilantro, for garnish
Brown or white basmati rice, *Roti*, or
 Naan (see recipes on pp. 230 and
 238), for serving

1. Place the raisins in a small mixing bowl and add the boiling water. Set them
aside to soak for at least 30 minutes as you prep the remaining ingredients.

2. Place the lamb in a large, shallow dish and sprinkle ½ teaspoon of the salt
and the turmeric over it. Set it aside at room temperature until you are ready
to cook.

3. Combine the cloves, cumin and coriander seeds, peppercorns, and cardamom in an 8-inch / 20-cm frying pan over medium–high heat and dry roast
for 3 minutes, until the seeds turn reddish-brown and become aromatic. During the entire cooking time, shake the pan every 15 to 20 seconds to prevent
the spices from burning. *When roasting spices, never leave the pan unattended—
they burn easily.* Remove from the heat, transfer to a plate, and set aside to cool
for 15 minutes.

4. Using a spice grinder or mortar and pestle, grind the roasted spices from Step 3 into a powder and place in a small mixing bowl.

5. In the bowl of a food processor, grind the ginger, garlic, and fresh chiles into a smooth paste. Transfer to the bowl containing the roasted, ground spices. Stir until combined and set aside.

6. In a heavy-bottomed, 6-quart/ 6-L sauté pan over medium–high heat, warm 3 tablespoons / 45 mL of the *ghee*. Add the lamb and sear, turning to cook each side, for 2 minutes on each side. Transfer to a plate and set aside.

7. Return the sauté pan to medium–high heat and warm the remaining 3 tablespoons / 45 mL of *ghee*. Add the cinnamon stick, onion, and the 1 pinch of salt and cook, stirring occasionally, for 3 minutes, until the onion is slightly browned.

8. Add the contents of the small mixing bowl last used in Step 5 to the sauté pan and cook for 1 minute. Add ½ cup / 120 mL of the room-temperature water and cook for 1 minute. Add another ½ cup / 120 mL of the room-temperature water, scrape the pan thoroughly, and cook for 1 minute.

9. Drain the raisins. Add them, along with the tomatoes, the tomato paste, the remaining 2 teaspoons of salt, and the red chile powder, to the sauté pan and cook for 2 minutes. Add the remaining 1 cup / 120 mL of room-temperature water and bring to a boil.

10. Reduce the heat to medium and simmer, uncovered, for 15 minutes, until the tomatoes break down and the mixture slightly thickens. *The spices will also come together and should merge with the tomatoes. Add a little more water if you prefer a thinner gravy.*

11. Slowly, carefully add the lamb pieces to the sauté pan. Reduce the heat to low and simmer for 1½ hours or longer, until the lamb is completely tender.

12. Add the cream to the sauté pan. Stir slowly and cook for 1 minute, until heated through. *If the mixture dries out a bit, just add a little water.* Remove from the heat.

13. Transfer to a serving bowl. Garnish with the cashews and cilantro and serve over the brown or white basmati rice or with the *Roti* or *Naan*.

Rogan Josh

YIELD: 2 CUPS / 470 ML

TOOLS: You'll need a food processor; a large mixing bowl; a whisk; a spice grinder or mortar and pestle; and a heavy-bottomed, 6-quart / 6-L sauté pan.

NOTE: You can easily make this dish with an alternative protein. Another popular version uses beef. Simply use the same cut and quantity as listed in the recipe and cook the beef longer, for 2 hours, until tender.

VEGANIZE IT! Substitute 24 to 28 ounces / 680 to 790 g of Baked Tofu (see recipe on p. 46), seitan, or tempeh for the lamb and coconut or soy yogurt or cashew or coconut cream for the dairy yogurt. Reduce the cooking time to 20 minutes in Step 7, and you may also want to cut back on the water a bit. Start with 1 cup / 240 mL and then work your way up if you need more.

The Persians introduced this hugely popular dish to Kashmir. *Rogan* means either "red" or "oil," while *josh* means "boiling" or "passionate." The dish's red hue is traditionally from deseeded Kashmiri red peppers. Here we use paprika instead. It's one of the tastiest dishes that descends from Moghul cuisine.

1 large yellow or red onion, roughly chopped
1 (2-inch / 5-cm) piece ginger, peeled and roughly chopped
2 cups / 470 mL plus 1 tablespoon water, divided (possibly more)
1 tablespoon ground coriander
2 teaspoons red chile powder or cayenne pepper
1 tablespoon plus 1 teaspoon unsmoked paprika
1 tablespoon salt
2 cups / 470 mL plain, unsweetened yogurt (whole milk, lowfat, or nonfat)
2 pounds / 910 g lamb (shoulder or leg), boned or boneless cubes

2 teaspoons *kalonji* seeds (nigella seeds)
1 teaspoon cumin seeds
2 teaspoons whole black peppercorns
½ teaspoon cardamom seeds
6 whole cloves
¼ cup / 60 mL *ghee* or vegetable oil
2 (3-inch / 8-cm) sticks cinnamon
3 cassia or bay leaves
6 cloves garlic, peeled and finely minced
½ cup / 120 mL half & half or heavy cream
Brown or white basmati rice, *Roti,* or *Naan* (see recipes on pp. 230 and 238), for serving

1. In the bowl of a food processor, grind the onion, ginger, and the 1 tablespoon of water into a smooth paste. *Take your time—this may take a few minutes. You'll likely have to stop and push the ingredients down from the sides and grind again.*

2. Transfer to a large mixing bowl and add the coriander, red chile powder, paprika, salt, and yogurt. Whisk until well combined.

3. Carefully add the pieces of lamb to the large mixing bowl and gently stir until all the pieces are evenly coated. Cover and refrigerate for 2 hours to overnight.

4. In a spice grinder or mortar and pestle, grind the *kalonji* and cumin seeds, peppercorns, cardamom, and cloves into a powder.

5. In a heavy-bottomed, 6-quart / 6-L sauté pan over medium–high heat, warm the *ghee*. Add the cinnamon and cassia leaves and cook for 40 seconds, until the spices are slightly brown and aromatic. Add the garlic and cook for 2 minutes, until browned. Add the *kalonji* spice mixture and cook for 40 seconds.

6. Slowly, carefully add the lamb pieces to the sauté pan (leaving the marinade behind) and cook, turning once to ensure even browning, for a total of 4 minutes. Add the leftover marinade and the remaining 2 cups / 470 mL of water and bring to a boil.

7. Reduce the heat to medium, cover, and simmer, stirring occasionally to prevent sticking, for 1½ hours. *The sauce will start to caramelize on the bottom, which will only add flavor. If, toward the end of the cooking time, you think you'd like to have more gravy in the dish, add another ½ cup / 120 mL of water or so, raise the heat to medium–high, and allow the dish to boil for 2 minutes, long enough for the gravy to thicken slightly.* Remove from the heat. Slowly fold the half & half into the mixture, cover, and set aside for 10 minutes, until the flavors pull together.

8. Transfer to a serving bowl and serve hot with the brown or white basmati rice, *Roti,* or *Naan.*

Egg Curry

YIELD: 4–6 SERVINGS

TOOLS: You'll need a small mixing bowl; a heavy-bottomed, 4-quart / 4-L sauté pan; a slotted spoon; a plate; and a food processor, a blender, or an immersion (stick) blender.

PICTURED ON P. 210

When I worked as a young staffer on Capitol Hill, one tradition my friends and I had—when we could afford it—was a champagne brunch at the infamous Bombay Club restaurant on Connecticut Ave. The dish I could never resist eating was the egg curry. I tried calling them for the recipe—with no luck. This is my attempt at replicating those days and that dish. I'm pretty happy with the turnout.

10 hardboiled eggs, peeled
¾ teaspoon turmeric powder, divided
2 tablespoons plus 2 teaspoons vegetable oil, divided
1 teaspoon cumin seeds
1 medium red onion, finely diced
1 (2-inch / 5-cm) piece ginger, peeled and grated
2 cloves garlic, peeled and grated or minced
6 medium tomatoes, diced
1–2 fresh Thai, serrano, or cayenne chiles, stems removed and thinly sliced
1 tablespoon *Garam Masala* (see recipe on p. 35)
1 tablespoon ground coriander
1 teaspoon red chile powder or cayenne pepper
1 tablespoon salt
1 cup / 240 mL boiling water
½ cup / 10 g chopped fresh cilantro
Roti or *Naan* (see recipes on pp. 230 and 238), for serving

1. Place the eggs in a small mixing bowl and sprinkle ¼ teaspoon of the turmeric over them. Rub lightly until they are evenly coated. *Thanks to my friend Naila for this tip.*

2. In a 4-quart / 4-L sauté pan over medium–high heat, warm the 2 teaspoons of oil. Add the eggs and sauté, gently moving the eggs around so they don't stick, for 2 minutes, until lightly browned. Remove with a slotted spoon and set aside on a plate to cool. *You can leave them whole for the final dish, or slice them in half before adding them back to the sauce. If slicing them, handle with care so the yolks stay intact.*

3. Return the sauté pan to medium–high heat and warm the remaining 2 tablespoons of oil. Add the cumin seeds and the remaining ½ teaspoon of the turmeric and cook for 40 seconds, until the cumin seeds sizzle and turn reddish-brown.

4. Add the onion to the sauté pan and cook, stirring occasionally to avoid sticking, for 2 minutes, until the onion is slightly browned. Add the ginger and garlic and cook for 1 minute.

5. Reduce the heat to medium–low and add the tomatoes, fresh chiles, *Garam Masala,* coriander, red chile powder, and salt to the sauté pan. Simmer for 12 minutes. Add the boiling water and cook for 3 minutes, until all the ingredients pull together and the tomatoes break down. Add the cilantro and cook for 1 minute. Remove from the heat.

6. Transfer the mixture to the bowl of a food processor or a blender or place an immersion blender in the sauté pan. Process until smooth.

7. Transfer the smooth mixture to a large serving bowl. Gently fold in the eggs (whole or sliced). Serve with the *Roti* or *Naan.*

Lamb *Vindaloo*

YIELD: 4 CUPS / 950 ML

TOOLS: You'll need an 8-inch / 20-cm frying pan; 2 plates; a spice grinder or mortar and pestle; a small mixing bowl; a food processor; a large glass or otherwise nonreactive mixing bowl; a medium mixing bowl; a heavy-bottomed, 6-quart / 6-L sauté pan; and tongs.

VEGANIZE IT! It's so simple to substitute veggies for lamb. I love making this dish with anything and everything from cauliflower and Baked Tofu (see recipe on p. 46) to tempeh and/or eggplant. If using chopped vegetables, you'll need about 4 cups / 600 g, and you should follow the recipe directions but reduce the cooking time in Step 8 to 15 to 20 minutes, depending on which main ingredient you choose.

Vin means wine, while *alho* is the word for garlic in Portuguese, the key language influence in Goa, India's smallest state. Located on the west coast, Goa is a former Portuguese colony—a fact most obvious in its cuisine. Classic *vindaloo* curry is bold and fiery, known as one of the spiciest dishes in India. Eventually the wine became vinegar, but the chiles remained, thankfully.

1 tablespoon whole black peppercorns
1 tablespoon cumin seeds
2 teaspoons mustard seeds
1 (3-inch / 8-cm) stick cinnamon
5 whole cloves
1 teaspoon fenugreek seeds
1 teaspoon poppy seeds
1 tablespoon unsmoked paprika
½ teaspoon turmeric powder
5 tablespoons / 75 mL vegetable oil, divided
1 medium yellow or red onion, minced
20 whole dried red chiles, soaked in hot water until soft, or 1 heaping tablespoon red chile powder or cayenne pepper
1 (2-inch / 5-cm) piece ginger, peeled and coarsely chopped

15 cloves garlic, peeled
2–4 fresh Thai, serrano, or cayenne chiles, stems removed and roughly chopped
1 medium yellow or red onion, roughly chopped
1 teaspoon *gur* (jaggery) or light brown sugar
2 tablespoons vinegar (cider or distilled white)
1 teaspoon tamarind paste
1 cup / 240 mL plus 1 tablespoon water, plus more as needed (divided)
2 pounds / 910 g lamb (shoulder or leg), boned or boneless cubes
1 tablespoon salt
Brown or white basmati rice, *Roti,* or *Naan* (see recipes on pp. 230 and 238), for serving

1. Combine the peppercorns, cumin and mustard seeds, cinnamon, and cloves in an 8-inch / 20-cm frying pan over medium–high heat and dry roast for 5 minutes, until the spices take on a reddish-brown color (the mustard seeds will be gray) and become aromatic. During the entire cooking time, shake the pan every 15 to 20 seconds to prevent the spices from burning. *When roasting spices, never leave the pan unattended—they burn easily.* Remove from the heat, transfer to a plate, and set aside to cool for 15 minutes. *If you grind them while still hot, they emit steam and clump up in the grinder.*

2. Transfer the cooled, roasted spices to a mortar and pestle or spice grinder. Add the fenugreek and poppy seeds *(I avoid roasting these 2 seeds in this recipe because fenugreek can turn bitter and poppy seeds burn easily)* and grind the mixture into a powder. Remove and discard any small pieces of cinnamon that aren't ground into powder form. Transfer the ground spices to a small mixing bowl, add the paprika and turmeric, and set aside.

3. In the same 8-inch frying pan over medium–high heat, warm 1 tablespoon of the oil. Add the minced onion and cook for 8 to10 minutes, until completely browned and caramelized. Remove from the heat.

4. Drain the dried chiles that have been soaking. In the bowl of a food processor, grind the onion from Step 3, the dried chiles, the ginger, the garlic, the fresh chiles, the chopped onion, the *gur,* the vinegar, the tamarind paste, and the 1 tablespoon of water into a red, watery paste. Transfer to a large glass or otherwise nonreactive mixing bowl and add the ground spices. Stir until well combined.

5. Transfer ½ cup / 120 mL of the *vindaloo* sauce to a medium-sized mixing bowl and add the lamb. Cover and refrigerate for at least 2 hours and up to 12 hours.

6. In a heavy-bottomed, 6-quart / 6-L sauté pan over medium–high heat, warm 2 tablespoons of the oil. With tongs, add the lamb (leaving the marinade behind) and sear, turning once to ensure even browning, for a total of 2 minutes. Transfer to a plate and set aside.

7. Return the sauté pan to medium–high heat and warm the remaining 2 tablespoons of oil. Add the remainder of the *vindaloo* sauce and the salt and cook, stirring occasionally to prevent sticking, for 4 minutes, until warmed through. As you cook, add the remaining 1 cup of water (plus more as needed) at a rate of 2 tablespoons at a time. *You never want to add too much at one time because it's difficult to get rid of moisture after adding too much. You can always add more if needed.*

8. Reduce the heat to medium and add the lamb to the sauté pan. Cook for 1½ hours, until the lamb is tender. Remove from the heat.

9. Transfer to a serving bowl and serve with the brown or white basmati rice, *Roti,* or *Naan.*

Breads

"What kind of bread do Indians typically eat?" It's a question I always ask in my cooking classes.

Without fail, the unanimous response is *"Naan!"* When I say, "No," the excited, eager faces fall.

I'm sorry to burst your bubble, but despite what you'll find showcased in most Indian restaurants and Western supermarkets, *Naan* (see recipe on p. 238) is not the go-to bread for most Indians. The first time I tried it was in high school, when one of the first Indian restaurants opened in Philadelphia.

Only in a restaurant will we splurge a little and order *naan,* a leavened bread typically made from all-purpose flour and cooked in a *tandoori* oven. Think about it: Do any of your friends own an oven that heats to 900°F / 480°C?

In North India, we usually eat *Roti* (see recipe on p. 230), an unleavened flatbread made simply from whole-wheat *chapati* flour and water. In South India, folks eat *Dosa* (see recipe on p. 253), which is a beautiful crepe made from soaked and fermented rice and lentils.

Other regions of India have dozens upon dozens of different breads. Some are made of wheat, while others are made from everything from chickpea and corn flour to rice and lentils. Many of these are perfect gluten-free alternatives for folks with gluten sensitivity or celiac disease.

The best tool for cooking your breads is a *tava,* a concave metal plate that you can find in Indian grocery stores. I use a heavy, cast-iron frying pan.

Experiment often. You'll be pleasantly surprised by the variety.

Roti-Chapati-Phulka

YIELD: 17 (6-INCH / 15-CM) *ROTIS*

TOOLS: You'll need a food processor or stand mixer; a deep, wide mixing bowl; 1 damp and 1 dry dish towel or paper towel; a plate; a rolling pin; a platter; a *tava,* flat griddle, or cast-iron frying pan; and tongs.

TIP: Make sure your *tava* stays clean! As dry flour falls from the *rotis,* it collects on the pan and burns from the heat. Avoid this by cleaning the pan out after every 3 *rotis* you make. I use a dry paper towel and carefully wipe the pan clean over the sink.

NOTE: In Punjab, where my family hails from, we use only flour and water to make *roti* or *chapati.* Cooks in other parts of India, like Gujarat, use 1 teaspoon of oil and 1 pinch of salt in the dough. Either way, you'll love this recipe.

Ask a group of Indians what *roti-chapati-phulka* mean to them (as I did recently on my Facebook fan page: Indian as Apple Pie), and you can bet there won't be universal agreement. Some will say *roti* refers to the bread we Indians eat, while others will say it refers to a meal that may or may not include bread. Some will say *chapati* is *roti* cooked flat, and that *phulka* refers to *roti* or *chapati* that puffs up with steam. Still others have never heard of the term *phulka.*

I'd say they are all right, in their own ways. In Punjab, where wheat is the key crop, *roti* is king. When Punjabis are called to eat a meal, we're often told to "eat our *roti,*" whether it's bread or rice on the table. It's kind of like the saying "breaking bread."

One side of my family hails from Chandigarh and the other is from the small village of Bhikhi, in the heart of Punjab. There, we typically use the words *roti, chapati,* and *phulka* interchangeably and we mean the bread you're about to learn about. Regardless of what you call it, know this beautifully simple flatbread, which is much like a tortilla, is essentially made of only two ingredients: finely milled, stone-ground whole-wheat flour and water. We use it for everything from scooping up veggies on our plates to mopping up curries.

Make them again and again, but know that it can take years to perfect the art of a perfectly round *roti.* I always joke that it only took me a decade. But not to worry—it's a delicious journey.

3½ cups / 480 g *chapati* flour *(atta),* divided*
1½ cups / 350 mL water (room temperature), plus more as needed

Butter, vegan margarine, or flaxseed oil, for stacking

1. In the bowl of a food processor or stand mixer, combine 3 cups / 410 g of the *chapati* flour and the water and blend until a dough ball forms. *You can do this by hand in a deep bowl, but it's messier—which is a big reason why many of us Indian–American moms dread making* roti. *If mixing by hand, put the flour in first and make a well in the center. Add the water and stir vigorously using 1 hand until the mixture comes together into a ball. This is where experience comes in handy. If the dough is sticky, add a little more dry flour. If it's too dry, add a little more water, 1 teaspoon at a time.*

2. Transfer the dough to a deep, wide bowl and knead by hand for 2 to 3 minutes, until the dough reaches the desired consistency. *Like any other bread, taking the time to knead the dough well is the key to successful* roti, *as kneading it develops a network of gluten, the principal protein in wheat. That helps it retain water, which turns to steam when cooking and lightens, or aerates, the* rotis. Cover with a damp dish towel or paper towel and set aside at room temperature for 20 to 30 minutes. Roti *dough can be used immediately, but I find that it helps to let it sit for a little while.*

3. Place the remaining ½ cup / 70 g of dry *chapati* flour on a plate. Pull off a golf ball-sized chunk (2 tablespoons) of the dough and roll it between your palms until it is as round as possible. *The rounder and smoother you can get the dough ball at this point, the better your results will be later, when you're rolling it out.* If it is too sticky to work with easily, roll the ball lightly in the plate containing the flour. *The trick to making perfectly moist* roti *is to use the dry flour sparingly. If you use too much, the* roti *will dry out when cooked.*

4. Press the ball between your palms until it is slightly flattened. Place it on a dry, lightly floured work surface. Using a rolling pin, roll the dough into a thin, 6-inch / 15-cm disc. *As you roll, practice pressing down on the rolling pin more one side. If done correctly, the* roti *will turn very slowly on its own, leading to a perfectly round* roti. *Don't worry if you have trouble, as this technique takes years to perfect. If you can't get it down, and the* roti *sticks to the surface while rolling, just pick it up, dip it very lightly in the dry flour on both sides, and roll it out again.*

5. Repeat the process until you have made 6 to 8 *rotis* and placed them on a platter. *The thickness and size of* roti *varies household to household. Generally, the thinner they are, the better they will puff up later. And not to worry—if you mess up, just roll the dough into a ball and start over.*

6. Warm an ungreased *tava*, flat griddle, or cast-iron frying pan over medium heat. *The key is to heat the pan enough that the* roti *will cook, but not so hot that it will sear as soon as you lay it in the pan. Test the heat level by flicking a drop of water onto the surface. If it evaporates right away, it is hot enough. Experienced* roti *cooks often just touch the pan quickly with their bare fingertips to assess the heat level. If you want to try this, just be sure your hand is completely dry. Any moisture will lead to a burn—I'm speaking from experience here.*

Continued

7. Carefully place 1 *roti* flat in the hot pan. Cook for 30 seconds and turn it over. *The roti will be barely cooked.* Cook on the other side for 30 seconds. *I've been perfecting my* roti *recipe for years, and find that cooking for 30 seconds on both sides first makes for a softer* roti *later.*

8. Turn over the *roti.* Ball up a dry paper towel or dish towel in 1 hand, use it to press down on the *roti,* and cook for 40 seconds, until the *roti* starts to puff up. *This is how the* roti *cooks best—with steam searing through it. The process is counterintuitive, because if you press gently where it puffs up, you'll see the rest of the* roti *blow up like a balloon.* Turn the *roti* over and press down again. Cook for another 40 seconds, until the *roti* is lightly browned on both sides and cooked through. *For even better results, after cooking it through (but not completely) in the pan and when it starts to puff up, transfer it to an open flame on another burner. Working quickly with the tongs, turn it, move it around, and flip until it puffs up for you. Be careful not to let it sit for too long, as it will burn. This is best done on a gas burner, but can also be done on an electric burner covered by a metal diffuser.*

9. Transfer the *roti* back to the platter and lightly apply the butter to the top side. *Don't butter* roti *that you plan to store; see the note below for storage information. If stacking and serving immediately, stack the* roti *with the buttered sides facing each other. This way, the butter stays contained and never touches both sides of any 1* roti.

10. Repeat Steps 7, 8, and 9 until you have made all the *rotis,* making sure to clean out the pan after every 3 *rotis* you prepare.

11. Clean the *tava* thoroughly. Repeat Steps 3 through 9 until you have used all of the remaining dough. I find that the best way to regulate the pan's heat level is to remove the pan from the heat (keeping the heat level steady on the cooktop) while you roll out the *roti.*

12. Serve immediately or store in the refrigerator for up to 1 week.**

*The key to making good *roti* is in using the correct flour. Typically, *chapati* flour is made from durum wheat, which is stone ground until it is very fine. It can be found in any Indian grocery store and is rarely found in mainstream Western grocers. When shopping for it, purchase *atta,* which is 100 percent whole-wheat flour rather than *maida,* which also contains bleached white flour. If you don't have a nearby Indian grocer, look for whole-wheat pastry flour, which is the closest you can come to traditional *chapati* flour. Using regular whole-wheat flour found in the West can result in hard, slightly bitter *roti* because it's a different type of wheat (typically hard red winter wheat). If that's all you have, mix 2 parts whole-wheat flour with 1 part all-purpose white flour to achieve the right taste and texture.

**Rotis* store well. If you are planning to store them, do not butter them. First, set them aside to cool completely. Place the cooked *roti* in stacks of 10 and wrap each stack in a dry paper towel or thin cloth. *The cloth absorbs extra moisture.* Enclose the stack in tightly sealed aluminum foil or plastic wrap and store in the refrigerator for up to 1 week or the freezer for up to 3 months. To reheat, warm the *rotis* on the stovetop in a dry cast-iron pan over medium heat for 2 to 3 minutes or place in the oven at 300°F / 150°C for 2 to 3 minutes, butter, and serve.

You can also store uncooked dough for later use. I freeze small batches for as long as 3 months. Defrost the dough the morning before you plan to cook them.

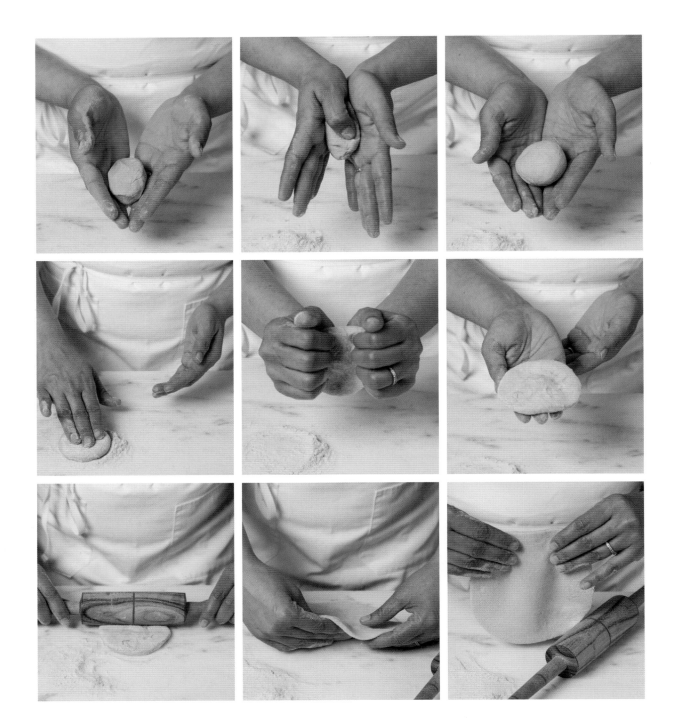

Aloo ka Paratha

YIELD: 11 (6-INCH / 15-CM) *PARATHAS*

TOOLS: You'll need a large mixing bowl; a heavy-bottomed, 4-quart / 4-L sauté pan; a rolling pin; a plate; a platter; and a *tava,* cast-iron frying pan, or flat griddle.

TIPS: The key to successful flatbreads is using a clean pan. As dry flour falls from the bread, it collects on the pan and burns. Avoid this by cleaning the pan out after every 3 *parathas* you make. I use a dry paper towel and carefully wipe the pan clean over the sink.

Parathas are the quintessential North Indian breakfast dish—savory and spicy at once. The best way to eat them is with a dollop of butter and a little bowl of yogurt sweetened with brown sugar or with some *achaar* (spicy pickle). My children have been raised on these, which are essentially *roti* stuffed with everything imaginable. This recipe is likely the most popular *paratha,* one stuffed with spiced potatoes, and my recipe is dedicated to my *Omi* uncle in Delhi. When I first made them for him over a decade ago and asked him how they were, he answered honestly: "Not so good." Thanks for the incentive to get it right, Uncle!

4 medium russet potatoes, boiled, peeled, and mashed
1 tablespoon vegetable oil
1 heaping teaspoon cumin seeds
1 teaspoon turmeric powder
1 small yellow or red onion, minced
2–3 fresh Thai, serrano, or cayenne chiles, stems removed, finely chopped
1 teaspoon red chile powder or cayenne pepper
1 teaspoon *amchur* (dried mango powder)
1 tablespoon *Garam Masala* (see recipe on p. 35)
2 teaspoons salt

¼ cup / 5 g *kasoori methi* (dried fenugreek leaves), lightly hand crushed to release flavor
1 batch uncooked *Roti* dough (see recipe on p. 230)
½ cup / 70 g *chapati* flour *(atta),* for rolling dough
Vegetable oil, as needed for frying
1 teaspoon butter or vegan margarine, for serving (optional)
1 small bowl of yogurt sweetened with brown sugar, for serving (optional)
Achaar (spicy pickle), for serving (optional)

1. Place the potatoes in a large mixing bowl and set aside.

2. In a heavy-bottomed, 4-quart / 4-L sauté pan over medium–high heat, warm the oil. Add the cumin seeds and turmeric and cook for 40 seconds, until the cumin seeds sizzle and turn reddish-brown. Add the onion and cook, stirring occasionally, for 2 minutes, until slightly browned. Remove from the heat.

3. Add the contents of the sauté pan to the bowl containing the potatoes. Add the fresh chiles, red chile powder, *amchur, Garam Masala,* salt, and *kasoori me-thi.* Stir, preferably using your hands, until well combined. *I prefer to stir with my hands to make sure the potatoes are thoroughly mashed and not lumpy, as chunks of potato will break through the dough when you stuff the* parathas. *If you want to avoid touching the chiles, you can use a large spoon or fork instead, or just wear kitchen gloves.* Set aside.

4. Pull off a golf ball-sized chunk (2 tablespoons) of the *Roti* dough and roll it between your palms until it is as round as possible. *The rounder and smoother you can get the dough ball at this point, the better your results will be later, when you're rolling it out.* If it is too sticky to work with easily, roll the ball lightly on a plate containing the dry *chapati* flour. *The trick to making perfectly moist* paratha *is to use the dry flour sparingly. If you use too much, the* paratha *will dry out when cooked.*

5. Press the ball between your palms until it is slightly flattened. Place it on a dry, lightly floured work surface. Using a rolling pin, roll the dough into a thin, 5-inch / 13-cm disc. *If you can't get it down, and the dough sticks to the surface while rolling, just pick it up, dip it very lightly in the dry flour on both sides, and roll it out again.*

6. Place 1 heaping tablespoon of the potato filling in the middle of the dough disc. Fold the sides of the dough inward so they meet in the middle and press the edges together, essentially forming a square. Place the dry *chapati* flour on a plate and dredge the square of stuffed dough in the flour.

7. Place the square of stuffed dough on the lightly floured work surface and roll it into a thin 6-inch/ 15-cm disc. *It may not be perfectly round, and some of the filling might come through slightly, but that's OK.*

8. Repeat the process until you have made 11 *parathas* and placed them on a platter.

9. Warm an ungreased *tava,* flat griddle, or cast-iron frying pan over medium heat. *The key is to heat the pan enough that the* paratha *will cook, but not so hot that it will sear as soon as you lay it in the pan.*

10. Carefully place 1 *paratha* flat in the hot pan. Cook for 30 seconds and turn it over. *This step is critical to making really delicious* parathas. *They will look like they're just about to cook through but still a little raw.* Cook on the other side for 30 seconds. *I've been perfecting my* paratha *recipe for years, and find that cooking for 30 seconds on both sides first makes for softer* paratha *later.*

11. Lightly oil the side of the *paratha* that is facing up. Turn it over and immediately lightly oil the other side. Cook, turning once to ensure even cooking, for a total of 2 minutes, until browned on both sides. Remove from the pan and transfer to a serving platter.

12. Repeat Steps 10 and 11 until you have cooked all the *parathas,* making sure to clean out the pan after every 3 *parathas* you prepare. Remove from the heat.

13. Serve immediately with the butter, sweetened yogurt, or *achaar* (spicy pickle), if using.

Naan

YIELD: 10 MEDIUM-SIZED *NAAN*

TOOLS: You'll need a small mixing bowl or measuring cup; 3 large mixing bowls; a whisk; a damp dish towel or paper towel; a large, ovensafe (to 500°F/ 260°C) casserole dish or baking pan filled with water; a pizza stone; and a plate.

TRY THIS! After buttering the *naan,* top the slices with a pinch of dried fenugreek leaves. Another delicious option is to fry minced onions and/or garlic in oil until browned and spread the mixture on each piece.

VEGANIZE IT! Just omit the egg and replace the dairy yogurt with plain, unsweetened soy, coconut, or alternative yogurt to make this bread vegan.

For most Indians, *naan* is a treat—a fluffy, leavened bread heated until very crispy in the steaming, fiery red pit of a traditional clay *tandoori* oven. You can make a close approximation at home, preferably using a pizza stone. Just know that no matter how hard you try, you won't be able to exactly replicate the experience of eating a *naan* seconds after it is pulled out of a *tandoori* oven. But you will come close enough.

¾ cup / 177 mL warm (110°F / 43°C) water
1 teaspoon active dry yeast
4½ cups / 563 g all-purpose flour, divided
1 teaspoon salt
½ teaspoon baking powder
2 teaspoons *kalonji* (nigella seeds)

1 egg, beaten
2 tablespoons *ghee* or vegetable oil
¾ cup / 177 mL plain, unsweetened yogurt
Vegetable oil, for greasing
Butter or vegan margarine, for serving

1. Place the water *(it should be about 110°F / 43°C in order to activate the yeast)* in a small mixing bowl or measuring cup. Sprinkle the yeast on top and set it aside for at least 15 minutes while you prep the remaining ingredients. *Make sure it's not too hot, as temperatures above 110°F / 43°C can kill the yeast.*

2. Sift 4 cups / 500 g of the flour into a large mixing bowl. Add the salt, baking powder, and *kalonji* and mix well.

3. In a separate large mixing bowl, whisk together the egg, *ghee,* and yogurt. *If your* ghee *is solid, you can warm it a bit in the microwave or on the stovetop to soften it.*

4. Add the wet mixture from Step 3 to the bowl containing the flour mixture from Step 2. Stir well, until the ingredients come together and the mixture is slightly crumbly.

5. Stir the yeast mixture from Step 1 until smooth and add it to the dough mixture in the large mixing bowl. Stir well until fully combined. Using your hands, knead the dough thoroughly until a smooth ball forms and the dough resembles and feels like pizza dough. *If you need to add a little more water, do so at no more than 1 tablespoon at a time.*

6. Lightly grease a large mixing bowl with the oil. Place the dough in the bowl, cover with a damp dish towel or paper towel, and set aside in a warm, dry place for 4 hours to allow the dough to rise. *If you live in a cold climate, heat the oven to 200°F / 90°C for 10 minutes. Turn off the oven, wait 10 minutes, and then place the covered bowl in the oven for the 4-hour rising period. The residual warmth of the oven will trigger the yeast, allowing the dough to rise.*

7. Set the oven rack at the highest position and place a large, ovensafe container filled with water on the bottom rack. *The water will prevent the* naan *from drying out as it cooks.* Place a pizza stone on the top rack of the oven and preheat the oven to 500°F / 260°C. *Remember, the pizza stone must go in the oven before you turn it on. If you put it in after the oven is hot, it may crack. If you don't have a pizza stone, use a greased baking sheet instead.*

8. Place the remaining ½ cup / 63 g of flour on a plate. Remove the dough from the bowl and punch it down, deflating the dough. Divide the dough into 10 equal-sized balls about 2½ inches / 6 cm in diameter.

9. Start with 1 of the dough balls. Press the ball between your palms until it is slightly flattened. Place it on a dry, lightly floured work surface. If it is too sticky to work with easily, roll the ball lightly on the plate containing the remaining flour. Using a rolling pin, roll the dough into a thin oval roughly 7 inches / 18 cm wide by 4 inches / 10 cm tall. Repeat until you have prepared all the dough ovals.

10. Place 3 of the dough ovals on the pizza stone and bake for 7 minutes on 1 side. Turn them over and cook for 5 minutes on the other side. Remove from the pizza stone and set aside on a warm serving platter tented with foil.

11. Repeat Step 10 until all the remaining dough ovals have been baked. Remove from the oven.

12. Lightly butter* each of the pieces of *naan* and serve hot or store in the refrigerator for up to 1 week or in the freezer for up to 3 months.

*If you are storing the *naan,* do not butter the pieces. Butter them only immediately before serving.

Bhatura

YIELD: 10–12 (4–6-INCH / 10–15-CM)
BHATURAS

This leavened, fried bread, paired with *Chana Masala* (a spicy chickpea curry), is a Punjabi classic. These days, it's also my older daughter Neha's favorite bread. I still remember childhood trips to New Jersey's Little India in Edison with one purpose, and one purpose alone: getting our hands on some *bhatura.* Every single calorie consumed is totally worthwhile.

TOOLS: You'll need a measuring cup or small bowl; a large mixing bowl; a damp dish towel or paper towel; a plate; a rolling pin; a small *kadhai,* wok, or saucepan; a wire mesh skimmer or slotted stainless steel spoon; and a tray lined with paper towels.

¾ cup / 180 mL warm water
2 teaspoons active dry yeast
2½ cups / 310 g plus 2 tablespoons *maida* (unbleached all-purpose flour), divided
2 heaping tablespoons plain, unsweetened yogurt (dairy or alternative)
1 tablespoon *ghee* or vegetable oil
1 teaspoon salt
2 cups / 470 mL vegetable oil, for frying
1 recipe *Chana Masala* (see recipe on p. 152), for serving (optional)
Any curry, *sabji,* or chutney, for serving (optional)

1. Place the water *(it should be about 110°F / 43°C in order to activate the yeast)* in a small mixing bowl or measuring cup. Sprinkle the yeast on top and set it aside for at least 15 minutes while you prep the remaining ingredients. *Make sure it's not too hot, as temperatures above 110°F / 43°C can kill the yeast. I sometimes put it in my unheated oven, which even when off is a little warmer than the counter.*

2. In a large mixing bowl, combine 2 cups / 250 g of the *maida,* the yogurt, the *ghee,* and the salt. *If your* ghee *is solid, you can warm it a bit in the microwave or on the stovetop to soften it.* Using your hands or a spoon, stir well until the ingredients come together. *I always use a spoon for this step—I don't like getting my hands dirty until I absolutely have to.*

3. Stir the yeast mixture from Step 1 until smooth and add it to the dough mixture in the large mixing bowl. Using your hands, stir until the mixture comes together into a sticky clump of wet dough.

4. Add 2 tablespoons of the flour to the dough and knead until the mixture forms a smooth ball of dough. Cover the bowl with a damp dish towel or paper towel and set aside for 30 minutes, until it rises slightly.

5. Place the remaining ½ cup / 60 g of flour on a plate. Remove the dough from the bowl and punch it down, deflating the dough. Divide the dough into 10 equal-sized balls about 2½ inches / 6 cm in diameter.

6. Start with 1 of the dough balls. Press the ball between your palms until it is slightly flattened. Place it on a dry, lightly floured work surface. If it is too sticky to work with easily, roll the ball lightly on the plate containing the remaining flour. Using a rolling pin, roll the dough into a thin, 4- to 6-inch / 10- to 15-cm round. *If you use too much dry flour, they won't fry properly. The dough will be spongy and will pull back. Just keep pulling at it until you have the right length. Do the best you can.* Repeat until you have prepared all the dough rounds.

Continued

7. In a small *kadhai,* wok, or saucepan, warm the oil over medium–high heat (it should be about 1 inch / 3 cm deep). *Test that the oil is hot enough by dropping in a pinch of the uncooked dough. If it rises immediately to the top, the oil is ready. If it sinks to the bottom, it's not quite hot enough.*

8. From the side of the pan, slowly slide a dough round into the hot oil and cook for 40 seconds on 1 side. As the *bhatura* is cooking, use a wire mesh skimmer or slotted stainless steel spoon to gently push it down and allow some of the hot oil to pour over it. Turn the *bhatura* over and cook on the other side for 40 seconds, until lightly browned. Gently bring the *bhatura* to the side of the pan and allow the excess oil to drip away. Transfer to a tray lined with paper towels to absorb the excess oil.

9. Repeat Step 8 until all the remaining dough rounds have been fried. Remove from the heat.

10. Serve the *bhaturas* traditionally with *Chana Masala* or with any curry, *sabji,* or chutney. You can also stack the *bhaturas,* let them cool, and wrap them first in a dish cloth and then tightly wrap with aluminum foil and store in the refrigerator for up to 1 week.*

*If you are storing the *bhaturas,* reheat them before serving by warming them on the stovetop in a dry cast-iron pan over medium heat for 2 to 3 minutes or place in the oven at 300°F / 150°C for 2 to 3 minutes.

Besan Poora

YIELD: 8 (5-INCH / 13-CM) *POORAS*

Usually, these thin North Indian pancakes are served with tea or a snack and eaten with a dollop of *achaar* (spicy pickle). When I was growing up, my mother often made them for breakfast. They were easy, nutritious, and exceptionally delicious. I now make these for my girls as a wonderfully healthy, protein-filled, and gluten-free meal or snack. Keep the batter handy—it will last for up to a week in the fridge.

TOOLS: You'll need a large mixing bowl or blender; a whisk; a *tava,* cast-iron frying pan, or griddle; a paper towel; a ladle; a spatula; and a warmed plate.

TRY THIS! The possibilities are endless with this recipe. Try jazzing up the batter by folding in anything from mashed or grated potatoes to grated zucchini, chopped spinach, mint, or scallions.

2 cups / 220 g *besan* (gram or chickpea flour)
1½ cups / 350 mL water
1 small onion, minced (about ½ cup / 80 g)
1 (1-inch / 3-cm) piece ginger, peeled and grated or minced
1–3 fresh Thai, serrano, or cayenne chiles, stems removed, finely sliced
¼ cup / 5 g *kasoori methi* (dried fenugreek leaves), lightly hand crushed to release flavor
½ cup / 10 g minced fresh cilantro
1 teaspoon salt
½ teaspoon ground coriander
½ teaspoon turmeric powder
1 teaspoon red chile powder or cayenne pepper
Vegetable oil, as needed for frying
Pudina ki Chutney (see recipe on p. 41) and *achaar* (spicy pickle), for serving (optional)
Hash browns spiced with cumin seeds, for serving (optional)

1. In a large, deep mixing bowl or a blender,* whisk together the *besan* and water until smooth. *I like to start off with a whisk and then use the back of a spoon to break up the small clumps of flour that normally form.* Set aside for at least 20 minutes.

2. Add the remaining ingredients, except the oil and the optional serving items, to the mixing bowl or blender and stir or process until thoroughly combined.

3. Warm a *tava,* cast-iron frying pan, or griddle over medium–high heat. Add ½ teaspoon of the oil, spreading it over the pan with the back of a spoon or a paper towel. *You can also use cooking spray to evenly coat the pan.*

4. Using a ladle, pour ¼ cup / 60 mL of the batter into the center of the pan. Using the back of the ladle, spread the batter in a circular, clockwise motion from the center toward the outside of the pan, creating a thin, round, 5-inch / 13-cm pancake. Cook for 2 minutes, until slightly brown on 1 side. Turn and cook for 1 to 2 minutes on the other side, pressing down a bit with a spatula to ensure that the middle cooks through. Remove the *poora* from the pan and set aside on a warm plate.

5. Adding oil as needed to prevent sticking, continue cooking until you have used all of the batter and stacked all the *pooras* on the plate. Remove from the heat.

6. Serve hot with a side of the *Pudina ki* Chutney and *achaar* (spicy pickle) or make some hash browns spiced with cumin seeds and use them as a filling.

*My mother prefers to make *poora* batter in a blender so all the ingredients combine really well and the result is a smoother *poora.* If using the blender, add the water first and then the remaining ingredients, and blend on the highest speed until smooth. I prefer a little crunch in my *pooras,* so I like to add another ½ onion, diced, to the batter just before cooking.

Moong Dal Poora

YIELD: 12–15 (5- TO 6-INCH / 13- TO 15-CM) *POORAS*

TOOLS: A powerful blender, such as a Vitamix; a medium and a small mixing bowl; a *tava,* cast-iron frying pan, or flat griddle; a ladle; a spatula; and a warm plate.

NOTE: To best balance and moderate the heat, pull the pan off the burner as you pour and shape the batter. As you move through the batter and the pan becomes hotter, the cooking time on each side may decrease slightly.

TRY THIS! I love using these *pooras* as gluten-free wraps stuffed with Indian stir-fries. You can also eat them for breakfast with an egg or tofu scramble.

As my husband and I have moved closer and closer to a gluten-free diet over the last year, these *pooras* have become my savior. Not only are they mega nutritious, they are tasty and completely addictive. I love making the batter and storing it in the fridge so we can make a fresh batch whenever we get hungry. The bonus? The kids love them too.

½ cup / 110 g *sabut moong dal* (whole green *dal* with skin), soaked overnight in warm water and drained (should yield 1½ cups / 350 mL)*
2 tablespoons *besan* (gram or chickpea flour)
¼ large yellow or red onion, roughly chopped
1 (1-inch / 3-cm) piece ginger, peeled and roughly chopped
1–2 fresh Thai, serrano, or cayenne chiles, stems removed

3 long, fresh cilantro stalks with leaves
½ teaspoon salt
½ teaspoon red chile powder or cayenne pepper
1 cup / 240 mL water
Vegetable oil, for frying
End of a raw onion, for prepping pan
Achaar (spicy pickle), for serving (optional)
1 tablespoon butter or almond butter and jelly, for serving (optional)

1. Add the ingredients, except the oil, the onion end, and the optional serving items, to the blender in the order listed. Blend on high until completely smooth (should yield 3 cups / 710 mL of batter). Transfer to a medium mixing bowl.

2. Place ¼ cup / 60 mL of the oil in a small mixing bowl and place the bowl beside the cooktop.

3. Warm a *tava,* cast-iron frying pan, or flat griddle over medium–high heat. Rub the cooking surface with the flat end of a raw onion. *The raw onion helps prevent the* poora *from sticking to the pan. Stick a fork into the onion end, with the flat side facing the pan, and rub down the pan each time before you place batter on the pan.* Using some of the oil in the bowl, lightly grease the pan.

4. Reduce the heat to medium–low. Using a ladle, pour ⅙ cup / 40 mL of the batter into the center of the pan. *Feel free to use a bigger ladle and dole out more, but less is better with these, because thinner* pooras *cook through better.* Using the back of the ladle, spread the batter in a circular, clockwise motion from the center toward the outside of the pan, creating a thin, round, 5-inch / 13-cm pancake.

5. Drizzle a small spoonful of oil from the bowl along the edges of the *poora.* Cook for 1 minute and 50 seconds, until the *poora* is browned on 1 side and turns over easily. Cook for 1 minute and 50 seconds on the other side, pressing down a bit with a spatula to ensure that the middle cooks through. Turn the *poora* over and cook for 5 to 10 seconds. *This second flip, I find, is important because the lentils are soft and need a few more seconds to cook through completely. Remember, the thinner the* poora, *the better.* Remove the *poora* from the pan and set aside on a warm plate.

6. Adding oil as needed to prevent sticking, continue cooking until you have used all of the batter and stacked all the *pooras* on the plate. Remove from the heat.

7. Serve hot with a side of *achaar* (spicy pickle) or 1 tablespoon of butter or almond butter and jelly.

*Before using the drained *moong dal,* be sure to sift through them and remove and discard any lentils that are still hard. If you are using a powerful blender, it should break down even the hardest lentils.

Puris

YIELD: 20–25 (5-INCH / 13-CM) *PURIS*

TOOLS: You'll need a food processor; a large mixing bowl; a damp paper towel or dish cloth; a rolling pin or a tortilla press; a *kadhai* or a small pot; a wire mesh skimmer or slotted stainless steel spatula; and a tray lined with paper towels.

PICTURED ON P. 246

To me, *puris* suggest a party. Whenever our family entertained large groups of Indian friends during my childhood, my mother would always set aside time to fry up some *puris,* and I would be her helper. My job was to press them thin in her tortilla press, and then she fried them to golden perfection. I could never resist those first few with a little *Pudina ki* Chutney (see recipe on p. 41). They spoiled my dinner, of course, but it was always worth it.

3 cups / 410 g whole-wheat *chapati* flour
½ teaspoon salt
3 tablespoons / 45 mL plus 1 teaspoon vegetable oil, plus more as needed for frying

1½ cups / 350 mL water
Any curry, *sabji,* or chutney, for serving (optional)

1. In the bowl of a food processor, combine the flour, salt, and oil. Process until the ingredients are well blended.

2. Slowly add the water as the food processor rotates and process until the mixture forms a dough-like consistency. Transfer to a large mixing bowl and knead well, until the dough is a large, smooth ball. *Instead, you can mix all ingredients in the bowl by hand, but of course this is more labor intensive and messier.*

3. Cover the bowl with a damp paper towel or dish cloth and set aside for 15 minutes. *Don't let it sit too long; if you do, the* puris *will soak up too much oil while frying and won't be light and airy.*

4. Divide the dough in half. Place ½ of the dough between the palms of your hands and work it until it forms a long, thin (about ¾ inch / 2 cm wide), snake-like strip. Slice the strip into a series of ¾- to 1-inch-long / 2- to 3-cm-long pieces, depending on how large you wish the *puris* to be.

5. Select 1 of the pieces of dough and roll it between your hands until it forms a smooth, round ball. Dip your fingertips into a little oil, if needed. *Don't use dry flour for* puris.

6. Prepare a clean work surface. Using a rolling pin or a tortilla press, roll (or, if using a press, 2 hard presses should do the trick) the dough into a thin, 5-inch / 13-cm circle. Repeat until you have 6 *puris* rolled out. *Be careful not to make them too thin, as they will crisp up too much when frying. Of course, if you make them too thick, they won't puff properly when cooking. Getting them just right may take a little practice, but not to worry. Keep trying and you'll be sure to perfect it. You can also make 3-inch / 8-cm rounds if you prefer a smaller* puri, *traditional in some parts of India.*

7. In a *kadhai* or small pot over medium–high heat, warm 1 inch / 3 cm of the oil (if it's any deeper, it won't get hot enough to fry the *puris* properly). *Test that the oil is hot enough by dropping in a pinch of the uncooked dough. If it rises immediately to the top, the oil is ready. If it sinks to the bottom, the oil needs to be heated longer.*

8. From the side of the pan, slowly slide the 6 *puris* into the hot oil and cook for 40 seconds on 1 side. As the *puris* are cooking, use a wire mesh skimmer or slotted stainless steel spatula to gently push it down and allow some of the hot oil to pour over it. Turn the *puris* over and cook on the other side for 30 seconds, until lightly browned. Gently bring the *puris* to the side of the pan and allow the excess oil to drip away. Transfer to a tray lined with paper towels to absorb the excess oil.

9. Repeat Steps 5 and 6 to roll out the remaining dough into rounds. Repeat Step 8 until all the remaining *puris* have been fried and stacked on the tray. Remove from the heat.

10. Serve the *puris* traditionally with any curry, *sabji,* or chutney. You can also stack the *puris,* let them cool, and wrap them first in a dish cloth and then tightly wrap with aluminum foil and store in the refrigerator for up to 1 week.*

*If you are storing the *puris,* reheat them before serving by warming them on the stovetop in a dry cast-iron pan over medium heat for 2 to 3 minutes or place in the oven at 300°F / 150°C for 2 to 3 minutes.

Makki ki Roti
Indian Corn Bread

YIELD: 10 TO 12 (4½–5-INCH / 11–13-CM) *ROTI*

There's likely no other bread that exudes nostalgia in India like *makki ki roti* does for Punjabis. It shows up in movies and television shows alike, always paired with *sarson ka saag* (spiced mustard greens). It's the one thing that I dream about having when my family returns to India to visit my father's village in Punjab. Now you can make them for yourself and your family, to be eaten the traditional way or as a change of pace.

TOOLS: You'll need a deep mixing bowl, a spoon, parchment paper, a small bowl filled with water, a *tava* or cast-iron skillet, and a tray.

PICTURED AT LEFT

1 *Makki ki Roti*
2 *Sarson ka Saag* (p. 160)

1 cup / 160 g corn meal
½ cup / 60 g corn flour
1 teaspoon salt
½ teaspoon red chile powder or cayenne pepper
2 tablespoons *kasoori methi* (dried fenugreek leaves), lightly hand crushed to release flavor
1 cup / 240 mL plus 2 tablespoons boiling water (it must be boiling)

Vegetable oil, for pan frying
Sarson ka Saag (spicy mustard greens; see recipe on p. 160) or *Dal Makhani* (black lentils; see recipe on p. 124), for serving (optional)
Butter or vegan margarine, for serving (optional)

1. In a deep mixing bowl, combine the corn meal, corn flour, salt, red chile powder, and *kasoori methi*. Stir until well combined.

2. Slowly add the water to the bowl, 1 to 2 tablespoons at a time. Stir well until the dough slowly starts to come together but is still slightly crumbly. *Be sure to use a spoon, as the water is very hot.*

3. Remove ¼ cup / 60 mL of the dough from the bowl, shape it into a ball, and place it on a 12-inch-long / 30-cm-long sheet of parchment paper. Remove another ¼ cup / 60 mL of dough, shape it into a ball, and place it next to the first piece, far enough apart that they will not touch when pressed down.

4. Dip your hand in a small bowl of room-temperature water and use it to slightly moisten the dough. Press down on each piece of dough with the palm of 1 hand. Place a second sheet of parchment paper over the dough and press down on each dough circle with the palms of your hands until they have flattened into 4½- to 5-inch-wide / 11- to 13-cm wide patties that are about ¼ inch / 6 mm thick.

5. Warm a well-oiled *tava* or cast-iron skillet over medium–high heat.

6. Remove the top sheet of parchment paper. Slowly, carefully, peel each *roti* off the bottom sheet of parchment paper.

7. Carefully place 1 roti on the *tava* and cook until brown on 1 side, about 2 minutes. Flip and cook the other side 1 to 2 minutes, until cooked through. Transfer to a tray.

8. Repeat Steps 3, 4, 5, 6, and 7 until all the remaining *rotis* have been pan fried. Remove from the heat. Clean the pan with a paper towel after you make every 3 *rotis*.

Continued

9. Serve the *rotis* traditionally with *Sarson ka Saag* (spicy mustard greens) or with *Dal Makhani* (black lentils), or with butter or vegan margarine for a quick breakfast. You can also stack the *rotis,* let them cool, and wrap them first in a dish cloth and then tightly wrap with aluminum foil and store in the refrigerator for up to 1 week.*

*If you are storing the *rotis,* reheat them before serving by warming them on the stovetop in a dry cast-iron pan over medium heat for 2 to 3 minutes or place in the oven at 300°F / 150°C for 2 to 3 minutes.

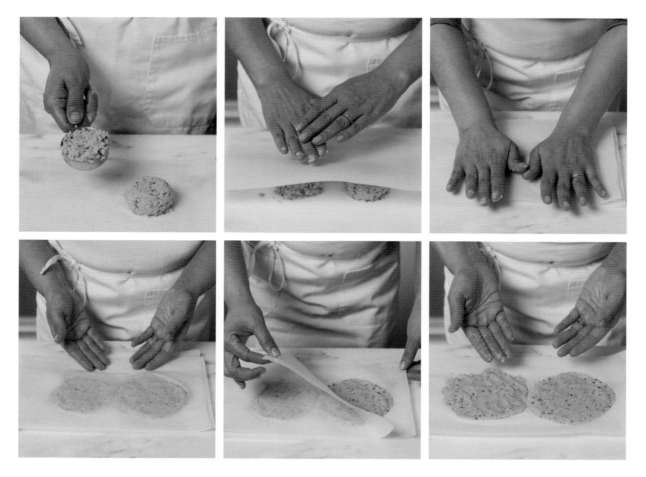

Traditional *Dosa*
South Indian Crepe

YIELD: 9 CUPS / 2.1 L OF FERMENTED BATTER, MAKES ABOUT 18–20 MEDIUM-SIZED *DOSAI*

TOOLS: You'll need 2 large mixing bowls, a blender, a damp dish towel or paper towel, a cast-iron frying pan or griddle, a dry paper towel, a small spoon, a ladle, a wide spatula, and a tray lined with paper towels.

NOTE: This batter will last for 3 days in the refrigerator, or you can freeze it and store it for as long as 3 months.

TRY THIS! Experiment by substituting brown rice, increasing the amount of *dal* used, or using other beans or lentils.

Dosa is one of the tastiest and healthiest breads around. A mainstay of the South Indian diet, this savory "crepe" is traditionally made from white rice and skinned *urad dal* and is often eaten for breakfast or brunch. Nonetheless, feel free to have *dosai* for dinner or as a snack. *Dosai* have become my go-to gluten-free wrap as I've started to cut out the gluten in my diet. I also like to use brown rice instead of white, and it works just fine.

3 cups / 560 g uncooked white or brown basmati rice
1 cup / 210 g *duhli urad dal* (whole or split black *dal* without skin), picked over
2 tablespoons *chana dal* (split and skinned gram or black chickpea), picked over
1 teaspoon fenugreek seeds
Water, to cover

3 cups / 710 mL room-temperature water
½ cup / 80 g cooked white or brown basmati rice
2 teaspoons salt
Vegetable oil, for frying, set aside in a small bowl
End of a raw onion, for prepping pan
Spiced potatoes and *Sambhar* (see recipe on p. 128), for serving (optional)

1. In a large mixing bowl, rinse the uncooked rice, *urad* and *chana dals*, and fenugreek seeds together. Add enough fresh water to cover the ingredients and set aside to soak at room temperature for 6 hours to overnight.

2. Drain the mixture and discard the water. Place the mixture in a blender with the room-temperature water and process. As the blender runs, slowly add the cooked rice. Continue blending until the batter is completely smooth. *Depending on the size of the blender, you may need to do this in 2 batches, and you may need a little more water to ensure that the batter is smooth.*

3. Transfer the batter to a separate large mixing bowl. Add the salt and stir using your hands. *Some say stirring the batter with your warm hands, rather than a cold metallic spoon, helps to trigger the fermentation process, which is key to a successful* dosa *batter. Use a large bowl because the batter will expand as it ferments.*

4. Cover the bowl with a damp dish towel or paper towel and set aside in a warm, dry place for 6 hours to overnight to allow the batter to ferment. *If you live in a cold climate, heat the oven to 200°F / 90°C for 10 minutes. Turn off the oven, wait 10 minutes, and then place the covered bowl in the oven for the fermentation process. You'll end up with a thin batter that is slightly bubbly, frothy, and sour. Perfect!*

Continued

5. Warm a cast-iron frying pan or griddle over medium–high heat. Place 1 teaspoon of the oil in the pan and spread it out with a paper towel (you can use cooking spray if you prefer). *The key here is to be sure not to use too much oil, which can make the batter soggy when you pour it in the pan. Also, make sure the pan isn't too hot when you pour the batter in, or it will stick and get clumpy.*

6. Once the pan is hot, stick a fork into the uncut, rounded end of the onion. Holding the fork handle, rub the flat side of the onion back and forth across the pan. The combination of the heat, the onion juices, and the oil will help prevent the *dosai* from sticking. Keep the onion with the inserted fork handy to use again between *dosai*. *This step is not necessary, but it does work.* Keep the small bowl of oil and a small spoon on the side to use later.

7. Using a ladle, pour ½ cup / 60 mL of the batter into the center of the pan. Using the back of the ladle, spread the batter in a circular, clockwise motion from the center toward the outside of the pan, creating a thin, round, 9-inch / 13-cm crepe. *Use slightly less batter if you want it to be thinner and crispier. I often use a wide spatula to spread the mixture out and make it as thin as possible around the edges, the way they do in the restaurants.*

8. Using the small spoon, pour a thin stream of oil from the small bowl in a circle around the outside edge of the batter. Cook for 1 to 2 minutes on 1 side, until lightly browned and pulled away from the side of the pan. Turn the *dosa* over and cook for 1 to 2 minutes on the second side, pressing down on the center of the *dosa* with a spatula to make sure the center cooks through. Transfer to a tray lined with paper towels to absorb the excess oil.

9. Repeat Steps 7 and 8 until all the remaining batter has been cooked. Remove from the heat. After you make every 2 to 3 *dosai,* rub the pan down with the onion as described in Step 6.

10. Serve the *dosai* traditionally, layered with spiced potatoes and a side of *Sambhar,* or simply use as a gluten-free substitute for bread. You can also stack the *dosai,* let them cool, and wrap them first in a dish cloth and then tightly wrap with aluminum foil and store in the refrigerator for 2 to 3 days.*

*If you are storing the *dosai,* reheat them before serving by warming them on the stovetop in a dry cast-iron pan over medium heat for 2 to 3 minutes.

Quinoa *Dosa*

YIELD: 10 CUPS / 2.4 L OF
FERMENTED BATTER, MAKES ABOUT
40 SMALL *DOSAI*

TOOLS: You'll need a large strainer, 2
large mixing bowls, a blender, a damp
dish towel or paper towel, a cast-iron
frying pan or griddle, a dry paper
towel, a small spoon, a ladle, a wide
spatula, and a tray lined with paper
towels.

NOTE: This batter will last for 3 days
in the refrigerator, or you can freeze it
and store it for as long as 3 months.

TRY THIS! Experiment by increasing
the amount of *dal* used or using other
beans or lentils.

I am always looking for ways to up the nutritional value of my food—I think
it's something my mother instilled in me growing up. So it only made sense to
try making a *dosa* with quinoa. Why not kick the rice out and add a protein-
rich component instead? Trust me, it's hands-down delicious—you may
never go back to the rice version.

3 cups / 510 g white or red quinoa
  (or a mix)
1 cup / 210 g *duhli urad dal* (whole
  or split black *dal* without skin),
  picked over
2 tablespoons *chana dal* (split and
  skinned gram or black chickpeas),
  picked over
1 teaspoon fenugreek seeds
Water, to cover

2 cups / 470 mL room-temperature
  water, plus more as needed
2 teaspoons salt
Vegetable oil, for frying, set aside in
  a small bowl
End of a raw onion, for prepping pan
Spiced potatoes and *Sambhar*
  (see recipe on p. 128), for serving
  (optional)

1. In a large strainer, rinse the quinoa, *urad* and *chana dals,* and fenugreek seeds
together. Transfer to a large mixing bowl and add enough fresh water to cover
the ingredients. Set aside to soak at room temperature for 6 hours to overnight.

2. Drain the mixture and discard the water. Place the mixture in a blender
with 2 cups / 470 mL of the room-temperature water and process. Continue
blending, adding more water as needed, until the batter is completely smooth.
*Depending on the size of the blender, you may need to do this in 2 batches, and you
may need a little more water to ensure that the batter is smooth. Just add ¼ cup /
60 mL at a time, so the batter doesn't get too watery.*

3. Transfer the batter to a separate large mixing bowl. Add the salt and stir using
your hands. *Some say that stirring the batter with your warm hands, rather than
a cold metallic spoon, helps to trigger the fermentation process, which is key to a successful dosa batter. Use a large bowl because the batter will expand as it ferments.*

4. Cover the bowl with a damp dish towel or paper towel and set aside in a
warm, dry place for 6 hours to overnight to allow the batter to ferment. *If you
live in a cold climate, heat the oven to 200°F / 90°C for 10 minutes. Turn off the
oven, wait 10 minutes, and then place the covered bowl in the oven for the fermentation process. You'll end up with a thin batter that is slightly bubbly, frothy, and
sour. Perfect!*

5. Warm a cast-iron frying pan or griddle over medium–high heat. Place 1 teaspoon of the oil in the pan and spread it out with a paper towel (you can use cooking spray if you prefer). *The key here is to be sure not to use too much oil, which can make the batter soggy when you pour it in the pan. Also, make sure the pan isn't too hot when you pour the batter in, or it will stick and get clumpy.*

6. Once the pan is hot, stick a fork into the uncut, rounded end of the onion. Holding the fork handle, rub the flat side of the onion back and forth across the pan. The combination of the heat, the onion juices, and the oil will help prevent the *dosai* from sticking. Keep the onion with the inserted fork handy to use again between *dosai*. *This step is not necessary, but it does work.* Keep the small bowl of oil and a small spoon on the side to use later.

7. Using a ladle, pour ¼ cup / 30 mL of the batter into the center of the pan. *Because the quinoa dough can cook a little soft, I use half as much batter as in the Traditional Dosai recipe.* Using the back of the ladle, spread the batter in a circular, clockwise motion from the center toward the outside of the pan, creating a thin, round, 5-inch / 13-cm crepe. *Use slightly less batter if you want it to be thinner and crispier. I often use a wide spatula to spread the mixture out and make it as thin as possible around the edges, the way they do in the restaurants.*

8. Using the small spoon, pour a thin stream of oil from the small bowl in a circle around the outside edge of the batter. Cook for 1 to 2 minutes on 1 side, until lightly browned and pulled away from the side of the pan. Turn the *dosa* over and cook for 1 to 2 minutes on the second side, pressing down on the center of the *dosa* with a spatula to make sure the center cooks through. Transfer to a tray lined with paper towels to absorb the excess oil.

9. Repeat Steps 7 and 8 until all the remaining batter has been cooked. Remove from the heat. After you make every 2 to 3 *dosai*, rub the pan down with the onion as described in Step 6.

10. Serve the *dosai* traditionally, layered with spiced potatoes and a side of *Sambhar,* or simply use as a gluten-free substitute for bread. You can also stack the *dosai,* let them cool, and wrap them first in a dish cloth and then tightly wrap with aluminum foil and store in the refrigerator for 2 to 3 days.*

*If you are storing the *dosai,* reheat them before serving by warming them on the stovetop in a dry cast-iron pan over medium heat for 2 to 3 minutes.

Idlis

YIELD: 30 *IDLIS*

TOOLS: You'll need 2 medium mixing bowls, a blender, a very large mixing bowl, a damp dish towel or paper towel, *idli* molds, an *idli* steaming pot, and a plate.

NOTE: This batter will last for 3 days in the refrigerator, or you can freeze it and store it for as long as 3 months.

To successfully make *idlis,* you need to do some planning, but the efforts are well worth it. These are the most delicious steamed rice–lentil cakes you'll ever eat. Better yet, they're a nutritious finger food the kids will devour.

2 cups / 344 g *idli* rice
½ cup / 100 g *sabut or dhuli dal* (whole or split and skinned black *dal*), picked over and washed
1 teaspoon fenugreek seeds
Water, to cover

¾ cup / 180 mL room-temperature water, plus more as needed, divided
1 teaspoon salt
Coconut Chutney and *Sambhar* (see recipes on pp. 43 and 128), for serving (optional)

1. Place the rice in a medium mixing bowl and combine the *dal* and fenugreek seeds in a second medium mixing bowl. Cover with water and set aside to soak at room temperature for 6 hours to overnight.

2. Drain and discard the water from both bowls. Place the drained rice in a blender and add ¼ cup / 60 mL of the room-temperature water. Blend until it becomes a frothy, loose batter. *I only needed this much water, but depending on how much you drain off, you may need a little more.* Transfer the batter to a very large mixing bowl. *Remember, the batter will expand as it ferments.*

3. To the same blender (no need to clean it), add the drained lentils and fenugreek seeds and the remaining ½ cup / 60 mL of room-temperature water. Blend until it becomes a loose, white, frothy batter. *Again, add a little more water if needed.* Add the mixture to the very large bowl containing the rice batter.

4. Add the salt and stir using your hands. *Some say that stirring the batter with your warm hands, rather than a cold metallic spoon, helps to trigger the fermentation process, which is key to a successful* idli *batter.*

5. Cover the bowl with a damp dish towel or paper towel and set aside in a warm, dry place for 6 hours to overnight to allow the batter to ferment. *If you live in a cold climate, heat the oven to 200°F / 90°C for 10 minutes. Turn off the oven, wait 10 minutes, and then place the covered bowl in the oven for the fermentation process. You'll end up with a thin batter that is slightly bubbly, frothy, and sour. Perfect!* After fermenting, the batter will rise in the bowl and will be loose and frothy.

6. Prep the *idli* mold by lightly oiling its metal trays. Add water to a pot for steaming the idlis, place the pot over medium–high heat, and bring the water to a boil.

7. Pour the *idli* batter into the half-circle molds. Place the molds in the pot, cover, and steam for 8 to 10 minutes. Remove from the heat.

8. Carefully remove the *idlis* from the molds and transfer them to a plate. Clean the mold and repeat Steps 6, 7, and 8 until you have finished with the batter.

9. Serve traditionally with the Coconut Chutney and *Sambhar,* or eat them as a finger food, like my girls like to do. *They love them in their lunch boxes or after school as a light snack.*

Desserts

Unlike the West, in India dessert isn't a given after every meal. We tend to gravitate toward seasonal fruits instead. But, whenever there are *puja* (prayers) or if there's an extra-festive occasion (and there are many), we always make or purchase our favorite *mithai*, or dessert.

Most Indian desserts can be labor intensive to make, which is why I think the art is slowly dying. Instead of laboring at home over all the different steps, most of us head to the local sweet shop and buy our sweets. That's why I have given you recipes in this section that are relatively easy to make at home. They're my children's favorites, and I suspect they'll become yours as well.

Kheer
Rice Pudding

YIELD: 5 CUPS / 1.2 L

TOOLS: You'll need a heavy-bottomed, 4-quart / 4-L stockpot or Dutch oven with a lid and a mortar and pestle.

VEGANIZE IT! It's very easy to make a vegan version of this dessert—I do it all the time. Just substitute unsweetened soy milk for the whole milk and sweetened coconut milk instead of the condensed milk. You'll never even notice the difference. If you use thinner milk alternatives, such as rice, almond, or hemp, just be sure not to simmer them too long. Simmer for no more than 10 to 15 minutes, until the rice cooks through. Turn the burner off, cover the pot, and let the pudding sit for about 10 minutes.

This delicately spiced rice pudding is comfort food, no matter what you were raised eating. Green cardamom pods give this dish a hint of spice without overwhelming it.

1 teaspoon vegetable oil
6 cups / 1.4 L whole milk
½ cup / 90 g uncooked white basmati rice
¼ teaspoon cardamom seeds, crushed in a mortar and pestle
⅓ cup / 60 g golden raisins

⅓ cup / 80 mL sweetened condensed milk
½ cup / 100 g granulated sugar (optional)
1 tablespoon ground almonds or pistachios, for sprinkling

1. Grease the inside of a heavy-bottomed, 4-quart / 4-L stockpot or Dutch oven with the oil. *This step is not essential, but it helps to prevent the* kheer *from sticking later.*

2. Combine the milk, rice, cardamom, and raisins in the stockpot over medium–high heat. Slowly bring the mixture to a boil, stirring occasionally.

3. Reduce the heat to low and simmer, stirring occasionally, for 25 minutes, until the mixture thickens. *Low heat and stirring are key here. Don't give the milk a chance to stick to the bottom of the pot. If it does, it can burn quickly, and you'll ruin the* kheer. *If a film forms on the top, just skim it off and discard it.*

4. Add the condensed milk to the stockpot. Stir well and cook for 5 minutes. Remove from the heat, cover, and set aside for 5 minutes to allow the pudding to thicken. If you are not using sweetened condensed milk, add the ½ cup / 100 g of granulated sugar. *I use an equal amount of agave nectar instead of the sugar, but you should only add agave at the end—otherwise it can discolor the* kheer. Transfer the pudding to a shallow container and refrigerate for at least 2 hours.

5. Sprinkle with the ground almonds and serve cold. *You can also serve it warm and garnish with anything you like. One night, my buddy Patrick Glenn and I got majorly creative and topped our guests'* kheer *with ground-up dark chocolate and peppermint candies. Yum!*

Gulab Jamun

YIELD: 20 PIECES

TOOLS: You'll need a wide, heavy-bottomed stockpot; a sifter; a shallow bowl; a plate; a small *kadhai,* wok, or saucepan; a slotted spoon; and a plate lined with paper towels.

If there's one dessert that Indians truly love, it's this one. I dedicate this recipe to my mother, who is known all over the East Coast for making some of the best *gulab jamun* ever. I also dedicate this recipe to my best childhood friend, Grace, who used to eat these like doughnut holes, popping one after another into her mouth. I wish my metabolism was the same today as it was back in high school! Now, I have to restrict myself to just one.

1½ cups / 300 g granulated or raw cane sugar, such as Sucanat
1½ cups / 350 mL water
1 pinch saffron (optional)
5 tablespoons / 40 g *maida* (unbleached all-purpose flour)
1 cup / 130 g powdered or dry milk
¼ teaspoon baking powder
¼ teaspoon ground cardamom
1 tablespoon *ghee*
7½ tablespoons / 110 mL heavy whipping cream
2 cups / 470 mL vegetable oil, for frying

1. In a wide, heavy-bottomed stockpot over medium–high heat, combine the sugar with the water. Stir well and cook for 10 to 15 minutes, until they are completely blended together. Remove from the heat. Add the saffron, if using, and set aside.

2. Sift the flour into a shallow bowl and add the powdered milk, baking powder, ground cardamom, and *ghee.* Stir well until all the ingredients come together. Slowly add the cream and stir well, until a dough forms.

3. Remove 1 teaspoon of dough from the bowl and roll it into a smooth ball. Place the ball on a plate. Repeat until you use all the dough (should yield about 20 balls).

4. In a *kadhai,* wok, or saucepan over medium–high heat, warm the oil. *I use a small* kadhai *because I don't like to use too much oil; the oil should be about 1 inch / 3 cm deep in the deepest part of the* kadhai. *You'll know the oil is hot enough when you drop in a tiny ball of dough and it rises to the top immediately. As soon as you see that it is ready, reduce the heat to low. If it starts to smoke, it's too hot. Just pull the* kadhai *away from the heat to let the oil cool down a bit.*

5. Slowly add the dough balls, 5 to 10 at a time, to the *kadhai* and cook, using a slotted spoon to move the balls around as they cook, for 2 to 3 minutes, until they are dark brown all over. Transfer to a plate lined with paper towels. Repeat until all the *gulab jamun* have been fried. Remove from the heat.

6. Add the dough balls to the stockpot containing the syrup from Step 1. Set aside at room temperature for 3 hours to overnight (overnight is ideal) so that they absorb the syrup and become very soft.

7. Remove from the stockpot. Serve at room temperature or warm in a small pan over medium heat for 1 to 2 minutes. You can also warm them for 30 seconds along with a little syrup in the microwave.

Kaju ki Barfi

YIELD: 35 (1-INCH × 2-INCH / 3-CM × 5-CM) DIAMOND-SHAPED PIECES

Barfi might sound funny in English but means "icy" in Hindi. It's a delicious confection made from a variety of ingredients traditionally cut into diamond shapes and served topped with a thin layer of edible silver. It often looks too pretty to eat. Try this recipe—a popular version made with cashews—as a nutritious after-school snack for the kids or as a pick-me-up for you.

TOOLS: You'll need a mortar and pestle; a blender; a medium mixing bowl; a medium stockpot; an overturned, well-greased *thali* or a greased baking sheet; a rolling pin; and a sharp knife or pizza cutter.

TRY THIS! For the kids or for a cocktail party, prepare small balls of *barfi* and roll them in finely ground pistachios. Serve skewered with toothpicks.

VEGANIZE IT! Substitute soy, coconut, or rice milk powder for the powdered or dry milk. For the butter, substitute Earth Balance or Spectrum spreads.

3 green cardamom pods, seeds removed and hulls discarded
2 whole cloves
1 cup / 140 g raw, unsalted cashews
3 tablespoons / 25 g powdered or dry milk
½ cup / 100 g granulated or raw cane sugar, such as Sucanat
½ cup / 120 mL water
2 teaspoons unsalted butter, plus more if needed

1. In a mortar and pestle, grind the seeds from the cardamom pods and the cloves to a fine powder.

2. In a blender, combine the cashews and the powdered spices from Step 1 and process until the mixture takes on a meal-like, almost powdery consistency. *You can also use a food processor, but the cashews may not reach the consistency you'll need for this recipe.*

3. Transfer the mixture in the blender to a medium mixing bowl. Add the dry milk and mix by hand. *The key here is to break down any lumps and remove any larger pieces of cashews that did not grind down.* Set aside.

4. In a medium stockpot over high heat, combine the sugar and water. Bring to a boil and continue boiling for 10 minutes, until the mixture thickens and becomes syrupy. *Be careful not to leave the stove at this point, as this mixture can dry up and burn very quickly. A great way to test the syrup for readiness is to put a tiny bit between your thumb and forefinger. When you pull them apart, sticky strings should form. When 2 strings form at a time, the syrup is ready. Be careful not to burn yourself.*

5. Add the butter to the stockpot, stir well, and cook for 1 to 2 minutes, until the butter has melted and the ingredients come together. Remove from the heat.

6. Add the mixture from Step 3 to the stockpot containing the mixture from Step 5 and stir very well, until the mixture hardens slightly, but not too much. *If the mixture seems too crumbly and not moist enough, add a little more melted butter—about a teaspoon at a time—until it has a consistency that can be rolled out.*

7. Spread the mixture into a greased baking sheet or ideally on the back of an overturned, well-greased *thali* (a stainless steel Indian tray). Grease a rolling pin and use it to press down the mixture into a 9-inch / 23-cm circle that is ⅛ inch / 3 mm thick. Set aside to cool for 40 minutes to 1 hour.

8. Using a sharp knife or pizza cutter, slice the *barfi* into diamond shapes and serve immediately. *To dress this up even more, you can purchase edible silver leaf from an Indian grocer and place it on top by inverting the sheets on the surface of the* barfi *and then removing and discarding the paper on the back of the silver sheets.*

Gajar ka Halwa

YIELD: 6 CUPS / 1.4 L

TOOLS: You'll need a food processor or hand grater; a heavy-bottomed, 6-quart / 6-L stockpot; a powerful blender, such as a Vitamix; and a mortar and pestle.

NOTE: Stored in an airtight container, *Gajar ka Halwa* will last 2 to 3 weeks in the refrigerator or as long as 3 months in the freezer.

VEGANIZE IT! This dessert can easily be made vegan by substituting vegetable, canola, or grapeseed oil for the *ghee* and using soy, almond, or other milk alternative for the dairy milk.

When I was a kid, making *gajar ka halwa* was always quite the project. My mom would pull out heaps of carrots and we'd spend the morning cleaning and grating them. Then, we'd boil them on the stovetop in a very large pot for hours. We'd be so excited to taste the results—it was always delicious and, thankfully, well worth the wait.

2 pounds / 910 g carrots, trimmed and peeled
¼ cup / 60 mL plus 2 tablespoons *ghee*
6 cups / 1.4 L milk (whole, lowfat, or nonfat)
1½ cups / 300 g granulated or raw cane sugar, such as Sucanat, finely ground in a blender or food processor

Seeds of 6 green cardamom pods, plus more if using for garnish
1 cup / 110 g coarsely ground raw, unsalted almonds
1 tablespoon golden raisins
1 tablespoon finely chopped pistachios, for garnish

1. In the bowl of a food processor, grate the carrots. (You can also use a hand grater.) *The texture of the grated carrot is very important when making quality* halwa. *You don't want it to be too coarse, which is why I don't recommend prepackaged grated carrots from the store. You'll be glad you spent the time to grate the carrots yourself.*

2. In a heavy-bottomed, 6-quart / 6-L stockpot over medium–high heat, warm the *ghee.* Add the carrots and sauté, stirring constantly to prevent sticking, for 4 minutes, until they soften. Add the milk and bring to a boil.

3. Reduce the heat to low and simmer, partially covered, for 3 to 4 hours, stirring occasionally to ensure that nothing sticks to the bottom of the pot. *The mixture is ready when all of the milk is absorbed, the carrots have swelled, and the mixture becomes fragrant. The heavier the pot, the less time it will take.*

4. Raise the heat to medium and slowly add the sugar. Cook for another 30 minutes, stirring occasionally, until the sugar melts and blends well. *Superfine sugar is best for this recipe, as it will melt through the carrots much better. That's why my mother recommends using a blender or food processor to grind the sugar a bit before adding it.*

5. Using a mortar and pestle, finely grind the cardamom seeds.

6. Add the cardamom powder from Step 5, along with the almonds and raisins, to the stockpot. Cook, stirring occasionally, for 15 to 20 minutes, until the *halwa* starts to pull away from the sides of the pot and starts to thicken and come together. *It should be very dry—that's precisely why you want to keep stirring. It can easily burn at this point.* Remove from the heat and set aside, uncovered, for up to 2 hours at room temperature.

7. Transfer the mixture to small serving bowls and garnish each bowl with a pinch of the ground pistachios. If you like, sprinkle a little more ground cardamom as garnish as well and serve warm or cold.

Besan Pinni

YIELD: 15–20 SMALL *PINNIS*

If there is one recipe that brings back well-loved memories of my mom's childhood home, it's this one. I can still see my grand-mother sitting on a low stool in the kitchen squeezing sugary dough balls in her wrinkled, shaking hand. Her *pinnis* were always exactly the same size and perfectly round—evidence of her years upon years of experience.

TOOLS: You'll need a heavy-bottomed, 4-quart / 4-L sauté pan; a blender or food processor; a large mixing bowl; and a platter.

TRY THIS! Skip making the balls entirely and keep the mixture in a container to eat with a spoon or sprinkled over oatmeal.

1½ cups / 160 g *besan* (gram or chickpea flour), sifted

½ cup / 120 mL *ghee* or vegetable oil, plus more if needed

½ cup / 50 g raw, unsalted almonds, finely ground in a blender or food processor

¾ cup / 150 g granulated or raw cane sugar, such as Sucanat, finely ground in a blender or food processor

1. Place the *besan* in a heavy-bottomed, 4-quart / 4-L sauté pan over medium–high heat and dry roast for 2 to 4 minutes, until lightly browned. Add the *ghee* to the sauté pan and stir well.

2. Reduce the heat to medium–low and cook, stirring occasionally, for 45 minutes to 1 hour. Once it's cooked through, the mixture will become very aro-matic. *The key here is to occasionally stir the* besan *so it cooks through but does not burn. The biggest mistake you can make at this stage is to leave the* besan *slightly raw by not cooking long enough. Be sure to keep a close eye on it, because it can burn easily. I have noticed quite a reduction in cooking time to 10 to 15 minutes when using cast-iron pots. The mixture should be cooked through, but as soon as it starts to brown too much, it's likely done.*

3. Add the almonds and cook for 5 minutes. *You're adding the almonds late in the cooking time so they don't burn.* Remove from the heat, add the sugar, and stir until well combined. *It's necessary for the sugar to be very fine so it blends well. It's also very important to add the sugar* after *you remove from the heat so the sugar doesn't immediately begin to melt.*

4. Transfer to a large mixing bowl and set aside for about 10 minutes, until the mixture is slightly warm but cool enough to handle. *If the mixture is dry at this point and does not bind, you can add more melted ghee, 1 teaspoon at a time. You are now ready to make the* pinnis. *Enlist your kids—they will love helping.*

5. Gather a handful of the mixture. While turning it slowly in 1 hand, squeeze it and bind the mixture together into a smooth ball. *Be patient, as this technique takes time to perfect. Some of the mixture will fall away, but after you work with it a bit, it should form a solid ball. Be sure the mixture remains warm. If it cools too much, it won't bind into a ball.* Place the ball on a large platter.

6. Continue making the balls until you finish the mixture. Set the *pinnis* aside on the platter to cool and harden slightly. Transfer to an airtight container and refrigerate for up to 1 month. You can also freeze them for up to 3 months.

Atta ka Halwa

YIELD: 2 CUPS / 470 ML

TOOLS: You'll need a medium stock-pot; a heavy-bottomed, 4-quart / 4-L sauté pan with a lid; and a mortar and pestle.

VEGANIZE IT! You can easily substitute vegetable oil (canola, vegetable, or grapeseed) for the *ghee*. The first time my mother and I tried substituting with oil, we were amazed at how much we preferred the taste. It tasted cleaner, but still felt authentic. We also tried substituting Earth Balance vegan margarine, but the result was a little salty.

MAKE IT GLUTEN FREE: I was hopping up and down when I successfully made my favorite dessert without wheat gluten. Substitute quinoa flour for the *atta* and follow the steps, but change the cooking time in Step 3 to 8 minutes. Quinoa flour is a little thinner and more delicate, so I found that I had to stir constantly during Step 3 to make sure it didn't burn. But, take it from me, it's delicious—I couldn't tell the difference.

The story goes that when my mother first visited my father's village as a new bride, she was surprised when she was offered this seemingly crass version of *halwa*. In her larger town, it was made from cream of wheat rather than just wheat flour. But, it took just a few bites to convince her that this village version of this dessert used in prayers and made during festivals is actually superior in taste to any other you will ever eat. My mouth still waters thinking about the hot, warm ball of sweet dough made sweeter by the occasional juicy raisin. Run—don't walk—to your kitchen to make this.

1½ cups / 350 mL water
½ cup / 100 g granulated or raw cane sugar, such as Sucanat
2 tablespoons golden raisins
½ cup / 120 mL *ghee* or unsalted butter
¾ cup / 100 g *chapati* flour *(atta)*

6–8 almonds, roughly chopped
½ teaspoon cardamom powder, ground as finely as possible in a mortar and pestle
Ground pistachios and/or almonds, for garnish
Fresh *Puris* (see recipe on p. 248) and a curry, for serving (optional)

1. In a medium stockpot, combine the water, sugar, and raisins. *Using Sucanat will give the* halwa *a brownish color.* Bring to a boil.

2. Reduce the heat to medium and gently simmer while prepping the remaining ingredients.

3. In a separate heavy-bottomed, 4-quart / 4-L sauté pan over medium–high heat, warm the *ghee*. Once the *ghee* has melted, stir in the *chapati* flour and cook, stirring occasionally to prevent sticking, for 10 minutes.

4. Add the almonds and cardamom powder and stir well. *It's best when the cardamom is ground into a very fine powder, so be sure to put some muscle into the mortar and pestle.* Cook, stirring constantly, for 2 minutes, until the mixture becomes very aromatic and begins to pull away slightly from the sides of the pan.

5. With the lid of the sauté pan handy, carefully and slowly pour the contents of the stockpot into the sauté pan containing the mixture from Steps 3 and 4. *Everything will initially steam and splash up, so be ready to quickly cover it.* Once the mixture begins to settle down, remove the cover and stir constantly as you cook for 5 minutes, until the mixture pulls away from the sides of the pan. Remove from the heat, cover, and set aside for 5 to 10 minutes to allow the *halwa* to settle (if you can wait that long, that is!).

6. Transfer to a serving bowl. Garnish with the pistachios and/or almonds and serve warm as a dessert or as a side dish with fresh *Puris* and a curry. *We love sweet and sour tastes, all in one bite.*

Sooji ka Halwa

YIELD: 2½ CUPS / 590 ML

TOOLS: You'll need a heavy-bottomed, 4-quart / 4-L sauté pan with a lid; a plate; a medium stockpot; and a mortar and pestle.

VEGANIZE IT! You can easily substitute vegetable oil (canola, vegetable, or grapeseed) for the *ghee*. We also tried substituting Earth Balance vegan margarine but the result was a little salty.

MAKE IT GLUTEN FREE: Substitute cream of rice cereal for the cream of wheat and follow the same instructions.

When most Indians think of *halwa*, they think of this version made from cream of wheat. It's delicious and a wonderful splurge after dinner or as a snack.

¾ cup / 130 g coarse cream of wheat
1½ cups / 350 mL water
½ cup / 100 g granulated or raw cane sugar, such as Sucanat
2 tablespoons golden raisins
¼ cup / 60 mL *ghee* or unsalted butter

6–8 almonds, roughly chopped
½ teaspoon cardamom powder, ground as finely as possible in a mortar and pestle
Ground pistachios and/or almonds, for garnish
Fresh *Puris* (see recipe on p. 248) and a curry, for serving (optional)

1. Place the cream of wheat in a heavy-bottomed, 4-quart / 4-L sauté pan over medium–high heat and dry roast for 2 to 3 minutes, until it is just toasted and lightly brown. During the entire cooking time, shake the pan every 15 to 20 seconds to prevent burning. *When dry roasting, never leave the pan unattended—the cream of wheat can easily burn.* Remove from the heat, transfer to a plate, and set aside to cool for 15 minutes. Wipe the sauté pan clean. *At most Indian grocers, you can purchase cream of wheat preroasted. If you do so, simply skip this step.*

2. In a medium stockpot over medium–high heat, combine the water, sugar, and raisins. *Using Sucanat will give the* halwa *a brownish color.* Bring to a boil.

3. Reduce the heat to medium and gently simmer while prepping the remaining ingredients.

4. Return the heavy-bottomed, 4-quart / 4-L sauté pan to medium–high heat, and add the *ghee*. Once the *ghee* has melted, stir in the roasted cream of wheat and cook, stirring occasionally to prevent sticking, for 10 minutes.

5. Add the almonds and cardamom powder and stir well. *It's best when the cardamom is ground into a very fine powder, so be sure to put some muscle into the mortar and pestle.* Cook, stirring constantly, for 2 minutes, until the mixture becomes very aromatic and begins to pull away slightly from the sides of the pan.

6. With the lid of the sauté pan handy, carefully and slowly pour the contents of the stockpot from Step 2 into the sauté pan containing the mixture from Steps 4 and 5. *Everything will initially steam and splash up, so be ready to quickly cover it.* Once the mixture begins to settle down, remove the cover and stir constantly as you cook for 2 minutes, until the mixture pulls away from the sides of the pan. Remove from the heat, cover, and set aside for 5 to 10 minutes to allow the *halwa* to settle (if you can wait that long, that is!).

7. Transfer to a serving bowl. Garnish with the pistachios and/or almonds and serve warm as a dessert or as a side dish with fresh *Puris* and a curry. *We love sweet and sour tastes, all in one bite.*

Mitha Sevian (Seviyan)
Sweet Vermicelli Pudding

YIELD: 6-8 SERVINGS (4½ CUPS / 1 L)

TOOLS: You'll need a small mixing bowl; a mortar and pestle; and a heavy-bottomed, 4-quart / 4-L sauté pan.

VEGANIZE IT! Like *kheer,* this recipe tastes even better when made using soy milk or another dairy alternative.

The first year of my marriage, my mother-in-law and I celebrated Karwa Chauth, a day of fasting for married Hindu women. We start the fast by eating before the sun is up, and *mitha sevian* is always a part of that breakfast. For me, this dish has come to represent special, festive days.

- 2 heaping tablespoons golden raisins
- 1 cup / 240 mL boiling water
- 1 teaspoon *ghee* or vegetable oil
- 6 green cardamom pods, lightly crushed in a mortar and pestle
- 4 whole cloves, lightly crushed in a mortar and pestle
- 2 cups / 210 g vermicelli noodles, broken in small pieces
- 4 cups / 950 mL milk (whole, lowfat, or nonfat)
- 2 tablespoons granulated or raw cane sugar, such as Sucanat; honey; or agave nectar, plus more to taste
- 1 teaspoon rosewater (optional)
- 2 tablespoons blanched almond slivers, for garnish*

1. Place the raisins in a small mixing bowl and add the boiling water. Set them aside to soak for at least 30 minutes as you prep the remaining ingredients.

2. In a heavy-bottomed, 4-quart / 4-L sauté pan over medium–high heat, warm the *ghee*. Add the cardamom and cloves and cook for 1 minute, until they just sizzle. Add the vermicelli noodles and cook for 2 minutes, until they are slightly browned. Stir well, breaking down the noodles a bit with the back of the spoon.

3. Drain the raisins, discarding the water. Add the milk and raisins to the sauté pan and bring to a boil.

4. Reduce the heat to low and simmer for 2 minutes. Remove from the heat.

5. Add the sugar and rosewater, if using, and stir well. Remove and discard the whole spices.

6. Transfer the mixture into 6 to 8 small serving bowls. Garnish with the almonds and more sugar, if desired.

*I like to soak the almonds overnight, peel them, and then thinly slice them lengthwise.

Moong Dal Payasam

YIELD: 5 CUPS / 1.2 L

TOOLS: You'll need a heavy-bottomed, 3-quart / 3-L stockpot or Dutch oven with a lid; a mortar and pestle; a slotted spoon; and a small sauté pan.

I was introduced to this dessert on an overnight cruise down the backwaters of Kerala. I was there to shoot cooking segments with chefs from across the state. I was completely amazed at the complexity of the flavors in the dishes made in the tiny kitchen at the back of the boat. This is one dessert you'll never feel guilty eating.

1 cup / 220 g *sabut moong dal* (dried whole green *dal* with skin), picked over, washed, soaked overnight, and drained
4 cups / 950 mL water
4 cups / 950 mL milk (whole or lowfat) or milk alternative (soy or coconut)
1 tablespoon *ghee,* vegan margarine, or vegetable oil
¼ cup / 35 g raw, unsalted cashews
¼ cup / 40 g golden raisins
¼ cup / 40 g granulated or raw cane sugar, such as Sucanat, or agave nectar
½ teaspoon cardamom powder, ground as finely as possible in a mortar and pestle, hulls discarded
1 tablespoon grated coconut, for garnish

1. In a heavy-bottomed, 3-quart / 3-L stockpot over medium heat, combine the *moong dal* and the water. Bring to a boil.

2. Reduce the heat to medium and simmer for 10 minutes, until the *dal* softens. Drain and discard the water. *You'll have 3 cups / 710 mL cooked.*

3. Return the drained *moong dal* to the same stockpot over medium–high heat. Add the milk and bring to a boil.

4. Reduce the heat to medium–low and simmer for 13 minutes. During the cooking process, use a slotted spoon to remove ½ cup / 120 mL of the *dal* from the stockpot and mash them. Return the mashed *dal* to the stockpot. If a light film forms on the milk, collect it with a slotted spoon and discard it. Remove from the heat. *As with my* kheer *recipe, I think using soy milk in this recipe instead of dairy milk makes it even better, because it gets thicker and creamier.*

5. In a small sauté pan over medium–high heat, warm the *ghee.* Add the cashews and raisins and sauté for 1 minute, until lightly browned. Remove from the heat and transfer the mixture to the stockpot containing the *moong dal.* Stir until well combined.

6. Add the sugar and cardamom powder to the stockpot and stir until well combined. Transfer the mixture to small bowls and garnish each with the coconut.

Kulfi
Indian Ice Cream

YIELD: 10–12 CONES

TOOLS: You'll need a heavy-bottomed, 4-quart / 4-L stockpot (preferably nonstick); a slotted spoon; a strainer; and a freezer container or *kulfi* or Popsicle molds.

In India, we love *kulfi*. It's similar to ice cream, but denser, creamier, and chewier. Unlike the ice cream you are probably used to eating, *kulfi* is not whipped, so it's more solid than ice cream. It's simple to make and decadent to eat. It's especially fun to freeze *kulfi* in cone-shaped, stainless steel *kulfi* molds, which you can find at any well-stocked Indian home goods store, or simply use Popsicle molds instead. Thanks to my dear friend Masha for lending me her *kulfi* molds from her hometown of Patiala, India.

8 cups / 1.9 L whole milk
10 green cardamom pods, crushed lightly
6 tablespoons / 75 g granulated or raw cane sugar, such as Sucanat

2 tablespoons blanched almond slivers, finely chopped
2 tablespoons unsalted pistachios, finely chopped, divided

1. In a heavy-bottomed, 4-quart / 4-L stockpot (preferably nonstick) over medium–high heat, combine the milk and the cardamom pods. Bring to a boil.

2. Reduce the heat to low and simmer, stirring occasionally to prevent sticking, for 2 hours. *Repeated stirring is very important, or it will stick to the bottom of the pot.* If a light film or skin forms on the milk, collect it with a slotted spoon and discard it or stir it back into the mixture. After the cooking time is complete, the reduced mixture will yield about 3 cups / 710 mL. *I find cooking milk to be tricky, as it can burn easily. Keep the heat very low and stir often and well.*

3. Add the sugar to the stockpot, stir well, and cook for 5 to 7 minutes, until the sugar dissolves into the milk. *I find that regular granulated sugar works best; no need to grind it to superfine.* Remove from the heat.

4. Pour the mixture through a fine strainer into a freezer-safe container with a very tight seal. Add the almonds and 1 tablespoon of the pistachios. Place in the freezer to chill for 40 minutes and also place *kulfi* or Popsicle molds in the freezer to chill.

5. Remove the *kulfi* from the freezer and mash it with a fork to break up any ice crystals that have formed. Return to the freezer for 20 minutes.

6. Repeat Step 5 at 20-minute intervals until the *kulfi* has stiffened. At that point, transfer it into the chilled molds and freeze for at least 3 to 4 hours, until it has hardened completely.

7. Remove the molds from the freezer and transfer each *kulfi* to a dessert plate. Garnish each with the remaining pistachios and serve immediately. *You may need to run the molds under hot water for a moment to release the* kulfi.

Acknowledgments

About six months after *Vegan Indian Cooking,* my second book was released, I received a Facebook message from a reader in Texas named Angela Marie Eaton. She owned my books, cooked from them, and loved the food. But, once in a while, Angela wrote, she also craved the Indian dishes she enjoyed at her local Indian restaurant. Angela wanted to make them in the comfort of her own home, so she asked if I would consider putting a few of those "comfort Indian" recipes on my blog?

I thought about it for a few minutes. My first and second books had been about making Indian food healthy. In fact, that's my whole platform—the foods Indian families eat at home are often not represented at typical Indian restaurants, and I want my readers to learn how to cook and enjoy traditional Indian home favorites. But Angela's question got me thinking: Why can't I have it both ways, and provide both to my readers? I could provide a little indulgence along with healthy sidebars, and give folks a single cookbook that provided all their favorite Indian recipes in one place.

The idea behind this book began with that one message. For that, I thank my village—Angela and all of my other online friends who have found me through my books, blog, and Facebook fan page. Every day, you give me new ideas about how to take Indian cooking and my books to another level. I am always listening, and your feedback helps me provide you with simple, practical options to make your time in the kitchen easier and more meaningful.

I would be remiss if I didn't thank my childhood friend, Jasmine Narula, for sending me my first Facebook friend request years ago. She is in part responsible for creating this social media monster.

I also want to thank my fellow moms who have helped me tremendously during the year it took me to write this book. They have been there for me, picking up my kids from school and whisking them away to play dates, both with or without me. Robin, Barbara, Elif, Karen, Naila, Mahtab, Brigitte, Mar, Patricia, Dimple, and so many others—thank you so, so much. I could not have done it without your support and vigilance over my girls. You all mean the world to me and to them.

And to my girls, Aria and Neha, who sometimes missed out on birthday parties (I often confused dates) and play dates because of "Mommy's writing"—don't worry. This year is about making it up to you! Now comes the fun stuff. And I also want to give thanks to your teachers, Miss Ioannou, Miss Harris, Mr. Biggs, and Miss Robinson, for often being willing to taste the dishes I prepared. Thank you for your feedback and for making my girls so comfortable in their own skin in your classrooms. It will mean the world to them in their lives.

I also have to thank my daughters' friends, who are as international as they come and always willing to try new foods and learn about our culture. Thanks especially to Alex, Marta, Matthew, Sid, Maya, Aysu, Chloe, Erik, Paul, Pariya, and Mirabel.

Thanks to my mom, Veena, for always being there for my recipe questions, and to my dad, Gian, for always adding his take on a recipe. I must also thank my wonderful in-laws, Santosh and Krishan, for their continued support. It's so wonderful that both Sandeep and I come from families who are dedicated to authentic Indian food.

Thank you to my extended family as well in India. Without the vigilance of my Sneh *massi* (aunt) I may not have kept my love of all things Indian when we left India back in the early 1970s. She dedicated my visits to India with Hindi lessons, books on Indian history, and trips with my cousins (her sons) all around Delhi to see and appreciate the sights. You, *massi,* are in large part why I can today do what I do—keeping one foot in each of my beloved countries. Thank you.

Thank you to my Hawaiian family. Though we are not related—it feels like we are. When I moved there for graduate school in the 1990s you taught me for the first time what it felt to be completely comfortable in my own brown skin. Kawika McKeague, Auntie Vicky Holt Takamine, and everyone else especially at the East West Center and the University of Hawaii, thank you for never making me feel like an outsider. It's made me who I am today and I always know I have a place there on the islands. *Mahalo.*

Writing cookbooks is not just about putting recipes together. It's also about getting the facts straight. In my case, that meant learning the true difference between a bean and a lentil, understanding that the scientific names of spices will help the readers know what they are using, and realizing that science plays a large role in cooking. Much of this knowledge came from my mentor and friend, food scientist Kantha Shelke, a principal at Corvus Blue LLC. Beyond the facts you've taught me, you've also shown me how to be a strong woman in what often can seem like a man's world. For all of this, thank you.

To Judith Dunbar-Hines and Toria Emas, I am humbled you asked me to join the sisterhood that is Les Dames d'Escoffier. Thank you.

Steven Fraser, thank you for your guidance. As my company grows and my products gain a foothold in the marketplace, I cannot forget how much I owe you for all of your feedback and guidance. Whenever I had a question or needed to meet with you, you were always there and always provided solutions. It's helped grow Indian As Apple Pie, my company, beyond my dreams.

I also want to thank the folks at the International Home and Housewares Show for connecting me to Steve when I was a mere blip on the screen. Susan Marzano, as always, thank you for including me in the cooking roundup year after year at this amazing show. I truly appreciate it.

Sarah Chrystal, thank you for your vision. Together, we have made Indian cooking a monthly staple at the Whole Foods Market in Lincoln Park. I appreciate your constant quest to work harder and forever find the proverbial silver lining. I like to say that we're almost the same person! Thanks for all that you do. And thank you to my two most dedicated students, LaTasha Gardner and David Acevedo. Your enthusiasm for learning, cooking, and eating this cuisine is contagious. (Not to mention your love of a good bottle of wine!)

Thank you, Patrick Glenn, for always being around when I need you. I just have to ask, and you somehow always show up, asking for nothing but knowledge in return. Your attitude is remarkable, with a focus on succeeding, no matter the odds, and always getting the job done right, with no excuses. I wish there were more like you in this world.

Thank you to the ladies (and man) of Chicagonista: MJ, Beth, Nancy, Duong, David, and, of course, Dwana. I appreciate that you have always gone out of your way to support my cause, even when I didn't really recognize that I had one. You are a true reflection of what can happen when folks (especially strong women) work together to build something bigger than ourselves.

Thank you to all of my early believers, especially the folks from my own community who understand my mission—to help Indian Americans preserve our roots through food. Raakhee Mirchandani, you fit that description perfectly! By day, you're the busy managing editor of the *Daily News,* yet somehow you're still able to get wholesome, healthy Indian food on the table every night. Don't worry: I promise I won't blow your cover with your mother-in-law. You are an ideal example of just the families I want most to reach—Indian Americans who want to pass along the traditions without having to give up their day jobs.

I also want to send a huge shoutout to my dedicated recipe testers! While I was working on this book, I posted requests on Facebook to find up to five testers for each developed recipe for this book. Each received a copy of a recipe to try. Not only did my wonderful testers find some simple errors—they also helped me write clearer instructions. The best part of all was that they made me think outside the box. Different sets of eyes interpret things in so many ways. I know I will likely miss some of you in this list, so my apologies if I have. Thanks to all of you: Mark Breta, Carolyn Lloyd, Keren and Ryan Roberts, Abby Cohen, Maria Masnato, Heather Koerber, Amanda McCutcheon, Courtenay

Verret, Tracey Beck-Campbell, Sarah Rajan, Subadra Varadarajan, April Carson, Angela Pinto, Yashvinee Narechania, Shailey Gupta-Brietzke, Elana Richman, Cheri Lash, Vandna and Shaan Ahluwalia, Rebecca Borges, Heather Demantes, Gregory Scott (your okra feedback in particular was priceless!), Meredith McGee, Julie Gordon, Joanne Mitchell, and Becki Whiskeyman-Smith, her daughter Grace, and Grace's Girl Scout Cadette Troop 1760 (for giving my *chai* recipe a thumbs-up).

Thanks to the Italian town of Castel di Casio, near Bologna, and to our dear friends Paul and Dahlia Magelli for inviting us to their home there. I was able to cook an Indian meal for the residents, some of whom had never tasted Indian food before. Your mountain town is simply heavenly. I cannot wait to return.

Big thanks to my Web designer, Crystal Kelly, and to Wendy Woodside, who did an amazing job on my makeup for this book. And an even bigger thanks to Sayuri at Charles Ifergan Salon, who keeps my short hair sharp.

Thank you to Mary Valentin. Your direction as photo art director was priceless, and your vision for this book was spot on.

A special thanks goes to the team at Agate Publishing. Doug Seibold, I appreciate your urging to "just write!" Perrin Davis, thank you for being an editor with vision. Eileen Johnson—you truly always, always, always come through for me. To Zach Rudin, Jali Becker, and everyone else at Team Agate—thank you. Time to celebrate!

About the Author

Cookbook author and journalist Anupy Singla is fast becoming one of the country's foremost authorities on Indian food and cooking. She is the author of three books. *Indian for Everyone* is a compilation of the most popular Indian recipes outside the Subcontinent. Her first two books, *The Indian Slow Cooker* and *Vegan Indian Cooking*, are top-selling Indian cookbooks in North America.

Anupy is a former business reporter and has worked in print, television, and radio. Her last job was as the morning reporter for *Chicago Tribune*-owned CLTV. She has also reported for Bloomberg News and WGN-TV. Anupy's food-related work has appeared in the *Chicago Tribune*, the *Chicago Sun-Times*, the *Wall Street Journal*, and various other newspapers and magazines.

Although not a trained chef, Anupy grew up cooking with her paternal grandfather who was from a small village in Punjab, India. She has traveled throughout India and worked with renowned chefs and home cooks alike.

Anupy and her growing food and housewares company, Indian As Apple Pie, have been featured in *Entrepreneur* and *Kiwi* magazines, and she has appeared on television stations across the country and in Canada. She teaches monthly classes at Chicago's Whole Foods Market in Lincoln Park and continues to blog and write about all things Indian food on her website, indianasapplepie.com.

Anupy was featured in the Smithsonian's Beyond Bollywood Exhibit, which showcases the impact of Indian Americans on this country's history. And, she is a member of the prestigious Les Dames d'Escoffier, the Asian American Journalist Association, and the South Asian Journalist Association. Anupy lives in Chicago with her husband, Sandeep Gupta, and their two young daughters.

Also by Anupy Singla

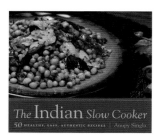

The Indian Slow Cooker

"The recipes are straightforward and, just as the subtitle claims, easy, healthy, and authentic." —Sarah Elton, *The Atlantic*, citing *The Indian Slow Cooker* as a "Top 10 Cookbook of 2011"

"My favorite new slow cooker book is *The Indian Slow Cooker* by Anupy Singla." —Genevieve Ko, *Good Housekeeping*

"If you love Indian food, have a look at Anupy Singla's *The Indian Slow Cooker*. Folded in with lush food photography are easy, healthful recipes with traditional flavors." —Lois White, *Better Homes and Gardens*

Vegan Indian Cooking

"Highly recommended, especially for fans of Madhur Jaffrey, Monica Bhide, and Suvir Saran." —*Library Journal*, starred review

"Chicago-based cookbook author Anupy Singla has cultivated a devoted following by showing readers how to master Indian spices and make great-tasting Indian food at home." —Sarah Terez-Rosenblum, *Chicago Sun Times*

1/24